Shakespeare, Midlife, and Generativity

Shakespeare, Midlife, and Generativity

KARL F. ZENDER

Louisiana State University Press

Baton Rouge

Published by Louisiana State University Press

Manufactured in the United States of America
First printing

Designer: Laura Roubique Gleason
Typeface: Tribute
Printer and binder: Thomson-Shore, Inc.

Library of Congress Cataloging-in-Publication Data

Zender, Karl F., 1937–
Shakespeare, midlife, and generativity / Karl F. Zender.
p. cm.
Includes bibliographical references and index.
ISBN 978-0-8071-3355-2 (cloth : alk. paper) 1. Shakespeare, William, 1564–1616—Criticism and interpretation. I. Title.
PR2965.Z46 2008
822.3'3—dc22

2008004136

The paper in this book meets the guidelines for permanence and durability of the Committee on Production Guidelines for Book Longevity of the Council on Library Resources. ♾

To My Students

This form, this face, this life
Living to live in a world of time beyond me; let me
Resign my life for this life, my speech for that unspoken.

—T. S. Eliot, "Marina"

Nobody remembers Shakespeare's children.

—William Faulkner to his daughter

Contents

Acknowledgments

My thoughts turn first to the dedicatees of this volume, whose enthusiasm for literature has helped to sustain my own during more than forty years of teaching. I think especially of the students in my undergraduate Shakespeare classes, of both the undergraduates themselves and the graduate students who have served as my assistants. Because most of my published scholarship has been on the fiction of William Faulkner, the conferences I've attended and the professional relationships I've developed have been mainly in that area, not in the area of Shakespeare studies. This has made me more than usually dependent on the classroom as a forum in which to develop my understanding and appreciation of Shakespeare's plays. To my good fortune, I've been assisted in this effort by many eager and intelligent students, several of whom have remained my friends, and to all of whom I owe a debt of gratitude.

I've been fortunate as well in the assistance given me by two members of my department—Michael Hoffman, who provided insightful comments on every chapter of this book, as he has on all of my work in the past, and Margaret Ferguson, who provided detailed comments on the first two chapters at a crucial stage in their development. I also wish to thank the members of my department who listened to me read the first half of chapter 5, and whose comments helped me see how to move forward into the second half. An anonymous reader at LSU Press also provided insightful comments, including important suggestions for further reading. I wish also to thank John Easterly, executive editor of the press, and the members of his editorial staff for the many forms of assistance they've given me.

To attempt to write on Shakespeare is to engage with (and be instructed by) a daunting amount of prior critical commentary. I've been assisted in locating this material by Diana King, humanities and social sciences reference librarian at Shields Library, University of California at Davis. Also, in the fall of 2004 a teaching fellowship at the University of California Washington Center allowed me to do sustained work at the Folger Shakespeare Library. I wish to thank the staffs of the center and of the library for making my stay both comfortable and profitable. (Like many visitors to the Folger, I spent some time contemplating the main reading room's stained glass window depicting the seven ages of man—particularly, for the purposes of this book, the middle panels.)

My thoughts turn now, as always, to my wife, Lynn, whose love, optimism, and faith in my abilities has comforted me and buoyed my spirits through all the years of our marriage. I think too of the other members of my family: my sons, Matthew and Jacob; Matthew's wife, Renée; Matthew and Renée's sons Zachary and Aaron; and my sister, Nancy Zender Kleinman. I think also, and sadly, of the many members of my family who can now visit me only in memory: my parents, Franz Josef and Rose Grimes Zender; my brother-in-law, James Kleinman; and my half-siblings, Ruth Hazelbaker Boyd, Robert Hazelbaker, and Patricia Hazelbaker Smith. *Lente, lente currite noctis equi.*

Shakespeare, Midlife, and Generativity

1

Introduction

How does Shakespeare represent the middle years of human life? To what extent are current understandings of the traumas, challenges, and opportunities of middle age useful in interpreting Shakespeare's plays? These questions, when posed, must immediately confront the objection of anachronism, for to what extent can the concept of middle age be relevant to an era in which life expectancy at birth was no more than 25 to 35 years, in which approximately a third of newborns died before their first birthday and half before their fifteenth, in which perhaps no more than 20 percent of the population was aged 40 or older, and in which the threat of plague and famine was ubiquitous? Awareness of these circumstances can lead to the supposition that middle age is primarily a modern concept, a product of the extraordinary increase in life expectancies of the last hundred years. Yet emphasis on the brevity and uncertainty of life in the Early Modern era must be counterbalanced by other considerations. It is a mistake, as Peter Laslett observes, "to suppose that if the period life expectation is 35 years, for example, as it was [around 1700], someone aged thirty could expect to live for 5 years more, someone aged twenty-five, 10 years more, and so on . . . In fact, . . . a woman of twenty in England before 1871 could expect to live about 36.5 years more; one of twenty-five about 33.5 years; one of thirty, 30.5, one of forty, 24.5."

In effect, individuals who survived the illnesses of infancy and childhood in Shakespeare's England could look forward to living into middle age with very nearly the same level of confidence as at present. "The life span in this sense," Laslett says, "has not lengthened appreciably since life expectation began its astronomical rise . . . a hundred years ago. Exactly as scripture tells us when it talks of three score years and ten, certain people always could and always did reach the maximum length of days, whatever the prevalent mortality."[1]

These demographic observations are consistent with evidence drawn from philosophic, literary, and iconographic traditions. Representations of the span of human life as extending into old age and as consisting of a series of stages long antedate the Early Modern era. The most frequent, tracing back to Hippocrates and famously expressed by Shakespeare in *As You Like It,* represents human life as consisting of seven ages; also prominent is the depiction, originating in Ovid's *Metamorphoses,* of human life as divided into four ages corresponding to the four seasons of the year; and, as Samuel Chew observes, other commentators—Aristotle, Marcus Varro, St. Augustine, Isidore of Seville, the Venerable Bede—argue for three or five or six divisions as well. All of these schemas identify a stage, variously called *gravitas,* manhood, *maturitas, media aetas,* middle age, *perfecta aetas,* corresponding approximately to the modern concept of middle age.[2] It should not surprise us, then, to find that representations of middle age, viewed not as an exceptional possibility but as an expected stage in ongoing life, occur throughout the Shakespearean canon, in forms ranging from Jaques' seven ages speech to Capulet's midlife nostalgia over the time thirty years prior when he had "worn a visor and could tell / A whispering tale in a fair lady's ear" (1.5.23–24) to Hamlet's shocked denial of the continuation into his mother's middle years of "[t]he heyday in the blood" (3.4.70) to Othello's concern over his having "declined / Into the vale of years" (3.3.281–82) to the emphasis, amounting almost to an obsession, on relations between the generations in *King Lear, Antony and Cleopatra, Macbeth,* and the late romances.[3]

What should immediately strike us in contemplating these depictions is the extent to which Shakespeare reoriented the representational traditions he inherited toward an interiorized understanding of midlife experience. As C. L. Barber has famously argued, Shakespeare "wrote at a moment when . . . a ceremonial, ritualistic conception of human life" was being modified "to create a historical, psychological conception."[4] Nowhere is this shift more evident than in depictions of midlife experience. The traditions mentioned in the paragraph above often depict the middle of life as fraught with sadness and conflict.

The Ovidian association of mature adulthood with autumn and hence with decline, for example, was extended in humoral theory to an association with earth, with the planet Saturn, and with the melancholy humor; and in the iconographic tradition, figures representing mature adulthood were depicted as carrying an hourglass, signifying the passage of time, or as standing near a tree with ripe fruit about to fall, or as having one winged and one chained foot. But these representations are limited in their ability to depict the interior experience of the middle years by their schematic character—by their adherence, in Mary Dove's words, "to a pre-known sequence of predictable ages and inevitable age-characteristics." In his jaundiced, nearly exclusively male representation of the seven ages, Jaques characterizes himself as a malcontent; but he does not, and cannot, truly characterize the ages themselves, for to do so would require that he abandon his schema and instead depict the ages from inside, in all of their intricacy and variety.[5]

Just such a reorientation is a major achievement of Shakespeare's drama when viewed as a whole. Understanding that achievement as it relates to one important aspect of the middle years—the transfer of power and authority between the generations—is the ambition of this book. How best to explore this topic requires some preliminary discussion of issues of methodology. Because of its centrality to current thinking about midlife experience, a consideration of the concept that developmental psychologists call "generativity" is a good starting point. The term *generativity* was introduced into psychological discourse in the 1950s by Erik Erikson, in his book *Childhood and Society.* Trained as a Freudian psychotherapist, Erikson broke with what Lawrence Wrightsman calls Freud's "early formation approach" to human development, which asserts "that personality structure is established—and then remains essentially unchanged—in the first years of childhood." Erikson instead formulated a theory of development as continuing throughout all of adulthood. In a modern variation on the notion of the seven ages, Erikson divided the life cycle into eight stages, with each stage defined by the main developmental "task" one confronts during this period of life, and with success or failure at each task characterized by an antinomy—"basic trust vs. basic mistrust" in the stage corresponding to Freud's oral phase, "autonomy vs. shame and doubt" in Freud's anal phase, and so on, culminating in "ego integrity vs. despair" in old age.

The antinomy for the seventh stage, extending broadly throughout the middle years of life, opposes "generativity" to "stagnation," with generativity defined as a shift from a preoccupation with achieving one's own position in the world to an interest in "establishing and guiding the next generation," and stagnation as "an obsessive need for pseudo-intimacy" in which individuals "indulge themselves as if they were their own—or one another's—one and only child."[6]

As the British psychologist Simon Biggs observes, and as many other commentators have noted, Erikson's emphasis on adult development expands "the role of the conscious ego and thereby link[s] the self more closely to the social world. . . . Erikson's model move[s] psychodynamic thinking on from a preoccupation with psycho-sexual development to psycho-social adaptation." This shift in focus has proven popular with many academic psychologists, who have sought to refine Erikson's eight stages and to subject the concept of adult development to empirical testing. Daniel Levinson, for example, subdivides Erikson's seventh stage into "early adulthood" and "middle adulthood" and inserts Early Adult, Midlife, and Late Adult transition periods at the intersections between the appropriate stages. Similarly, George Vaillant, working with data gathered in a long-term study of adult development at Harvard University, subdivides Erikson's fifth as well as his seventh stage, creating two new stages labeled "Career Consolidation vs. Self-Absorption" and "Keeper of the Meaning vs. Rigidity." And John Kotre has sought to distinguish between two forms of generativity: *agentic,* which is inwardly oriented, and *communal,* which is outwardly oriented.[7]

In contrast to these elaborations, which basically accept the validity of Erikson's schema, Eriksonian ego psychology has recently been subjected to a number of negative critiques, with objections often raised to what Kathleen Woodward calls Erikson's "proscriptive or prescriptive stance." As Wrightsman observes, "value judgments abound in Erikson's conception," to the point where one must ask whether it is "a scientific theory or a philosophy of life." Commentators espousing postmodern theoretical orientations have extended the critique of Erikson's theory, and of ego psychology in general, along several fronts. Individuals writing from cultural materialist, feminist, and gay studies perspectives have objected to the implicit assumptions of universality, gender neutrality, and heterosexual normativity in Erikson's theory, arguing, in the first instance, that "generativity is not a universal psychological principle but rather a cultural construct . . . [that] must be analysed as a product of American culture and its embeddedness in individualism"; in the second, that Erikson's emphasis on "independence and adulthood overlook[s] aspects most important to women's identity development, specifically communion, connectedness, relationships, and spirituality"; and, in the third, that the diverse styles of modern life are not well accommodated within Erikson's assumption of the preferability of "the heterosexual, the nuclear, and the work-determined." Further, postmodern commentators adhering to constructivist theories of the human personality have challenged Erikson's assumption of a single coherent chronologically developing self, preferring instead, in Biggs's words, an understanding of the human psyche as including "a multiplicity of options, . . . with [i]dentity no longer contingent on the organizing principle of the lifecourse" but instead capable of being "adopted or discarded over time."[8]

At the heart of the cultural materialist version of these critiques is a challenge to the concept of generativity itself. Although some developmental psychologists doubt the importance of the midlife crisis—or, phrased more neutrally, the midlife transition—most acknowledge its centrality to the experience of the middle years. Those who do so characterize the transition as dominated by a sense of finitude, a sudden activation, in the words of Daniel Levinson, of "our deepest anxieties about decline and dying." For cultural materialist commentators, viewing the midlife transition in this fashion opens the idea of generativity to the possibility of deconstruction, for in relation to the certainty of physical decline and death, Erikson's optimistic view of generativity as the ego's triumph over midlife "stagnation" and self-absorption can be read as a culturally specific form of psychic evasion. If "[t]he urge for generative action" arises out of "a matrix of culturally specific beliefs about the self, death, the nature of giving, nurturance, and economic and gender issues," says Baine Alexander, then generativity itself is "a cultural solution to the paradox of individuality within finitude." To the extent that generativity aims at "creating an enduring and infinite self through an investment in the other," it can be interpreted as "self-absorption in a culturally sanctioned form." Further, as Simon Biggs argues, viewing generativity in this fashion aligns the concept "with other ageist beliefs in contemporary society," for "the story that psychoanalysis tells us about mature adulthood is that its centre of gravity [always] lies elsewhere." Thus, "while generativity rests at the heart of ego psychology, it is . . . difficult to find an authentic adult subjectivity inside [the concept]. . . . As the wrappings of the Eriksonian lifecourse unravel, it appears . . . as a series of Chinese boxes. Each stage, at least in mid and late adulthood, is essentially empty of meaning except insofar as it contains another."[9]

This theoretical give-and-take offers a useful perspective on representations of middle life in Shakespeare's plays. Awareness of the cultural specificity of generativity—its contingent status as a modern American concept—can alert us to the equally contingent status of ideas of middle life in Shakespeare's own time. In *Romeo and Juliet,* while urging Juliet to consider marriage, Lady Capulet says, "By my count / I was your mother much upon these years / That you are now a maid" (1.3.72–74). There are reasons for declining to interpret these lines as indicating that Lady Capulet is literally 27 or 28 years old at the time of the play's action, most notably her final speech, in which she calls Romeo's and Juliet's deaths "a bell / That warns my old age to a sepulcher" (5.3.206–7). But the fact that Shakespeare can present Lady Capulet's earlier statement as plausible suggests a greater malleability to the *terminus a quo* of middle age in the Early Modern period than would be true today. And in the same fashion, the *terminus ad quem* of middle age, which in the contemporary world continues to be pushed forward as life expectancy increases, in Shakespeare's time tended to move in the other direction. As Philippe Ariès observes, "old age started early in the society of the past. . . . [T]he iconography of old age does not always represent it in the guise of a decrepit invalid: old age begins with the losing of one's hair and the wearing of a beard, and a handsome old man sometimes appears simply as a man who is bald."[10]

As with the chronological definitions of middle age, so with the material and social conditions and cultural presuppositions within which all of the ages of life, including middle age, were lived in the Early Modern era. As Ariès notes, in the classical, medieval, and Early Modern schemas, "[t]he ages of life did not correspond simply to biological phases but also to social functions," and they were interpreted "in accord with the universal system of correspondences" "which joined the destiny of man to that of the planets." Hence Jaques can associate several of his seven ages with particular social roles—schoolboy, lover, soldier—even though those roles could in reality occur at other points in the life cycle, and each of the ages would necessarily include individuals occupying an immense variety of other roles. Hence too what Ariès terms the "long duration of childhood" in pre-modern times and the absence of the concept of adolescence: "[N]obody would have thought of seeing the end of childhood in puberty," Ariès argues, for "[t]he idea of childhood was bound up with the idea of dependence. . . . One could leave childhood only by leaving the state of dependence, or at least the lower degrees of dependence."[11]

The responsibilities and privileges of middle life as these relate to gender, social status, religious belief, and familial role were of course also understood considerably differently in the Early Modern era than today. The nearly universal assumption in the Early Modern era, as Susan Amussen observes, "that all relationships were hierarchical," placed wives to husbands, and children to parents, in a stringently defined subordinate status, one that authorized physical punishment for misbehavior by children and, in the view of some commentators, by wives as well. Also, the closing of the nunneries in England during the Reformation meant that in Shakespeare's time there were essentially no approved social roles available to women outside of marriage, with the result, as F. H. Mares says, that while Shakespeare's plays offer "sympathetic insight into the way women suffer in a world where men control all the property," they include "no advocacy of change" nor any suggestion of an alternative "career for a woman." Similarly, the reliance on primogeniture as the governing principle for the transmission of property meant that younger sons faced a more uncertain future than may be the case in the modern era. And in a number of other areas—the obligation of fathers to ensure regular church attendance by family members, for example, or the role of shaming rituals in enforcing communal norms of behavior—the relation of the nuclear family to the larger society was considerably more intimate than it is today.[12]

These observations have a beneficial effect insofar as they challenge what Catherine Belsey calls "the humanist complacency that finds its guarantee in a metaphysics of universal human nature." Looming behind such challenges is the larger issue of the relationship between psychoanalytic—or, more generally, psychologically oriented—and New Historicist/cultural materialist modes of interpretation. As Stephen Greenblatt says in advancing a New Historicist critique of "the universalist claims of psychoanalysis," the notion that "the self is at its core a stable point of reference, a given upon which to construct interpretations, . . . is achieved . . . only by repressing history, or, more accurately, by repressing *histories*." Viewing the liberal subject—autonomous, integral, self-regulating—as an invention of post-Descartian philosophy and nineteenth-century bourgeois culture, Greenblatt and other New Historicist commentators have challenged Jacob Burckhardt's famous claim that, whereas in the Middle Ages "man was conscious of himself only as a member of a race, people, party, or corporation," in the Renaissance "man became a spiritual *individual* and recognized himself as such." Countering this claim, they have explored the ways in which the Early Modern experience of subjectivity is itself socially constructed, produced by (and constrained by) structures of power, ideology, and social coercion, both the ones mentioned in the paragraph above and others: profound shifts in religious belief and practice; spectacles of terror and forgiveness cultivating what Greenblatt calls "salutary anxiety"; sumptuary laws, laws against vagabondage, and homilies against disobedience enforcing hierarchical economic and class relationships; and a tradition of homophobic and misogynistic discourse designed to regulate sexual and gender deviance.[13]

This book seeks to strike a balance between assimilating this New Historicist critique of a universalist psychology and resisting its more radical implications—its implication, for example, in Jonathan Goldberg's words, that thinking "our way into the multiple forms of Shakespearean experience" requires giving up "notions of character as self-same, owned, capable of autonomy and change . . . [and] the notion that biological difference is an *a priori* fact." In seeking this middle ground I have been greatly aided by Robert N. Watson's *The Rest Is Silence*, a book to whose argument I return in chapter 3, and also by the work of a number of historians who emphasize continuities rather than discontinuities between Early Modern and present-day social and psychic life. Acknowledging that there are "fluctuations in the degree and configuration of psychological individualism, as domestic arrangements and religious practices change," Watson nonetheless argues that in important ways over the past five hundred years the experience of selfhood has remained invariant. Most notable among these ways for his purposes are continuities in the fear of personal extinction. Arguing that only "a facile and even patronizing reading of human psychology, as well as an incomplete reading of the historical record, can insist that Renaissance minds were incapable of registering the fear of personal annihilation," Watson develops a subtle and convincing argument concerning "the mortality-crisis of Jacobean England," one that restores the analysis of subjective experience to primacy of place without reverting to universalist assumptions about human psychology.[14]

As with the fear of death, so with the developmental challenges of the middle years, in particular those involving generativity. In its positive familial manifestations, generativity is a name for parental love; at a broader level, the word designates a concern for the future well-being of a larger community. The social forms within which these impulses manifest themselves (or fail in their realization) have changed substantially over the centuries, but the underlying substructure of need and desire remains recognizable. Consider in this regard an extreme example. When Leonato repudiates Hero for her supposed infidelity in *Much Ado About Nothing,* he fantasizes having taken up "a beggar's issue at my gates," rather than having fathered a daughter, so that he could say "'[n]o part of it is mine; / This shame derives itself from unknown loins.'" He then laments the impossibility of his fantasy, saying, "But mine, and mine I loved, and mine I praised, / And mine that I was proud on, mine so much / That I myself was to myself not mine, / Valuing of her—why, she, O she, is fallen / Into a pit of ink, that the wide sea / Hath drops too few to wash her clean again" (4.1.132–41).

In Leonato's repeated "mine" we hear an ideology of possessive father-daughter relations less prevalent (one hopes) in our own age than in Shakespeare's. We hear also a patriarchal culture's anxieties about unregulated female desire in the rush to judgment not only of Leonato but of every male character except Benedick and the Friar, despite the implausibility of the charge that Hero, who has slept every night save one in Beatrice's company, has engaged in "vile encounters . . . /A thousand times in secret" (4.1.93–94). But we truncate our experience of the play if we do not hear as well an authentic expression of fatherly affection. As Leonato's insistent phrasing reveals, not only his daughter but he himself has become "not mine"; and significantly, Leonato's loss of himself does not *follow* from Hero's supposed infidelity but *precedes* it, in the overwhelming fullness of his "[v]aluing of her." Here, as in his subsequent serio-comic threat to "prove" Claudio's villainy "on his body if he dare, / Despite his nice fence and his active practice" (5.1.74–75), a familiar emotion reveals itself within an alien social form.

Like most of the other examples cited thus far, the example of Leonato and Hero is taken from a play written in the first half of Shakespeare's career. It is important to observe that these early depictions differ in a fundamental way from the later ones that are the subject of this book. Although empathetic depictions of midlife experience occur throughout the early plays, primary emphasis falls on the influence of middle-aged characters on characters younger than themselves, most often on their children. Several of the romantic comedies follow the conventions of Roman New Comedy in depicting a father or a father-surrogate—the Duke of Milan in *The Two Gentlemen of Verona,* Egeus in *A Midsummer Night's Dream,* Duke Frederick in *As You Like It*—as a blocking agent whose opposition must be overcome or reversed if the younger generation is to achieve romantic fulfillment. Similarly, although the *Henriad* displays in precise detail the effects on Henry IV's personality and behavior of his guilt over Richard II's murder, this display is less important in its own regard than in its influence on Prince Hal's gradual willingness to assume "the debt I never promisèd" (*1 Henry IV,* 1.2.203). Only in *Hamlet* does this emphasis shift, as the play divides almost schizophrenically between Hamlet's struggle to replicate his father's identity by enacting revenge and his shocked discovery of his mother's existence as a desiring being independent of her maternal function. From this point forward in the Shakespearean oeuvre, the struggles of the child to outwit (or assimilate) parental demands recedes in importance, as attention shifts instead to the struggle of a parent—with the exception of Cleopatra, always a father—either to retain or to relinquish his sense of his child as "mine."

It is scarcely an exaggeration to say that the theme just identified is ubiquitous in Shakespeare's plays from *Hamlet* forward. In *Othello* Shakespeare explores a different aspect of midlife experience than the one studied here, of "the young affects / In me defunct" (1.3.266–67);

in *Coriolanus* he reverts to the theme of the child's quest for autonomy, displaced here into Coriolanus's adult relationship with his mother; and in *Timon of Athens* and *The Famous History of the Life of King Henry the Eighth,* the nature of his subject matter prevents much concern with relations between the generations. But in all of the other plays, the theme is prominent, and in most of them it is dominant. Chapter 2 of this book, "Lear's Age," inaugurates study of the theme by arguing that *King Lear* folds together the concerns of extreme age with those more characteristic of the middle years. At its center is the claim that underlying Lear's relationship with Cordelia is a midlife fantasy of literal rebirth, one in which Cordelia is assigned the role of a surrogate bride in an effort on Lear's part, never consciously acknowledged, at incestuous self-renewal. Building on feminist challenges to earlier humanist interpretations of the play, the chapter asks how far such a de-idealizing reading can be carried, whether even in the scenes of Lear and Cordelia's reunion and in the final death scene we do not detect an inability on Lear's part to release his daughter to a separate existence, and even to understand the full nature of his own anguish. Answering this question in the affirmative, the chapter ends by meditating on the significance of the absence of anagnorisis to interpretation of the play and to an understanding of the relation the play bears to Shakespeare's subsequent career.

The next two chapters, "The River of Blood" and "Cleopatra's Children," carry the study of resistance to generativity in different directions. Starting from the question of why Macbeth persists in the violent course of action initiated with the murder of Duncan, despite its ineffectuality, "The River of Blood" argues that here Shakespeare depicts an even more intransigent struggle against temporal decline than the one depicted in *King Lear.* After establishing two cultural contexts that render repentance problematic for Macbeth—the ambiguities of monarchical succession as depicted in the play and the challenge posed by Protestant reformers to the sacrament of auricular confession—the chapter explores the psychology of resistance enacted in the play's pervasive references to children and childlessness. Agreeing with Robert Watson that in Protestantism generational succession emerges as a substitute form of immortality, I see in *Macbeth* a pervasive skepticism regarding the adequacy of this alternative, rendered, in the failure of

Macbeth's efforts to achieve an alternative immortality through self-creation, as tragedy. In *Antony and Cleopatra,* by contrast, the struggle against generativity moderates, as Shakespeare depicts a longer chronology of midlife experience than in either of the preceding plays. *Antony and Cleopatra* not only depicts experiences that can be interpreted as versions of a midlife crisis, it portrays subsequent attempts to reconstitute identity through the memorialization of lost status and power. Starting from the question of how the play's representations of real and specular children relate to one another, the chapter proceeds through a discussion of performative conceptions of identity to a consideration of the crises themselves and their aftermaths. It ends by returning to the topic of children, reflecting on the relation between the play's emphasis on retrospection and the hopes invested in both Shakespeare's age and our own in generational succession.

Not surprisingly, the final chapter, "Hermione's Wrinkles" explores the turn toward a positive acceptance of generativity characteristic of the late romances. But the terrain to be traversed before this turn can be achieved is arduous. Unlike the other plays examined here, and indeed, unlike any other of Shakespeare's mature plays, *The Winter's Tale* depicts a normative nuclear family, one in which both parents are present and there are multiple children. Yet by the middle of the play, it appears that this family has been entirely destroyed. "Hermione's Wrinkles" explores the psychology at work in Leontes as he brings about that apparent destruction, seeing at the core of his paranoia fantasies of infantile omnipotence, and viewing the death of Mamillius and the expulsion of Perdita as a symbolic enactment of the resistance to generativity that those fantasies logically entail. The chapter then raises the question of why the paranoia emerges when it does, arguing the importance to that emergence of the changed parent-child dynamic implicit in the birth of a second child. Only then does the chapter turn, as the play does, to the journey toward a final reconciliation between Leontes, Perdita, and Hermione. Confronting the objections raised in much recent criticism to positive interpretations of that reconciliation, the chapter ends by finding in Leontes' behavior in the fifth act an abbreviated reenactment, and successful revision, of the fantasy of literal rebirth dramatized in *King Lear.* The study as a whole then ends with an epilogue exploring the further move into generativity in *The Tem-*

pest and the way in which this move is inhibited, but not entirely countermanded, by Prospero's anxieties concerning aging and debility.

Each of the chapters just described places primary emphasis on interpretation of the play under examination as a separate work of art. A subordinate topic is the arc of development by which Shakespeare moves from the resistances of *King Lear* to the resolution of *The Winter's Tale* and *The Tempest.* It is tempting to think of that arc in biographical terms, as a developmental crisis confronted and resolved by Shakespeare himself. But despite some enlightening recent biographically oriented studies—Stephen Greenblatt's *Will in the World,* James Shapiro's *A Year in the Life of William Shakespeare*—the biographical record remains too sparse to allow speculations about Shakespeare's inner life to be voiced with much confidence. And even if that record were fuller, reading the plays in biographical terms risks confusing the thing represented with the act of representation. A better approach, pursued here, is the one recommended by C. L. Barber and Richard Wheeler in their study of Shakespeare's artistic development, of viewing Shakespeare's "art as the endeavor of a human sensibility that can be known only from what the art accomplishes, the directions in which it moves, the recurrent crises it encounters, and the patterns that emerge from the different kinds of artistic resolution by which those crises are mastered."[15] Approached in this fashion, each of the plays under examination in this book can be seen as a stage in a continuing meditation on midlife issues, with each succeeding play affording clarifications and resolutions (and exposing complications) not evident in the preceding plays in the sequence.

In their discussions both of individual plays and of the arc of development relating the plays to one another, the following chapters more often emphasize the distresses of the middle years than their pleasures and successes. In part this emphasis is a matter of temperament, an inclination to see the glass as (at least) half empty. But it is also, and I think more important, a reflex of an ethics of interpretation. The constructivist challenge to the universality of generativity noted above has been advanced in broader terms as a deconstruction of the "naturalness" of the consciousness of decline characteristic, for many people, of the middle years. In the words of Margaret Morganroth Gullette, a leading advocate of this deconstruction, "'the midlife' is a cultural fiction," and belief that entry into the middle years must be accompanied by a fear of finitude and of the onset of debility "is actually a socially constructed disease." In contrast to the view of "aging" as "natural, biological, prenarrativized, ahistorical, [and] universal," Gullette advocates developing alternatives to what she calls the "narrative of decline," ones that emphasize the positive potential for emotional, intellectual, and spiritual growth in the middle years and afterward.[16]

At the heart of Gullette's argument lies a quarrel with the politics of aging in contemporary America, as manifested in social policies and practices and cultural representations. Anyone who has visited a nursing home will, I imagine, share some amount at least of Gullette's indignation; when Old Adam in *As You Like It* speaks of "unregarded age in corners thrown" (2.3.42), he describes a practice not only of Shakespeare's time but of our own. But a nearly exclusive emphasis on aging as a social construction, on the body not as biological but as "biologized," to use Gullette's word, runs the risk of creating its own forms of denial. In their popular manifestations, constructivist challenges to the reality of aging have simply displaced that reality forward in time, so that, as Gail Sheehy says, "Fifty is what 40 used to be" and "Sixty is what 50 used to be."[17] Sooner or later, though, some age will be only itself, and death will happen. Rather than marginalize or downplay the intimations of this prospect as they manifest themselves in the middle years, it seems better to look the Gorgon in the face. In doing so, in acknowledging the fundamentally tragic character of human life in time, we may in fact increase our ability to live happily in concordance with more positive narratives, of which a commitment to generativity is one. It is in service of this belief that the following chapters were written.

2

Lear's Age

I

King Lear, with its insistent emphasis on Lear as advanced in years, on "[n]ature in [him]" as standing at "the very verge / Of his confine" (2.4.147–48), may seem an odd point of entry for a discussion of Shakespeare's mid- and late career representations of the middle years.[1] But a moment's reflection will remind us that Lear's extreme age is occupied with concerns characteristic of a man thirty or so years younger. If Lear is fourscore and upward, not an hour more nor less, his youngest daughter is nonetheless barely of marriageable age; and his other two daughters are young enough to be (it appears) childless and to be imagined as still capable of bearing children. Similarly, the nature of Lear's interactions with his daughters overlays the anxieties of age with those of middle life. In his hope to "[u]nburdened crawl toward death," to "set [his] rest / On [Cordelia's] kind nursery" (1.1.41, 123–24), Lear could be any elderly man intent upon cajoling his most-loved child into caring for him in his dotage. But accompanying this need are sexual and generational conflicts and jealousies more characteristic of a man in his middle than in his declining years. The opening ploy of reserving "[a] third more opulent" (1.1.86) for Cordelia and of favoring Burgundy over France as her prospective husband can be read as an oblique attempt, if not to forestall Cordelia's marriage entirely, at least to ensure that she will remain in Britain and hence within geographical (and emotional) proximity of Lear himself.[2] And in its ferocity, the curse Lear levels against Goneril's fecundity (1.4.274–88) can be read as extending well beyond its immediate provocation, into a rage at the transfer of power and identity implicit in having children old enough to become parents themselves, a rage exacerbated in this instance by the fact that the transfer is not only personal but dynastic.

As these two examples suggest, at the heart of any interpretation of Lear as a middle-aged man *manqué* lie struggles over issues of generativity. Attention to these struggles can augment our understanding of Lear's relations with his daughters, in particular with Cordelia, as they have been interpreted in a number of recent critiques. A strong tradition of feminist- and psychoanalytically oriented criticism has worked to expose the psychic urgencies underlying Lear's scheme to divide the kingdom in a way that will provide Cordelia with "[a] third more opulent" (1.1.86). As Janet Adelman observes in an outstanding contribution to this body of work, in Lear "father and son are collapsed into one figure: for Lear is simultaneously the father who abdicates and the son who must suffer the consequences of this abdication." This doubling of identity, Adelman argues, introduces into the play "the immense fear and longing of a son's relationship with a mother," for when Lear says that he had "thought to set [his] rest / On [Cordelia's] kind nursery" (1.1.123–24), he "revisions as plenitude the death toward which he is crawling, attempting to replace its nothingness with the *all* that fusion with her idealized maternal body seems to promise."[3] But when Cordelia denies this attempt by refusing "[t]o love [her] father all" (1.1.104) and is banished as a result, Lear finds himself subjected instead to a nightmarish alternative version of maternity, as manifested in Goneril and Regan—the daughter-as-mother as a source not of nurture but of deprivation and punishment, of the whippings the Fool envisions when he says "e'er since thou mad'st thy daughters thy mothers . . . thou gav'st them the rod and putt'st down thine own breeches" (1.4.169–71).

Adelman's reading produces strong interpretations of a wide variety of aspects of *King Lear,* ranging from reading the storm as a "sign of the female place of origin" to viewing Lear's obsession with illegitimacy and adultery as an attempt to forestall awareness that he himself is "intolerably implicated in . . . femaleness."[4] But in its reliance on an early-formation approach to psychic development—an approach derived for Adelman more from objects relation theory than from Freud—this reading tends to occlude the midlife dimension of Lear's opening psychodrama. The play begins with a parodic variation on a wedding ceremony, in which the groom-to-be is not only absent from the stage but has not yet been decided upon, and the bride-to-be is asked to express her love not for her future husband but for her father. Both ego psychology and common sense tell us that, for the father, the *form* of a successfully conducted wedding ceremony seeks to reinforce a psychic transference that must take place if the move into generativity is to occur. As Coppélia Kahn observes, the ritual of the father handing his daughter "directly to her husband" "dramatizes the bond between father and daughter even as it marks the severance of that bond."[5] In Eriksonian psychology this transference, if successful, is envisioned as complete and unconflicted. But is it? Can it be? No less than any other concept, parental love can be subjected to deconstructive scrutiny. As Jacques Derrida says, speaking of erotic love but in terms equally applicable to parental love, affection for another cannot provide an experience of unmediated presence "without symbol or suppletory." This is so because "pure presence itself, if such a thing were possible, would only be another name for death. . . . [H]etero-eroticism can be lived . . . only through the ability to reserve within itself its own supplementary protection."[6]

In the parent-child relationship as experienced in the parent's middle years, this supplementary protection takes the form of reserving *from* generativity a desire to undergo rebirth not in the sublimated form of nurturing one's children (and subsequently, it is imagined, future generations of descendants) but directly and literally, as a regeneration of the parental self in its own form. Arguing that Lear displaces the feared nothingness of death into the fantasized "all" of an idealized maternal presence tells only part of the story, for this displacement contains a progressive as well as a retrogressive element. In a landmark essay, Stanley Cavell demonstrates the importance of "the shame of exposure, the threat of self-revelation," to an understanding of Lear's behavior in the play's opening scene. But in characterizing this shame in exclusively ideational and emotional terms, as originating in Lear's inability either to accept or to return love, Cavell declines to locate its source where a materialist psychology teaches us to look: in the body and in bodily manifestations of desire. It may be true, Cavell acknowledges, that Lear's love for Cordelia "is . . . far from plain love of father for daughter"; yet he nonetheless applauds the tendency of readers and spectators to "resist seeing in it the love of lovers." In approving this tendency, Cavell continues a long tradition of humanist criticism (Christian and secular), in which the incestuous impulses underlying Lear's opening love-ritual are acknowledged to exist, but it is argued that in the rest of the play—in Lear's anguished descent into madness and his subsequent regeneration—these impulses are transcended or worked through and resolved.[7]

When viewed from a materialist orientation, by comparison, the cause of Lear's shame can be seen to be somatic as well as psychic. Simon Biggs argues that in viewing the self as capable of continuous reinvention and the past as simply "a metaphor for current concerns," constructivist versions of ego psychology repeat the Eriksonian avoidance of an awareness of finitude. To the extent that individuals involved in a midlife transition see themselves as comprising "youthful potential trapped in an ageing container," Biggs contends, they avoid confronting "experience[s] intrinsic to maturity." "In answer to the question of how age should be thought of," he says, "postmodernity at first denies its relevance, then sees it as a threat to unlimited hedonism." Approached in this way, Lear's journey backward reveals an underlying forward-looking purpose. He seeks to return to infancy not only to shelter there in a timeless fashion but to find a starting point for a movement into a second adulthood, one that can supplant the rapidly depleting existence he is actually experiencing. For Lear, as, one imagines, for most people undergoing a midlife transition, the adult subjectivity concealed inside the Chinese box of generativity can be said to be "authentic" only in its inauthenticity—only, that is, in its adherence to the elemental (if delusive) fantasy that rebirth can be literal. In contrast to the ideal of generativity, which endorses moving forward in time via a sublimated investment in offspring, the rebirth fantasy envisions experiencing again—and possibly even more intensely, because knowingly—both infantile nurture and the pleasures of adulthood.[8]

Because the fantasy of literal rebirth resists releasing one's offspring to their own independent futures, it has at its core an element of incest. When Lear encounters Regan in 2.4, he says, in his only reference to his wife in the play, that he "would divorce me from thy mother's tomb, / Sepulch'ring an adultress," "[i]f thou shouldst not be glad" (2.4.129–31). In a large sense, this divorce has already taken place, for

Lear seeks in his daughters—in Cordelia most of all—not only mothers but brides. Evidence in support of this claim is strewn throughout the middle scenes of the play, in the pattern of shame, guilt, projection, and denial with which Lear addresses issues of sexuality and, specifically, of incest. Shakespeare establishes this pattern at the outset of the storm scenes, as Lear alternates between invoking the storm's assistance in enacting his anger and viewing himself as its victim. The anger, tellingly, is directed toward sexuality, first generally, then specifically, as Lear first demands that the storm "[c]rack nature's molds, all germens spill at once / That makes ingrateful man" (3.2.8–9)—an image which, if taken literally, entails simultaneous sexual climax by all male humanity—then demands that punishment be meted out against "[t]hou perjured, and thou simular of virtue / That art incestuous" (3.2.54–55). The specification of incest in the second of these invocations suggests that Lear is projecting his own illicit urges outward, first onto "ingrateful man," then onto the "simular of virtue." But in twice turning from calling for punishment of sexuality to asserting his own innocence, by describing himself as "[a] poor, infirm, weak, and despised old man" (3.2.20), and as "a man / More sinned against than sinning" (3.2.59–60), Lear persists in denial, resisting awareness of the urges that his examples suggest he possesses.

This pattern of projection and denial continues, even accelerates, throughout the subsequent storm and mad scenes. If we ask why Lear takes Poor Tom to be his "philosopher" and insists on remaining in his company, a plausible answer can be found in Poor Tom's response to Lear's question, when first they meet, "[w]hat hast thou been" (3.4.83). That response, combining as it does a fictional history of Poor Tom's having "served the lust of my mistress' heart" with moralizing injunctions to "[l]et not the creaking of shoes nor the rustling of silks betray thy poor heart to woman" (3.4.85–86, 93–95), speaks to both halves of Lear's struggle: it provides expert information, instruction as it were, in how to enact illicit passion while at the same time enjoining against doing so. It is worth noting, in fact, that Lear's question, "[w]hat hast thou been," is provoked by a brief speech of Poor Tom's that contains the admonition "commit not with man's sworn spouse" (3.4.80–81)—an admonition which, like all mentions of adultery in the play, can have personal reference for Lear only in relation to his daughters, since the play contains no other "sworn spouse," indeed, no other female character with whom an illicit sexual liaison could be imagined to occur.

Throughout the remainder of the encounter with Poor Tom, Lear's struggle over his illicit desires is alluded to in such sly sexual innuendoes as the Fool's comparison of "a little fire in a wild field" to an "old lecher's heart" (3.4.110–111) and his joke that Bessy's "boat hath a leak" (3.6.26).[9] When Lear returns to the stage after the long absence between 3.6 and 4.6, this struggle resumes with startling intensity, as if both the repressed desire and the need for its repression had grown to unmanageable proportions. The topic of illicit sexuality reemerges here in a personalized form, with Lear veering between invoking his kingly authority to legitimate adultery—"Die for adultery? No./The wren goes to 't, and the small gilded fly/Does lecher in my sight" (4.6.111–13)—and using that same authority to command the beadle whom he imagines as whipping a whore to "hold thy bloody hand" because "[t]hou hotly lusts to use her in that kind/For which thou whipp'st her" (4.6.160–63). Simultaneously, his imagination focuses on the physical site (from a heterosexual male point of view) of desire and denial, for when he calls for "an ounce of civet" to "sweeten [his] imagination," the image he seeks to expunge from his mind is of "the sulfurous pit, burning, scalding, stench, consumption" that lies beneath "the girdle" of the "simpering dame"—Goneril? Regan? Cordelia? Lear himself in a projective act of self-rejection?—who "minces virtue and does shake the head/To hear of pleasure's name," yet in comparison to whom not even "[t]he fitchew nor the soilèd horse goes to 't/With a more riotous appetite" (4.6.131, 128–29, 118–23). Hence it is reasonable to believe that when Lear exits this scene running, he is attempting to escape less from his supposed captors than from himself. And it is surely significant, as evidence that this effort is not succeeding, that he ends the scene claiming, in a notorious use of the "die" pun, that he "will die bravely, like a smug bridegroom" (4.6.198).[10]

II

How thoroughly does Lear's fantasy of incestuous self-renewal inhabit the text and meaning of *King Lear?* Is it present not only in the opening scene of the division of the kingdom and in the storm and mad scenes, but subsequently, in the reunion scene and its aftermath? I believe that the fantasy *is* present in those scenes, to an extent and in a fashion that should profoundly affect our interpretation of their significance. To show how this is so, I need to reflect for a bit on the role Cordelia occupies in relation to her father, primarily in the reunion scene and afterward, but also earlier. In the long tradition of humanist critiques, Lear's awakening in Cordelia's presence, his subsequent "[c]ome, let's away to prison" speech, and his anguished attempt to deny the reality of Cordelia's death have called forth an extraordinary, often very deeply moving, affirmation of the value of transcendence and spiritual regeneration. "In the scene of his reunion with Cordelia," says G. Wilson Knight, "[Lear] wakes to music, like a mortal soul waking to immortality, to find his daughter bright as 'a soul in bliss'; now both find the richness of love more rich for the interval of agony, misunderstanding, intolerance." "Cordelia dies," says Michael Holahan, in a recent commentary, "so that Lear can learn familial love." "The quality of [Cordelia's] voice," he says, "has passed to Lear as an authoritative sign of her rule in his ethical growth. . . . The value *of* Cordelia is now a function *in* Lear's speech, a last 'trick of that voice.'" As for Lear himself, he dies, says Maynard Mack in a memorable locution, "with his whole being launched toward another." "[W]hat we are and may be," Mack says, asserting the memorability of the play itself, "was never . . . more memorably fixed upon a stage than in this kneeling old man whose heartbreak is precisely the measure of what, in our world of relatedness, it is possible to lose and possible to win."[11]

The power of this rhetoric bespeaks a corresponding power in the play itself, one for which ample textual evidence can easily be found: to cite examples only from the awakening scene and earlier, we find such evidence in the Gentleman's description of Cordelia's tears as "holy water from her heavenly eyes" (4.3.31; quarto only); in the echo of Luke 2:49 in Cordelia's "O dear Father, / It is thy business that I go about" (4.4.23–24); in the humility of Lear's attempt to kneel and in his referring to himself not as king but as "a very foolish, fond old man, / Fourscore and upward" (4.7.61–62); in Cordelia's "[n]o cause, no cause" (4.7.78) in response to Lear's claim that she has reason not to love him; and in Lear's pathos-laden scene-ending request, "[p]ray you now, forget and forgive" (4.7.89). Over the span of the last thirty years, however, cultural materialist, psychoanalytic, and (especially) feminist critics have mounted an equally powerful counterargument. No longer willing to accede to the humanist dictum, as expressed by Paul Jorgensen, that "even we that are young see the whole [drama of self-discovery] through Lear's aged and bewildered eyes," postmodern critics have called into question the patriarchal and masculinist presuppositions underlying this way of reading the play. Feminist critics in particular have reoriented critical interpretation toward an awareness, in Lynda Boose's words, of "the cost of both the daughter's life and of the future life of the family" that accompanies "the beauty of Lear's reunion with Cordelia." Similarly, after calling attention to the Gentleman's characterization of Cordelia as the "one daughter / Who redeems nature from the general curse / Which twain have brought her to" (4.6.205–7), Janet Adelman argues that while Cordelia is "remade as the second Eve, the Virgin Mother who can undo harm," this can only happen "insofar as [Cordelia] gives up every sign of the marital sexuality that had epitomized her disturbing otherness in 1.1, the sexuality that in effect mobilized Lear's fantasy-creation of [Goneril and Regan as] the malevolent mother."[12]

For a time, and to considerable degree still, these contending claims created an impasse in interpretations of *King Lear,* as commentators hesitated, like Balaam's ass, between the twin imperatives of acknowledging the play's artistic power and of resisting its apparent political and ethical obtuseness. For some materialist feminist critics, most notably Kathleen McLuskie in an influential and wide-ranging essay, commitment to a belief that "the alternative to the patriarchal family and heterosexual love is not chaos but the possibility of new forms of social organization" requires that the interpretative impasse be resolved in favor of resistance to the play's emotional appeal. Acknowledging that not even "the most stony-hearted feminist could . . . withhold her pity" from the scene of Lear's entry "bearing his dead daughter in his arms," McLuskie nonetheless argues that "feminist criticism must . . . assert the power of resistance, subverting rather than co-opting the domination of the patriarchal Bard." "Feminist criticism of this play," she says, referring to *Measure for Measure* but foreshadowing her discussion of *King Lear,* "is restricted to exposing its own exclusion from the text." "A feminist reading of [*Lear*]," she argues, cannot even be content with "assert[ing] the countervailing rights of Goneril and Regan, for to do so would simply reverse the emotional structure of the play, associating feminist ideology with atavistic selfishness and the monstrous assertion of individual wills."[13]

In contrast to McLuskie, Janet Adelman, in what Kiernan Ryan characterizes as "a bold final twist of her argument," "refuses," in his words, "to gender as exclusively male a mother-complex by which women, including Adelman herself, are just as afflicted as men." In Adelman's own words, "[e]ven while I understand the urgency of Cordelia's refusal to be all to her father, I share with Lear—and with Shakespeare—the stratum of desire that brings her back all his. . . . For I too inhabit the terror of finitude and the desire for merger with the infinitely kind nursery that can undo the pain of separation; I too long for her return." These are indeed bold, and, I would add, generous words. In refusing to "mobilize anger against both the fathers—literal and literary—that require Cordelia's sacrifice," Adelman avoids what Ann Thompson, herself a feminist, identifies as "some sort of dead end for feminism" in McLuskie's radical intransigence. Yet as Adelman's interpolated phrase—"and with Shakespeare"—indicates, she too accedes to the belief that Shakespeare is the patriarchal bard, for "at the same time that Shakespeare seems to analyze Lear's need, and hence to distance himself from it, his representation of Cordelia is deeply complicit with that need. . . . Shakespeare too requires the sacrifice of [Cordelia's] autonomy." Calling this a "very painful recognition . . . for any reader who reads as a daughter," Adelman argues that the primary task for feminist critics of *King Lear* "is simultaneously to acknowledge this place of common need [i.e., for infantile nurture] and to measure its cost to the woman forced to bear its burden."[14]

In discussing her own entanglement in Lear's fantasy of infantile nurture, Adelman engages in one of the characteristic practices of postmodern criticism, for a fundamental tenet of postmodern theory is that the positionality of the interpreter is always implicated in the act of interpretation.[15] Because Adelman reads as a daughter and as a feminist, she understandably does not explore the question that troubles the edges of all male-centered interpretations of *King Lear,* including this one: what it means to identify with Lear in his need for Cordelia not only as mother but as bride. There is, however, a further, daughter-oriented question that deserves to be posed, one that Adelman could have raised, had she wished, but did not. In her willingness to identify across gender lines, Adelman interprets Cordelia's role in the play exclusively in external terms, viewing Cordelia as the object successively of Lear's, then of Shakespeare's, and finally of her own desire. She asks what it means to *need* Cordelia as the embodiment of unstinting nurture; she does not ask what it means to *be* Cordelia—what it means, that is, to accord Cordelia agency as a character in her own right and to explore the opportunities, and perils, for identification that understanding Cordelia in this fashion affords female and (in a different way) male spectators and readers.

Evidence for the importance of this question to an interpretation of the Lear-Cordelia dyad can be found in a seemingly remote location: Janet Bottoms's study of the ways in which nineteenth-century editors and adapters of Shakespeare turned "Cordelia into a heroine for girls." Recognizing the limited opportunities for identification afforded by *King Lear* to female readers, these commentators drew out of the play a moral about the importance of female filial piety. If even Cordelia's "well-intentioned deviation from absolute submission could produce . . . anarchy," they argued, "must not unquestioning filial obedience . . . be a girl's first duty?" And in Cordelia's "redemptive martyrdom, . . . feminine delicacy[,] and modest reserve," these commentators claimed to have discovered the best model for girlish emulation in the entire roster of Shakespeare's female characters. Furthermore, as Bottoms herself argues, this effort at ethical instruction appears to have been successful, for identification with Cordelia as "the impersonation and the symbol of perfect love," was evidently not only imposed on Victorian young women from without but was responded to from within. Agreeing with Sally Mitchell in her observation that a "'fantasy of martyrdom and posthumous vindication' . . . holds a strong attraction for women in a patriarchal society," Bottoms concludes that "[t]he suffering Cordelia, who sacrifices her personal security and happiness" to her filial obligations "was well suited to the psychological fantasy needs of dutiful Victorian daughters."[16]

Because Bottoms's essay is primarily a reception study, she does not explore the extent to which the fantasy of redemptive martyrdom might meet Cordelia's needs as a character no less than those of youthful female members of the play's audience. In a provocative reading of *King Lear,* Harry Berger Jr. examines exactly this issue. Accepting with radical thoroughness Coleridge's dictum that Shakespeare's characters always speak "in character," and that they are therefore liable to being misunderstood not only by other characters but by themselves, Berger explores "the social resources available to self-deception" in *King Lear.* "How," he asks, do the play's characters "*use* the roles and relationships of love, courtship, and marriage, of family, court, and kingdom, of race, religion, and gender, to validate their pursuits of power or pleasure or pain or self-interest or love?" Arguing that any Shakespeare play "may offer the audience a model of the ethical range [occupied by its characters] that differs from any particular character's version of it," Berger says that "[a]t the ethical poles of *King Lear* are two scenarios": one in which "the mixed and good characters try to make others and themselves believe 'I am more sinned against than sinning,'" another in which "[t]he bad characters try to make others and themselves believe 'I am more sinning than sinned against.'" Claiming that whenever a "character pledges allegiance to one of these two scenarios, his [or her] language betrays the presence of the second," Berger asserts that the language of the play consistently reveals "the complementary pressures of a self-justifying function and a scapegoating function," as "characters . . . avoid recognizing their own contributions to the difficulties they face, while magnifying the complicity of others."[17]

Applying this line of interpretation to Cordelia allows Berger to resolve to his own (and to my) satisfaction the question of whether her behavior throughout the play is psychologically self-consistent. In her obduracy in 1.1 and her selflessness in 4.4, 4.7, and 5.3, Berger detects a young woman maneuvering as best she can among the limited and dysfunctional options afforded her by her role in what he calls "the Lear family romance." "[T]he thought of Lear's setting his rest on her kind nursery," he says, "must surely be oppressive to [Cordelia], though she is not likely to admit it to herself." Hence "she [presumably] would like to break free of the parental bondage . . . if she could find a way to do it that wouldn't jeopardize her self-respect and her sense of obligation to [her father]." And she "*does* find a way" when "she senses the value of the victim's role" in her asides after her sisters' protestations of love. By choosing to "[l]ove and be silent," to think of herself as "poor Cordelia," and to mimic Lear's own flawed understanding of the nature of love in her assertion that the "lord whose hand must take my plight shall carry / Half my love with him, half my care and duty" (1.1.62, 76, 101–2), Cordelia discovers a way to "renounce, without really renouncing, the name and additions of daughter."[18]

This renunciation, however, carries with it an element of unacknowledged guilt, insofar as it makes Cordelia complicit in relegating Lear to Goneril's and Regan's "professèd bosoms" and to the suffering that follows, even though, as she says to her sisters when leaving, "I know you what you are" (1.1.276, 273). Hence when she returns in the fourth act, she faces the problem of how to situate herself emotionally in relation to the consequences of her prior behavior. Although, as Berger says, "[w]hen [Cordelia] returns . . . her language remains—unlike Lear's—pure of conflicting voices," it is nonetheless possible to detect in her statements and in her actions an effort to protect herself against an awareness of her role in contributing to her father's suffering. Her careful rehearsal of her good intentions in 4.4—"O dear Father, / It is thy business that I go about / . . . . / No blown ambition doth our arms incite, / But love, dear love, and our aged father's right" (4.4.23–28)—can be read, Berger argues, as "part of her persistent habit of publishing her unpublished virtues." In denying any personal political motivation and in echoing Christ's words in Luke 2:49, Cordelia presents herself, he says, "as a merciful redeemer, one who was more sinned against than sinning but [one who has] forgiven her tormentors and [who] now returns to restore them from their crimes and woes." And in her "[n]o cause, no cause" in the reunion scene (4.7.78), Cordelia simultaneously expresses her deep affection for her father and "triumphantly refine[s] the victim's role to a Christlike perfection," for denying that any cause exists for her not to love her father allows her to ignore not only what he did to her but what she did to him. Like Isabella in *Measure for Measure,* a character she in many ways resembles, Cordelia is not a saint. She is a young woman who for good and sufficient cause chooses to act as if she were one.[19]

III

Ascribing agency to Cordelia does not exempt Shakespeare from the charge of complicity directed at him by Adelman and others, for there is a politics of genre no less than of character and theme. It is Shakespeare, not Cordelia, who chooses to rewrite the Lear story as tragedy and who ends the play, in contradiction to earlier versions of the story, with Cordelia's death, rather than with her and her father's reconciliation.[20] Nonetheless, asserting that the role of redemptive martyr is not only assigned *to* Cordelia but is internalized *by* her affords an important advantage to the argument under development here, for it clears the way for a de-idealized and sexualized reading of Cordelia and Lear's reunion and its aftermath. If Cordelia is simply the passive embodiment of an ascribed identity, whether as innocently-loved-and-loving daughter, beneficent mother, or bride, then Lear's awakening to their reunion faces no obstacle internal to her being. However touching in its enactment, their reconciliation consists merely of a movement toward the predetermined goal of Cordelia's renunciatory "[n]o cause, no cause." But if Cordelia is not a saint but a young woman enacting saintliness, then Lear does not awaken to a situation in which he can simply accept his daughter's unstinting love, now miraculously made available to him by authorial fiat. He awakens instead to a situation in which he (or he and Cordelia together) must seduce that love into being.

The sense that Lear is engaged in an effort at fatherly seduction emerges first in the reunion scene, then again, more strongly, in the "[c]ome, let's away to prison" sequence. Humanist commentators, committed to a view of Lear as struggling painfully but successfully toward ethical and emotional regeneration, emphasize the symbolic elements of 4.7, finding evidence in various details—Lear's "heaviness of sleep" and "fresh garments" and (in quarto only) the presence of the Doctor and the playing of music—that Lear has undergone a character-altering experience of death and rebirth. But the fundamental argument of this chapter, that Lear's effort at "rebirth" enacts a malign form of midlife fantasy, leads me to question both the extent and the innocence of this transformation. Also, in the style of reading I am using here the scene's symbolic elements, while not unimportant, must be weighed in the balance against more mundane considerations. Lear awakens newly clothed, yes, and perhaps to the playing of music. But he awakens also uncertain of where he is and in the company of a daughter he has not seen since he banished her and who he has no reason to suppose will behave any differently toward him now than before. He awakens as well to a recurrence of the fear that he will lose (now has lost), through marriage, the "all" of Cordelia's love. For at the core of his four-times-reiterated uncertainty about "[w]hat place this is" stands its culminating question, "Am I in France?" (4.7.67, 79)—am I, that is, in the place where the love I wished to retain for myself is now claimed by another. Similarly, when he says "[m]ethinks I should know you, and know this man" (4.7.65), his seemingly inconsequent mention of "this man"—in fact either the Gentleman or the Doctor—gains significance if we assume that he may be imagining, and fearing, that Cordelia's companion is France himself, her husband.

These considerations produce in Lear a form of behavior—a performance of debility—found only once elsewhere in the play, in his half-scornful, half-fearful kneeling before Regan in 2.4. It is puzzling why so many commentators are eager to see a breakthrough in understanding in Lear's self-characterizations in the reunion scene. Certainly there is a newfound access to humility here. But accompanying this humility is a series of self-descriptions—"I am a very foolish fond old man"; "I fear I am not in my perfect mind"; "I am old and foolish" (4.7.61, 64, 90)—that differ little if at all from Lear's earlier scornful "[d]ear daughter, I confess that I am old; / Age is unnecessary" or Regan's cold-hearted "I pray you, Father, being weak, seem so" (2.4.154–55, 202). There is an implicit ageism in the assumption that Lear's breakthrough in understanding need consist of nothing more than an acknowledgment of his frailty.[21] Equally to the point is the fact that this self-characterization stands in sharp contrast to Lear's self-representations everywhere else in the play, including the scenes surrounding the reunion scene. In 4.6, just prior to the reunion scene, Lear imagines himself as capable of engaging in a duel in which he will "prove it on a giant" and of stealing upon "these son-in-laws" in order to "kill, kill, kill, kill, kill, kill" (4.6.90, 186–87). And in his two subsequent appearances, both occurring in the play's final scene, he first depicts himself as capable of resisting those who would seek to separate him from Cordelia, then exhibits sufficient strength to carry her dead or dying body on stage unaided, then pauses during his anguish to proclaim that he "killed the slave that was a-hanging [her]" and to take pride in his former prowess with his "good biting falchion" (5.3.279, 281).

Viewed in this light, Lear's self-characterization in the reunion scene, however authentic as a newfound access to humility, can also be seen as strategic. Bereft of his foolish former assumption that his older daughters, themselves unloved, will nonetheless love and care for him as he wishes, he awakens to the uncertain prospect of a reunion with his rejected younger daughter. And Cordelia's behavior at the outset of the scene compounds this uncertainty, for as Alexander Leggatt observes, Cordelia exhibits "a moment of shyness at Lear's waking. As he sleeps she kisses him and speaks eloquently of her pity. . . . But when he wakes her first impulse is to ask her attendant to speak to him, and [the attendant] has to tell her, 'Madam, do you; 'tis fittest'" (4.7.44). Similarly, while Cordelia refers to Lear in his absence and while he is still asleep in affectionate, daughterly terms, as "this child-changèd father" and "my dear Father" and "poor Father" (4.7.17, 27, 39), in all of her speeches after he awakens, her references are always to his identity as king, not as father—"royal lord," "[y]our Majesty," "[s]ir," "sir," "sir," "[y]our Highness," "oppressèd King" (4.7.45 [2], 49, 58, 80, 87, 5.3.5). Hence Lear must present himself in a self-denigrating fashion that disarms this formality of reference and that solicits the pity that we have heard Cordelia express, but he has not. As C. L. Barber and Richard Wheeler observe, Lear thus "compels by his helplessness what he has been unable to command from his daughter by his power." But he does so at no little cost to a full, true self-understanding, for as Leggatt says, Lear's "'old and foolish' does not quite sum up the character we have seen or the reasons he needs forgiveness."[22]

The darker reasons for that need—Lear's hidden desire to make Cordelia his mother and his bride—are latent presences in the reunion scene, evident primarily in Lear's sidelong anxiety about his (and France's) whereabouts. In the "[c]ome, let's away to prison" sequence, these impulses emerge more strongly. At the center of the speech with which Cordelia opens the scene lies an ambiguity consistent with an interpretation of her as a character possessing independent agency. "We are not the first," she says, "[w]ho with best meaning have incurred the worst. / For thee, oppressèd King, I am cast down; / Myself could else outfrown false Fortune's frown" (5.3.3–6). "For thee," one asks, in what sense of the phrase? In the sense of "in your service," as your selfless and loving daughter? Or in the sense of "because of you," as the victim of your folly? The urgency of Lear's rejoinder, "[n]o, no, no, no!"

(5.3.8), suggests a desperate effort to forestall the second of these possibilities. As Adelman observes, Lear's intervention effectively silences Cordelia, who never speaks again in the play, a fact that lends symbolic weight to the choking off of "her potentially troublesome voice" by strangulation when she is hanged. As Adelman also observes, the fantasy that Lear constructs further forestalls Cordelia's independence, substituting for the "thee" and "I" of her "[f]or thee, oppressèd King, I am cast down" the "we" of "[w]e two alone will sing like birds i' the cage" (5.3.5, 9). Also, as several commentators have noted, Lear's image of his and Cordelia's life together in prison works against his daughter's independence in yet another fashion, for his "[w]e two alone" excludes France just as surely as it does those who have just defeated Cordelia's army.[23]

For Adelman, Lear's prison fantasy reenacts his "dream of maternal plenitude," for by "[r]ecasting the walled prison in the image of the walled garden, complete with birds and butterflies, Lear in effect transforms it into a spatialized form of the unfallen maternal body." This reading should be augmented by an awareness that the prison fantasy also embodies Lear's dream of incestuous self-renewal, for as Alan Dundes observed some years ago, the birds in Lear's "birds i' the cage" can plausibly be interpreted as lovebirds. The implicit sexualization of this image of Lear and Cordelia alone in joy together continues throughout the remainder of the "away to prison" speech, masqueraded as childlike innocence. Few observers of the play, I imagine, have failed to be at least momentarily surprised by the examples Lear provides of the activities in which he and Cordelia will engage during their life in prison. Why this sudden interest in "[w]ho loses and who wins; who's in, who's out" (5.3.15)—this from a man whose former "out" consisted of the "[h]ence, and avoid my sight!" (1.1.124) of banishment, and whose "in" consisted of the belief that his own monarchical identity was indestructible? And what court is this, in reference to which Lear and Cordelia will "laugh / At gilded butterflies, and hear poor rogues / Talk of court news" (5.3.12–14)? Is it Lear's own court, mentioned by him at the outset of the play, when he says that "France and Burgundy / . . . / Long in our court have made their amorous sojourn"(1.1.46)? Or is it Goneril's and Regan's courts, one of which is mentioned by Goneril when she says that because of the "debauched and bold" behavior of Lear's hundred knights "this our court . . . / Shows like a riotous inn" (1.4.239–41)? Or is it perhaps yet another court, never directly mentioned in the play but present nonetheless, the one in France that Cordelia left to return to her father's aid?[24]

Among these options, the most plausible referent for Lear's comments would seem to be the courts of his elder two daughters, for it is there that the forms of activity Lear alludes to are depicted—the Oswald-like affectation of the "gilded butterflies," the "ebb and flow" of status seen in Edmund's rise and in Albany's resistance to his rise. But the likelihood of a consciousness as well on Lear's part of the court Cordelia recently has left should not be dismissed. Lear has no direct knowledge of the intrigues that have taken place in Goneril's and Regan's courts, except to the extent that he might have noticed something—an unseemly closeness between Oswald and Goneril, for example—during the time that he sojourned with his eldest daughter.[25] But he does have access to information about courtly behavior from another source: his conversations with Poor Tom, a dim memory of which may be present in his characterization of the conveyors of "court news" as "poor rogues" (5.3.14, 13).[26] And that information, we recall, focused on the prevalence in courtly settings of sexual licentiousness, of how Poor Tom, when a "servingman, . . . served the lust of my mistress' heart, and did the act of darkness with her" (3.4.84–87). Folding together these considerations, one arrives at an interpretation of the prison fantasy as a continuation of Lear's dream of incestuous self-renewal, under the guise of an offer of recompense to Cordelia for the losses she has suffered as a result of her having been "cast down." You have lost your husband, the speech says in effect, but you have me instead. You have lost the innocent pleasures of your life in the French court, but I give you in their place the innocent pleasures of our praying and singing and telling old tales. And should the pleasures you have lost prove over time not to be so innocent, should you develop into a simpering dame like your sisters, a mistress the lust of whose heart needs to be served, well, then too, you have me.

IV

As with the reunion and the prison scenes, so with Lear's final encounter with the dead or dying Cordelia. Lear's entry with Cordelia in his arms has been called by Barber and Wheeler "a Pietà with the roles reversed, not Holy Mother with her dead Son, but father with his dead daughter"; but as Adelman observes, the image can also be read as Lear carrying "the dead Cordelia onto the stage like a bridegroom carrying his bride." Looming behind these opposed but equally plausible interpretations is a larger air of undecidability and irresolution, "a radical instability," in R. A. Foakes's words, "that permits no confidence in any particular reading." We cannot know with certainty whether Cordelia is already dead at the beginning of the scene or momentarily revives; we cannot know (although a choice must necessarily be made in performance) whose button Lear asks to have unfastened, or who performs this service; most important, we cannot know whether Lear dies believing Cordelia to still be alive or shattered by an awareness that she is in fact dead. Because of these and similar uncertainties—is the feather real and does it stir, does Lear recognize Kent, is Lear deluded in believing that Cordelia speaks, does "my poor fool is hanged" refer to Cordelia, to the Fool, or to both?—Lear's state at the moment of his death invites, and has received, an extraordinarily wide range of interpretations. As Thomas Clayton observes, "[t]his state may be seen . . . as clinical senility . . . , as childlike—or childish—innocence, as grace through forgiveness, as age transfigured by traces of the white radiance of eternity, or as a moment of simple—and fleeting—reunion and reconciliation." So too with the overall effect of the play, which seems to hold in unresolved opposition affirmative and despairing meanings, A. C. Bradley's claim that Lear dies in "unbearable *joy,*" Judah Stampfer's claim that the play invites its audience to believe "that we inhabit an imbecile universe."[27]

To this range of interpretations the argument advanced here adds the likelihood that even in his moment of maximum agony, as he confronts what in *Antony and Cleopatra* is called "the very heart of loss" (4.12.29), Lear does not break free of his dream of incestuous self-renewal. In *Shakespeare's Bawdy,* Eric Partridge cites Lear's "I will die bravely, like a smug bridegroom" (4.6.198) as one of two examples of Shakespeare's use of "die" to mean "experience a sexual orgasm." He does *not* cite Lear's statement at the outset of the death scene, "I know when one is dead and when one lives; / She's dead as earth" (5.3.265–66), as containing a similar allusion; nor, so far as I know, does any other commentator. This absence is understandable, for the literal meaning of the statement is far from erotic. But the statement is metaphoric as well as literal, invoking the overarching question of whether Lear even yet understands the nature of life and death and the limited extent to which it is possible to be "reborn."[28] And a moment's reflection will remind us of how freely Shakespeare avails himself of variations on the "die" pun in those of his death scenes that explicitly involve romantic lovers: in Romeo's question in Juliet's tomb, "Shall I believe / That unsubstantial Death is amorous, / And that the lean abhorrèd monster keeps / Thee here in dark to be his paramour" (5.3.102–5); in Othello's smothering of Desdemona on their nuptial bed, a bed on which Emilia has lain, by Desdemona's own command, the "wedding sheets" (4.2.109); in the Clown's extended double-entendre byplay with Cleopatra as she prepares for her highly eroticized suicide, byplay concerning "the pretty worm of Nilus" from whose bite "[t]hose that do die of it do seldom or never recover" (5.2.243, 247–48).

Armed with this reminder, we are enabled to see not only Lear's "I know when one is dead and when one lives" but the final moments of the death sequence as well as containing a libidinal undertone. Hearing Lear's "[p]ray you, undo this button," Berger says that he thinks not only of "Lear's earlier '[o]ff, off you lendings! Come, unbutton here'" (3.4.107–8) but of "the smug and incestuous bridegroom" (4.6.198), as if Lear were disrobing either himself or Cordelia for a marital bed. So also with Lear's final outcry, "Do you see this? Look on her, look, her lips, / Look there, look there!" (5.3.316–17; folio only). If we wish to believe, with A. C. Bradley, that Lear dies in "unbearable *joy*," with "his whole being," in Maynard Mack's phrase, "launched toward another," how innocently shall we interpret that joy and that discovery of the importance of human relatedness? Does not our present skepticism concerning idealizing readings incline us to see what Keats calls "the fierce dispute / Betwixt damnation and impassion'd clay" as continuing even in this final moment? As Lear gazes down on Cordelia's lips (her "ripe lip," as the Gentleman earlier describes it [4.3.20; quarto only]) and, I am compelled to imagine, on her now-unbuttoned bodice, his urgent desire that his daughter continue to live should not be segregated from what Barbara Everett calls "his infinitely pathetic threnody for his own waning powers." Even here, as Lear resists awareness of

Cordelia's finitude, he continues to resist awareness of his own. And as he gazes down at Cordelia, his joy, if it be joy, remains contaminated by an element of scopophiliac (and now perhaps necrophiliac) incestuous yearning.[29]

V

And yet . . . after such knowledge, what forgiveness? I have taught *King Lear* for nearly forty years, and for the first twenty-five or so of those years, I situated my class presentations quite firmly inside the humanist paradigm, often teaching the reconciliation and death scenes with tears in my eyes and always with as much emotional and rhetorical force as I could muster. In the subsequent fifteen years, the reading I have just advanced developed quite slowly and confusedly, as if it were emerging from behind a strong wall of internal resistance. Insofar as I understand its causes, this resistance stems from a reluctance to lose the profound experience of catharsis that the humanist reading had afforded me (and, in many instances, I know, my students). And that catharsis was fated to be lost, it seemed to me, because the reading I was developing simply reenacted in a different set of terms the Balaam's-ass dilemma mentioned above, in which contemporary trends in interpretation hesitate over the choice between beauty and truth, between appreciating the play's artistic power and challenging its political and ethical implications. Why, after all, should spectators and readers—most immediately, myself and my students—continue to be moved by Lear's anguish, if his quest for personal self-renewal not only wreaks such havoc but remains unassuaged even at the moment of his own and his daughters' deaths?

There is some comfort in knowing that I am not alone in my ambivalence and feelings of resistance. In a footnote, Adelman speaks of the "intense anxiety and guilt" caused by her "standing aside from this most patriarchal text . . . as though by that gesture [she] was attempting to kill not only Shakespeare but all the much-loved fathers who first gave him to [her]." Speaking more broadly and impersonally, A. D. Nuttall explores a similar response. Commenting on the absence of anagnorisis in the play (particularly in the folio version), the sense provided by Lear's final "Do you see this? Look on her, look, her lips, / Look there, look there!" (5.3.316–17; folio only) that he dies "an uncomprehending death," Nuttall asks, bluntly, "What, then, can be the pleasure of *this* tragedy?" Citing with sympathy Dr. Johnson's and Tolstoy's reservations about the play, Nuttall considers the possibility "that there is a short answer to [his] question, namely that this is a great work but it does not please; it hurts too much." And while he himself ultimately rejects this answer, he terms Dr. Johnson's shock at Cordelia's death and his reluctance to reread the play "a wholly *honourable* response," one that he respects more than "much facile praise which has been set down since the time of Johnson."[30]

It may be, then, that Lear's inability to abandon his fantasy of incestuous self-renewal is simply one more of the many ways in which, as Stephen Booth says, "the impossibility of finality permeates the play." Yet I wish to resist this conclusion. Underlying my reluctance to let go of the experience of catharsis afforded by a humanist interpretation of *King Lear* may be a resistance to acknowledging my own implication in the fantasy of entire rebirth and in the modes of generational and sexual imperialism implicit in its pursuit. Because my wife and I have no daughters, I had imagined myself to be exempt from Lear's emotional dilemma, only to discover, when our older son married, that the wish to retain the "all" of a child's affection is not gender-specific. Working my way through and beyond this surprising (and humbling) discovery was difficult, but doing so had the benefit not only of enriching my relationship with my son and daughter-in-law but of enhancing my understanding of the ways in which "incest" is not only a subject of fantasy and a fact of behavior but a trope. And it had the benefit as well of allowing me to understand generativity—both the concept itself and my own experience of it—not as a state but as a process, one fated, it appears, never to be unambiguously completed.[31]

It is worth bearing in mind that the incestuous feelings Lear exhibits toward Cordelia are not *wrong*. What is *wrong* is the behavior he engages in as a consequence of those feelings. And it is worth bearing in mind as well that Lear does undergo profound ethical and emotional growth: as is so often observed, the "[t]hank you, sir" that follows his "[p]ray you, undo this button" (5.3.314) "are not the words of a despot accustomed only to giving orders . . . but the words . . . of a man who can now feel gratitude for the humblest service he would once have taken for granted."[32] Finally, it is worth insisting on the interdependence of these observations. In adult development no less than in development occurring during childhood, the oedipal struggle cannot be successfully resolved through either repression or transcendence. Here, as always, ethical growth originates in libidinal desire, in our necessary habitation inside what Yeats calls the foul rag-and-bone shop of the heart. Only because Lear desires so strongly is he able to change so profoundly. But the frustration of the play, its clotted, surging, baffled quality, particularly when considered in developmental terms, is that this painfully acquired growth occurs only intermittently and at a tangent to the paramount concern of Lear's relations with Cordelia and with his other two daughters. As Stanley Cavell says, the play shows "that the *reason* consequences furiously hunt us down is . . . that we go on doing the thing which produced these consequences in the first place. What we need is not rebirth, or salvation, but the courage, or plain prudence, to see and to stop." This lesson Lear only incompletely learns. We learn it more fully, if in fact we do (or can), only by watching him fail to do so.[33]

King Lear, though, is one play, not an entire corpus. Shakespeare's decision to fold together the concerns of advanced age with those of the middle years allows the first of these chronologies to reinforce the second, as if Lear's nearness to death were a lens magnifying the play's concern with a midlife fear of finitude. But this symbolic intensification also narrows the play's range of social representation. One need not agree with A. C. Bradley's claim that the play is "too huge for the stage" to nonetheless see some justice in his comments about "the vagueness of the scene where the action takes place, and of the movements of the figures which cross this scene." In relation to the topic explored here, this vagueness consists of a relative absence of depictions of dimensions of midlife experience *other than* the fantasy of literal rebirth. We see in Goneril and Regan's competition for Edmund a behavior that can plausibly be thought of as a sexual reflex of midlife discontent. And in the Gloucester subplot, we see the main plot's relations between parent and child enacted in a different form, as Gloucester's anxiety over the possibility that Edgar intends to usurp his power. But other dimensions of midlife experience remain unrepresented. In Shakespeare's subsequent engagements with the dilemmas and challenges of the middle years, his attention turns to several of these dimensions: the relation between guilt, denial, marriage, and violence; the texture of life subsequent to the midlife crisis; the psychodynamics of the nuclear family. To see how this is so, we need next to consider a play whose central character, we are told, "has no children." We need to consider *Macbeth*.[34]

3
The River of Blood

How much freedom of choice does Macbeth have, once he has murdered Duncan? Macbeth's own characteristic answer to this question is that he has only one option, which is to continue in the bloody course that the murder initiated. If the first murder did not work, in the sense of making him "perfect, / Whole as the marble, founded as the rock, / As broad and general as the casing air" (3.4.21–23), then perhaps more murders will. "Things bad begun," he says, anticipating the murders of Banquo and Fleance, "make strong themselves by ill" (3.2.58). And when this effort fails, resulting instead in Fleance's escape and the visitation by Banquo's ghost, Macbeth repeats the same belief. "My strange and self-abuse," he says, in one of the most chilling speeches in the play, "[i]s the initiate fear that wants hard use. / We are yet but young in deed" (3.4.143–45). Rejecting the possibility that "self-abuse" may be inherent in the experience of murder, Macbeth hopes through more murders to make "murder" mean differently. In a fashion entirely consistent with his ambitious, future-oriented, anxiety-laden manner of being, he seeks release from his agony of guilt by repeating the experience that is its source.

This obsessive pattern of repetition has led many commentators to view Macbeth as incapable of change. "It never occurs to us," says Helen Gardner, "that Macbeth will turn back, or indeed that he can." As the play progresses, says James Calderwood, Macbeth "suppresses conscience altogether," until he becomes a "perfect tyrant, a murderous reflex action." The "[t]omorrow, and tomorrow, and tomorrow" speech, says Paul Jorgensen, constitutes "an exact and binding commitment to despair." "The final Macbeth," says A. P. Rossiter, "is a human mind dwindled down to one faculty: faith in force, against all sense and conscience." Yet just prior to his comment about the initiate fear, even if only dismissingly, Macbeth suggests a different possibility. "I am in blood / Stepped in so far," he says, "that, should I wade no more, / Returning were as tedious as go o'er" (3.4.137–39). Implicit here is the possibility, raised nowhere else by Macbeth, of turning back rather than of moving forward, of rescinding or revising in some way the error that the murder of Duncan is revealing itself to be.[1]

Both the existence of this statement and its singularity merit reflection. Its existence conforms to an argument advanced on broader grounds by Wilbur Sanders. Calling the "[t]omorrow, and tomorrow, and tomorrow" speech "not a philosophical position so much as an intellectual by-product of behaviour," Sanders says that "we may wonder whether [Macbeth's] sensation of fatality is not equally something proceeding indirectly from choice." Yet if Macbeth implies a wider domain of choice in pausing over the possibility of turning back, he does so only this once; elsewhere he looks back toward the past as if across an impassable gulf, and he contemplates the future with equal intransigence. Combining these observations suggests the importance of denial, in the clinical sense of the term, as an element of Macbeth's character, while at the same time raising the question of its sources. Exploring the cultural contexts that enable this denial, along with some of its more prominent manifestations in Macbeth's behavior, will lead ultimately to an argument that in this play Shakespeare dramatizes an even more radical form of midlife resistance to generativity than the one presented in *King Lear*. Whereas Lear's rebirth fantasy acknowledges the ubiquity of temporality by attempting to co-opt it, Macbeth tries to deny temporality itself. He may momentarily consider returning to the shore of the river of blood from which he departed, but his core fantasy is not of regeneration but of resistance.[2]

I

A traditional answer to the question of how Macbeth might return to a state of existence prior to the murder cites as a model the behavior at the time of his death of the Thane of Cawdor, the second of the play's three rebels against Duncan. "Very frankly he confessed his treasons, / Implored Your Highness' pardon, and set forth / A deep repentance," says Malcolm. "Nothing in his life/Became him like the leaving it. He died/As one that had been studied in his death/To throw away the dearest thing he owed/As 'twere a careless trifle" (1.4.5–11). In this behavior, an earlier generation of commentators claimed to find a norm against which Macbeth's intransigence might be measured and judged. For Roy Walker, "[t]he deep repentance of the guilty and condemned Thane of Cawdor . . . deepens the final infamy of Macbeth, who succeeds to the title of Thane of Cawdor and to the treachery, but not to the remorse." Similarly, for G. R. Elliott, even at the end of the play, in Macduff's intention to allow Macbeth to live as "the show and gaze o' the time" (5.8.24), "Macbeth is providentially offered the chance to suffer repentantly the flagrant degradation called for by his flagrant self-glorification. . . . But that purgatory is rejected. . . . Unlike the first Cawdor [Macbeth] does not, at the end, 'set forth a deep repentance.'"[3]

These comments arise out of a critical tradition in which *Macbeth* is read as a warning against the dangers of ambition and (at times) as a defense of the divine right of kings and even as an act of flattery offered to King James. For a more recent generation of critics, working primarily from the tenets and assumptions of cultural materialism, both this overall interpretation and the exemplary status of the first Thane of Cawdor's repentance have been cast into doubt. The Thane's repentance is a version of the *amende honorable,* the ritual of confession at the foot of the scaffold whereby, as Peter Brooks says, "the condemned were required . . . to proclaim their crimes and to beg forgiveness of the community they had offended." Far from seeing this ritual as an authentic expression of a condemned person's remorse, recent critics (most famously Michel Foucault) see instead a political tactic, a form of state-sponsored theatrics of power. As J. A. Sharpe argues, quoting Mervyn James, "the weakness and uncertain operation of the order-keeping forces at the disposal of the state" in earlier eras meant that "[c]ivil order depended, to a much greater extent than in the bureaucratized societies of a later age, on the effective internalization of obedience." And one of the best ways of demonstrating (and inculcating) that internalization was through the speeches of repentance preceding the execution of even the most lowly of convicted felons. Hence "the public execution," in Foucault's words, "belongs, even in minor cases, to the ceremonies by which power is manifested. . . . It is a ceremonial by which a momentarily injured sovereignty is reconstituted. It restores that sovereignty by manifesting it at its most spectacular."[4]

For many contemporary commentators on *Macbeth,* this critique of the meaning of the *amende honorable* is accompanied with a skepticism about the value of the social order against which Macbeth rebels. Not content, as David Norbrook says, to accept "the more authoritarian currents of Renaissance thought as absolute truths about human nature," these critics seek to expose the ideological underpinnings of readings interpreting Duncan, in Kenneth Muir's words, as a "venerable and saintly" monarch presiding over "an orderly and closely knit society." As Harry Berger Jr. argues, interpreting the social order over which Duncan presides as "natural" and Macbeth's rebellion as "unnatural" is less a given of the play than a "view entertained and articulated by all the 'good' characters," a view they use to "justify themselves and their society." In contrast to these characters' "persistent praise of Duncan as an ideal king, the head of a harmonious state," Berger notes that by the middle of 1.4, Duncan "has run into two rebels, a foreign foe, and a budding regicide," and he argues that "something intrinsic to the structure of Scottish society, something deeper than the melodramatic wickedness of one or two individuals, generates these tendencies toward instability, conflict, sedition, and murder." Far from seeing Macbeth's rebelliousness as "unnatural," Berger suggests that it should be seen as "a structural component of [the existing] social order, inextricable from the positive energy that sustains the order."[5]

If this line of interpretation renders problematic the question of how (and whether) Macbeth should repent, so also do considerations arising from the larger history of repentance as a state of mind and of confession as a social act. Confession is by its nature both a juridical and a religious phenomenon. Considered in either of these aspects, to whom should Macbeth express repentance, and in what fashion? The juridical difficulty arises from Macbeth's status as an elected monarch. Although a regicide, Macbeth is not a usurper, even though Macduff at the end of the play claims to be placing on display "[t]h' usurper's cursèd head" (5.8.55), and this fact reveals itself in the uneasy way in which characters slide between referring to Macbeth as "king" and as "tyrant." Furthermore, Macbeth is in part induced to rebel by Duncan's nomination of Malcolm as heir, an act which, as A. R. Braunmuller explains, replaces tanistry, the "traditional system of royal succession" in Scotland, in which "a ruler's successor was elected from a parallel family line," with "a system half-way between tanistry and primogeniture." And the disruption introduced by this nomination continues throughout the play, for an implication of Ross's "'tis most like / The sovereignty will fall upon Macbeth" and Macduff's "[h]e is already named and gone to Scone / To be invested" (2.4.29–32) is that the nomination of Malcolm has been overridden or ignored by the nobles, presumably because his and Donalbain's flight "puts upon them / Suspicion of the deed" (2.4.26–27). Also, as William Carroll observes, "[t]he play never suggests that Macbeth is overthrown as king because he had murdered his predecessor . . . but because he had become a 'tyrant.'" Hence, although Malcolm's right to the kingship is called "the due of birth" (3.6.25) and he is said to be "the truest issue of [Scotland's] throne" (4.3.107), he nonetheless "becomes king through an act of regicide, as well as by election and inheritance."[6]

In these ambiguities regarding monarchical status and succession, the play palters with us in a double sense, lending a political coloration to behavior on Macbeth's part that might otherwise seem mere stubbornness or bravado. In the final scenes of the play, Malcolm and the other rebels attempt to establish the legitimacy of their actions through claims that "[t]hose [Macbeth] commands move only in command, / Nothing in love" and that "none serve with him but constrainèd things" (5.2.19–20; 5.4.13). Macbeth too recognizes that "honor, love, obedience, troops of friends, / I must not look to have" and that "the thanes fly from me" (5.3.25–26, 51). But in calling those who "mingle with the English epicures" "false thanes" and in saying that the English army has been "forced with those that should be ours" (5.3.7–8; 5.5.5), he exposes a disjuncture at the heart of the mechanism of monarchical succession, one that Malcolm and his followers are anxious to conceal. Similarly, when Macbeth first refuses to "play the Roman fool and die / On mine own sword," then refuses "[t]o kiss the ground before young Malcolm's feet / And to be baited with the rabble's curse" (5.8.1–2, 28–29), he expresses a political as well as a personal defiance. The drumbeat of restored order is sounded insistently at the play's close, in Macduff's "[t]he time is free" and in the repeated "Hail, King of Scotland" with which Macduff and the others salute Malcolm

(5.8.55, 54, 59, 60). But like the presence of his severed head on stage, Macbeth's final intransigence serves to remind us of the fragility of this restoration and of the ways in which its legitimacy follows after, rather than precedes, the attainment of power.[7]

II

If politics provides a context in which to interpret Macbeth's intransigence, so also does religion, for in Shakespeare's time the primary religious means for the expression of repentance—the sacrament of auricular confession—was facing significant challenge. In his book *Hamlet in Purgatory,* Stephen Greenblatt explores the implication for Shakespearean tragedy (and for *Hamlet* in particular) of a parallel challenge to established religious practice: the attack by sixteenth-century Protestant reformers on the rituals and ceremonies surrounding Roman Catholicism's belief in the existence of purgatory. Viewing purgatory as a fiction, based on no biblical authority, Protestant reformers emphasized its role in sustaining the vast system of "prayers, fasts, almsgiving, and masses . . . that could in effect be purchased . . . on behalf of specific dead persons." "[V]irtually obsessed," as Greenblatt says, "with the amount of wealth wasted in the vain belief that [the celebration of] masses can shorten [purgatorial] torment," Protestant polemicists argued that "generations of pious Christians have been lured by a fiction into handing over their wealth to clerical drones."[8]

Yet belief in purgatory, however potentially corrupt in its economic effects, also could produce important psychic benefits. In Greenblatt's words, "[w]ith the doctrine of Purgatory and the elaborate practices that grew up around it, the church had provided a powerful method of negotiating with the dead. . . . The Protestant attack on the 'middle state of souls' and the middle place those souls inhabited destroyed this method for most people in England, but it did not destroy the longings and fears that Catholic doctrine had focused and exploited" (pp. 256–57). In effect, Greenblatt argues, the ideological struggle of the Reformation "turned negotiations with the dead from an institutional process governed by the church to a poetic process governed by guilt, projection, and imagination" (p. 252). And Shakespeare, more than any other playwright of his age, understood that unsettling "the institutional moorings of a crucial body of imaginative materials" made those same materials "available for theatrical appropriation" (p. 249). In the instance of *Hamlet,* by causing "a young man from Wittenberg, with a distinctly Protestant temperament, [to be] haunted by a distinctly Catholic ghost" (p. 240), Shakespeare found a way to explore the tragic potential of a vast ideological and social transformation.[9]

As with purgatory, so with confession. In theory, the Christian rite of auricular confession, mandated as a yearly requirement by the Fourth Lateran Council in 1215, offers to the repentant sinner spiritual consolation and reintegration into the community of believers. But for Protestant reformers, as Geoffrey Rowell observes, "the perceived abuse of the penitential system of the medieval church" was "[o]ne of the proximate causes of the Reformation." Viewing auricular confession to a priest less as a source of consolation and communal reintegration than as a mode of social and ideological control, "[t]he Protestant reformers," Thomas Tentler argues, "did not agree on what institutions of discipline and consolation should replace medieval sacramental confession; but they agreed that it had to be replaced." And this was so because the Catholic practice of auricular confession, with its attendant system of penances and its arrogation of power over the granting of absolution to the priest, seemed to the reformers a particularly egregious form of the "works" against which Martin Luther had posed as a radical alternative "grace alone, faith alone, the word alone." For the Protestant reformers, in Tentler's words, "absolution is an objectively unconditional offer of forgiveness . . . [and it] is subjectively certain." It depends for its efficacy on the faith of the sinner seeking forgiveness, and it can neither be authorized nor withheld by a priest or any other human agent.[10]

Like their critique of purgatory, the Protestant reformers' critique of auricular confession had mixed social and psychic consequences. For the first wave of reformers, releasing themselves from the mandated disciplinary surveillance of the established church must have seemed but one part of a larger onset of spiritual and emotional freedom. "God has now separated my salvation from my will," said Luther. "He has promised to save me not because of my good works and not because of my efforts but because of His grace and His mercy." Hence "I am sure . . . that no demon and no adversity will be able to . . . tear me from Him." For those convinced of their own election, arriving at this certitude must have seemed, in C. S. Lewis's words, like waking "from nightmare into ecstasy. . . . All the initiative has been on God's side; all has been free, unbounded grace. . . . Bliss is not for sale, cannot be earned." In the view of the early reformers, the doctrine of predestination, as Lewis says, quoting the XVIIth Article, is "'full of sweet, pleasant and unspeakable comfort for godly persons.'"[11]

But what of those, Lewis goes on to ask, who are not godly? What of those for whom the conviction of having been elected is uncertain, or worse? Inside the "original experience [of catastrophic conversion]," Lewis says, "no such question arises." When it does arise, "very troublesome problems . . . appear." As Peter Brooks has observed, in the movement from the public penitential exercises of the early church to the Lateran Council's insistence on individual confession, "one grasps the emergence of a key element in the modern sense of selfhood, of inwardness." The Protestant devaluing of auricular confession carries this process a step further, by replacing an interpersonal ritual with various forms of private self-scrutiny—prayer, diary-writing, spiritual autobiography.[12] However liberating this shift might have seemed to the godly, for those less certain of election it must have seemed less than satisfactory. A question for all penitential systems, as Thomas Tentler says, is how sinners know that they have been forgiven. In auricular confession, this question is answered objectively (if legalistically), in penances performed and absolution granted. But the Protestant interiorization of the rituals of repentance makes the answer to the question uncertain, subject to the vagaries of individual thought and emotion. With confession, as with purgatory, the Reformation converted (in Greenblatt's words) an "institutional process governed by the church [in]to a poetic process governed by guilt, projection, and imagination."

III

These observations about the history of auricular confession are relevant to *Macbeth* because they suggest a cultural corollary to Macbeth's (and the play's) ambivalent relation to the world of religion. If "this blow / Might be the be-all and the end-all!—here," Macbeth says, when contemplating the murder of Duncan, "[w]e'd jump the life to come" (1.7.4–7), only to reveal, even before the end of the soliloquy in which this statement occurs, that the concern he has consciously discarded remains powerfully active within his imagination. A similar doubleness, if with an opposite emphasis, appears in the play's representations of a supernatural order of good and evil. The witches apparently possess some form of supernatural power, and after the murder of Duncan, we are told that "the heavens, as troubled with man's act, / Threatens his bloody stage," in the form of daylight not returning when it should, a "mousing owl" killing a falcon, and Duncan's horses eating each other (2.4.5–18). But these evidences of the existence of an intervening supernatural order are accompanied by a persistent tendency toward naturalism. The witches can predict the future but not control it; the dagger that Macbeth sees prior to the murder of Duncan, like the later appearance of Banquo's ghost, seems to be "a false creation, / Proceeding from the heat-oppressèd brain" (2.1.39–40); and the arrival of Birnam Wood at Dunsinane, like Macduff's caesarean birth, is effected by human agency, not by divine intervention.[13]

This tendency toward naturalism manifests itself in the striking absence from the play of almost all references to institutional religion; and this absence places Macbeth in a situation analogous to that of a Protestant sinner, fearful of damnation, yet unable any longer to avail himself of the consolation afforded by auricular confession. The play contains two doctors, but no priest, and a primary effect of the doctors' appearances on stage is to underscore the inadequacy of merely secular responses to human ills. The English Doctor says that the "crew of wretched souls" awaiting the king's touch are beyond medical help, but "at his touch— / Such sanctity hath heaven given his hand— / They presently amend" (4.3.142–45). Similarly, the Scottish Doctor, the one who observes Lady Macbeth's sleepwalking, says that "[i]nfected minds / To their deaf pillows will discharge their secrets. / More needs she the divine than the physician. / God, God forgive us all!" (5.1.72–75). And when Macbeth, ostensibly inquiring about Lady Macbeth's "thick-coming fancies," asks the same doctor "[c]anst thou not minister to a mind diseased, / Pluck from the memory a rooted sorrow," the Doctor answers, "[t]herein the patient / Must minister to himself" (5.3.42–43, 47–48).

The inadequacy of the Scottish Doctor's responses to both Lady Macbeth's sleepwalking and Macbeth's questioning gains salience if we think of him as a confessor *manqué,* placed in the situation of listening to confessions, yet unable either to recognize them as such or to offer solace. In the *Oxford English Dictionary,* the third and the fourth senses of *minister* used as a verb are "to dispense, administer (a sacrament, the 'elements' or the like)" and "to apply or administer (something healing)." In the exchange between Macbeth and the Doctor the second of these meanings is clearly primary, as Macbeth's response, "[t]hrow physic to the dogs! I'll none of it," suggests (5.3.49). But the first, religious meaning adds an ironic resonance, as does the Doctor's earlier description of Lady Macbeth's pillow as "deaf." The patient must minister to herself, the infected mind must speak to the unhearing pillow, because the sacramental form of ministering to sinners' afflictions, auricular confession, has fallen into disrepute. Because the Doctor attends to Lady Macbeth only as a patient, not as a sinner, he is unable to offer her (or Macbeth) any solace.[14]

Looming behind the inability of the Doctor to offer solace is the larger issue of the play's dissociation of psychic and social reality. From the immediate aftermath of the first encounter with the witches onward, Macbeth and Lady Macbeth repeatedly enact this separation. We see it in Macbeth's "rapt" inattention to Angus and Ross, his "function . . . smothered in surmise," as they wait impatiently to begin the journey back to Duncan (1.3.144, 142); we see it as well in the soliloquy beginning "[i]f it were done when 'tis done," a speech requiring for its delivery Macbeth's potentially self-incriminating absence from the banquet with Duncan (1.7.1). As the play progresses, this separation widens and deepens, until it encompasses not just Macbeth's withdrawal from occasions for social interchange but his self-deception during them. The encounter with the Scottish Doctor—indeed, each of Macbeth's conversations in the fifth act prior to the final encounter with Macduff—conveys the sense that Macbeth is speaking at, not to, his interlocutor and that the true topic of his comments is unknown to either of them. It is Macbeth's own "thick-coming fancies," not Lady Macbeth's, that truly concern him, his "rooted sorrow," not hers, for which he wishes the doctor to prescribe "some sweet oblivious antidote" (5.3.40, 43, 45).

The Scottish Doctor can scarcely be blamed for failing to detect the hidden topic of Macbeth's comments. But one wonders whether a differently trained listener might not have fared better. Psychoanalysis is often viewed as a secular descendant of religious confession, and it is commonly supposed that this form of intervention into the experience of guilt and remorse commands a greater methodological sophistication than did its religious ancestor. Yet as Thomas Tentler has shown in a discussion of the pre-Reformation advice literature regarding the proper conduct of the sacrament of penance, a priest hearing confession was expected to display a considerable level of psychological acuity. In an anticipation of the famous Freudian couch, for example, "the practice of [the priest's] looking directly at any penitent . . . [was] discouraged because of the tendency to inhibit and confuse the telling of sins." Similarly, confessors were expected to encourage what is now called transference, by instructing the confessant "that the more openly he confesses, the more fully he will be pardoned and the more the confessor will esteem him." Also, the model confessor was expected to display something resembling a modern analyst's ability to guide a patient toward a discovery of the hidden sources of shame and guilt, for one of his most prized skills was the ability "to question prudently and effectively, . . . in order to get a complete confession from [the confessant]."[15]

It may not be entirely fanciful, then, to imagine Macbeth as achieving some degree of cathartic self-recognition, were he speaking to a different interlocutor. The pathos engendered in the latter part of the play arises in large measure from the sense conveyed of a submerged desire in Macbeth for some form of confessional interchange, combined with an agonized awareness of its unavailability. Subsequent to the long speech beginning "[t]o be thus is nothing" (3.1.49), Macbeth has no speech that can properly be called a soliloquy. All of his fifth-act speeches of regret, despair, and longing are spoken in the company of another character—the Scottish Doctor, Seyton, the servant he calls a "cream-faced loon" (5.3.11)—and all suggest a balked groping after response. Macbeth's eloquent assertion of universal meaninglessness, "Life's but a walking shadow . . . / . . . a tale / Told by an idiot" (5.5.24–27), is a coded statement, an oblique reconfiguration of the ways in which his own life, not necessarily life in general, has lost its significance. But as Macbeth recognizes, the nature of his relationship to the individuals in whose company he speaks ensures that they will remain silent, or at best provide only "mouth-honor, breath / Which the poor heart would fain deny and dare not" (5.3.27–28). "Were I from Dunsinane away and clear," says the Scottish Doctor as he leaves the stage for the last time, "[p]rofit alone should hardly draw me here" (5.3.63–64). An economic model of relationship—"wretched kerns, whose arms / Are hired to bear their staves" (5.7.18–19)—has supplanted the forms of humane interchange—with a spouse, with loyal followers, with a priestly confessor—in which some amount of cathartic unburdening might be possible.

IV

Yet I hesitate in pressing this line of analysis further. Emphasizing the incapacities of Macbeth's interlocutors runs the risk of sentimentalizing the play, of reducing Macbeth's tragedy to an Early Modern version of the difficulties involved in finding a really good therapist. My wife is a psychiatric social worker with extensive experience in therapeutic settings. She has said occasionally that a therapist sometimes has to decide whether to take the money—has to decide, that is, whether to accept as a client someone whose system of defenses may be so extensive as to forestall effective intervention. A client who enters therapy saying that life is a tale told by an idiot would cause a therapist, I imagine, to question whether to take the money. Macbeth's intransigence is not merely situational, it is personal, an effect not only of absence of opportunity but of the deep-seated resistance that he himself brings to the scenario of confession. As Harry Berger Jr. says, situating his critical method relative to Stanley Cavell's, "'fear of what is revealed' to others presupposes a fear of what has been revealed to oneself, and the avoidance of the sight of others presupposes—and is presumably part of—a strategy of self-avoidance." In *Macbeth,* as so often in Shakespeare's tragedies, circumstance conspires with character: the inadequacies of Macbeth's interlocutors reinforce, but do not fully explain, the underlying avoidances that block and disable his utterances.[16]

A bridge between these two dimensions of the play, cultural context and individual attitude, can be found in Robert N. Watson's study of what he calls "the mortality-crisis of Jacobean England." Asserting that fear of death as personal extinction is not exclusively a modern, secular phenomenon, Watson argues that several "changes in English Renaissance culture would . . . have accentuated the primal fear of annihilation." Most notably, he says, in an argument anticipating

Greenblatt's, the Protestant Reformation played a role in "heightening the psychological burdens of mortality. Both the inscrutable determinism and the systematic iconoclasm of Calvinist theology created a blank wall between the living and the dead, encouraging the ominous inference that all might be blankness or darkness beyond it." Emerging alongside this increased fear of personal annihilation, Watson argues, was a form of compensation directly pertinent to the concern in this book with issues of generativity, one still widely believed in today. Observing that Catholicism's valorization of celibacy implies "an absolute confidence in the afterlife, a certainty that the Christian devotee would be abundantly compensated for abjuring worldly pleasures," Watson argues that the contrasting Protestant valorization of "fruitful marriage" had as one of its motives a "desire to reconstruct the Catholic promise of immortality in a doctrinally acceptable form. Procreation became, in part, a displacement of sacramentalism and transubstantiation: a tangible and communal form of immortality tied to the cycle of human life, a consuming of the body in the hope of rendering life eternal [in the form of one's descendants]."[17]

Yet "while procreation might have offered Protestants at least a biological simulacrum of immortality," Watson says, "it could offer little promise of preserving their precious interiority"; and this inability produced in turn an intermittent skepticism regarding the adequacy of genetic survival as a substitute for personal immortality. In a brilliant reading of *Measure for Measure* and a less extensive one of *Macbeth,* Watson explores how this skepticism manifests itself in Shakespeare's plays. It is characteristic of Renaissance marriage comedies to offer in their conclusions an implicit endorsement of "the figurative immortality offered by procreation." But in *Measure for Measure*'s challenge to the assumptions of its genre, Watson argues, "Shakespeare . . . seems intent on exposing procreation as a means of perpetuating, not the individual, but a group and a genotype that exploit the illusion of personal immortality." Duke Vincentio's specious consolation offered in response to Claudio's fear of personal annihilation, Isabella's forced and uncertain move from celibacy to marriage, a fifth-act denouement in which (as I have argued elsewhere) "no member of the presumed happy ending speaks to any other member of his or her happiness"—these elements align the resolution of *Measure for Measure,* as Watson says, not with the triumph of romantic love and future parenthood but with "what Michel Foucault calls 'biopower': . . . the need of the state, under the guise of personalized benevolence, simply to keep the procreative machine running." And this alignment exposes procreation as less a form of personal immortality than "a mechanism of biology manipulated by the state."[18]

Perhaps because he had written extensively on the play in an earlier book, Watson does not develop the implications of his argument for *Macbeth* as fully as I would like. In his earlier study, Watson joins with numerous other commentators in depicting the surface structure of *Macbeth* as enacting "a basic talionic myth of the ambitious person, a pattern of punishment reflecting the crime." Because Macbeth and Lady Macbeth attempt to preempt temporal process, to "feel now / The future in the instant" (1.5.57–58), the cycles of time that they disrupt, day and night, sleeping and waking, planting and harvesting, rise up to punish them. At a basic level, this talionic punishment consists of retaliation against Macbeth and Lady Macbeth for their defiance of the cycle of human generation. In invoking the "spirits / That tend on mortal thoughts" to "unsex me here," to "[m]ake thick my blood," and to "take my milk for gall," Lady Macbeth quite literally asks that her menstrual cycle be intermitted and that her (stereotypical) female capacity for providing nurture be replaced by the "keen knife" of a phallic form of murderousness (1.5.41, 43, 48, 52). When Macbeth accedes in this transformation, accepting his wife's definition of manhood as requiring daring beyond mortal limitation (1.7.50–52), the stage is set, Watson says, for the talionic punishment first described by Sigmund Freud, when he said that "[i]t would be a perfect example of justice in the manner of the talion if the childlessness of Macbeth and the barrenness of his Lady were the punishment for their crimes against the sanctity of geniture."[19]

At the level of conscious thought and expectation, Macbeth certainly experiences his and his wife's childlessness as a form of punishment. When he agrees to Lady Macbeth's plan for the murder of Duncan, he says "[b]ring forth men-children only" (1.7.73), as if an expectation of future fecundity were a shared but unstated assumption between them. And when he turns his attention to the witches' prophecy concerning Banquo, he complains that "[u]pon my head they placed a fruitless crown / And put a barren scepter in my grip, / Thence to be wrenched with an unlineal hand, / No son of mine succeeding" (3.1.62–65). But to accept this interpretation of Macbeth's attitudes without qualification, as Watson at times seems to do, runs counter to his own richest insight, for it implies the validity of a solution to the perils of mortality that his overall argument challenges. It may be, as Watson says, that with the death of his wife, Macbeth loses "his last hope for a procreative future," but the larger question is how thoroughly this hope, were it in fact to be realized, would conform to Macbeth's deepest desires. The answer, by Watson's own logic, is not thoroughly enough. If Macbeth's "obsession with controlling future generations [is] a desperate compensation for mortality," then his hope for posterity should itself be seen as an expression of the "common tendency to submerge fears of personal mortality in fantasies of progeny," and hence as part of a "futile struggle to give his life meaning and justification." It should be seen, that is, not as an authentic expression of desire in its own right but as a displaced expression of an underlying fear.[20]

Macbeth's fundamental quarrel is not with childlessness but with children. A long tradition of criticism has explored the ways in which the murder of Duncan constitutes an effort on Macbeth's part at parthenogenesis. For critics relying on an oedipal developmental model, the play presents us, as James Calderwood says, "with a Macbeth who incarnates the infantile desire to kill the father and possess the mother at the same time, thereby becoming, as Lady Macbeth would have Macbeth become, a 'man.'" For critics emphasizing feminist and preoedipal developmental theories, Macbeth's fantasy of self-generation entails as well an effort to break free of the maternal matrix. In Macbeth's quasi-caesarean self-creation, when he "carve[s] out his passage" by unseaming Macdonwald "from the nave to th' chops" (1.2.19, 22), as in his retreat from Lady Macbeth's (maternal) anger into an acceptance of her transformation of herself into an "all-male mother," Macbeth enacts, as Janet Adelman says, a "radical excision of the female site of origin." And for critics of various persuasions, the murder of Duncan combines these two modes of attempted autogenesis, for Duncan's androgyny, his combination of paternal power and female gentleness and softness, suggests, in David Willbern's words, that he is "a magical composite parent, both father and mother," so that "his murder then becomes a complete parricide."[21]

When Macbeth's attempt at self-creation turns from the past to the future, it enacts itself as a war against the young. The passage in which Macbeth complains of a future in which there will be "[n]o son of mine succeeding" exhibits a curious slippage, for his claim that the weird sisters "put a barren scepter in my grip, / Thence to be wrenched by an unlineal hand" (3.1.63–64) makes best sense if he is imagining himself as somehow still alive, still grasping the scepter, when the transfer of the kingship to either his own son or Banquo's takes place. This slippage suggests that the son Macbeth here imagines—like, perhaps, the babe to whom Lady Macbeth claims to have given suck (1.7.55)—is specular, not someone endowed (in Macbeth's imagination) with an independent identity, but instead a fantasized embodiment of Macbeth's own fears and desires. The passage in which Macbeth imagines the scepter as being wrenched from his grip begins "[t]o be thus is nothing, / But to be safely thus" (3.1.49–50), and "safety" here, like "success" elsewhere in the play, is too all-encompassing an aspiration to align itself comfortably with a desire for progeny. At a conscious level, Macbeth may fear a coup d'état on the part of Banquo and Fleance; but underlying this practical concern is his struggle against temporality, a struggle in which any son, his own no less than Banquo's, presents himself as a threat.

The play's often-remarked-upon oneiric quality, its tendency to unfold its action by the logic of dream and nightmare rather than by strict causality, is thoroughly colored by Macbeth's war against generational succession, in the form of repeated images of miscarriage, caesarean and other forms of difficult delivery, and child-murder. Accompanying these images is a pervasive association of sexuality with violence, an association which, as James Calderwood observes, inverts Shakespeare's "usual figurative practice of likening the sexual act to various forms of violence" by instead likening murder to copulation. As many commentators have noted, when Macbeth associates himself with "withered Murder," advancing "[w]ith Tarquin's ravishing strides, towards his design" (2.1.53, 56), he transforms the impending regicide into a rape, with himself as the assailant and Duncan as his feminized victim.

And as Calderwood nicely demonstrates, the assassination is depicted as sexual not only in relation to Macbeth and Duncan but to Macbeth and Lady Macbeth as well. Interpreting Lady Macbeth's "unsex me here" as a rechanneling of libido into violence and emphasizing the sexual double-entendres at work throughout the play in the words *do* and *done* and *deed,* Calderwood arrives at a reading of the murder as "a metaphorically displaced act of copulation between Lord and Lady Macbeth." As he says, the scene of Lady Macbeth outside Duncan's bedchamber, made bold by drink, "is surely a strange, perverted moment, with Macbeth 'about it' in the bedchamber and the emboldened Lady Macbeth physically outside listening but imaginatively inside 'doing the deed' with her husband. Then Macbeth comes forth to announce 'I have done the deed,' and she cries 'My husband!' and the two of them conduct their harrowing aftertalk."[22]

In displacing copulation into murder, Macbeth and Lady Macbeth pervert the relationship of lovemaking not only to love but to the engendering of progeny as well. Yet as Calderwood goes on to argue, "Macbeth's act, however shameful, is not sterile," for in a further inversion, "this uncreating act is procreative. . . . It generates unforeseeable reactions in [Macbeth] and his world . . . [and it] propagates subsequent acts which have as their aim the murder of offspring."[23] These subsequent acts appear throughout the remainder of the play as both image and behavior. The cauldron around which the witches dance in 4.1 is a parodic, anti-fecund womb, the ingredients of which have connotations of lust, violence, and the slaughter of offspring. During Macbeth's visit to the witches, the ingredients of the cauldron—"[f]inger of birth-strangled babe / Ditch-delivered by a drab," "sow's blood, that hath eaten / Her nine farrow"—merge by a dream-logic into the apparition of the bloody child and into the promise that "none of woman born / Shall harm Macbeth" (4.1.30–31, 64–65, 80–81). Then when the show of eight kings reveals a line of Banquo's descendants that seems to "stretch out to th' crack of doom" (4.1.117), this dream-logic undergoes a further transformation. "From this moment," says Macbeth, "[t]he very firstlings of my heart shall be / The firstlings of my hand," and the first of these "firstlings" will be the slaughter of Macduff's "wife, his babes, and all unfortunate souls / That trace him in his line" (4.1.146–48, 152–53), an action that has no practical benefit relative to Macbeth's fears of Macduff's insubordination but that makes perfect sense as a displaced act of revenge against Banquo's descendants and the power of generational succession that they represent.[24]

In the fifth act, Macbeth's phantasmagorical war against the young emerges into the light of day, in the form of his battle with Malcolm and his companions, who are described as being mainly youthful. The "file / Of all the gentry," says Lennox of the assembled troops, contains "many unrough youths that even now / Protest their first of manhood" (5.2.8–11), and this cadre of youthful warriors includes Malcolm himself, as Macbeth himself acknowledges when he says "What's the boy Malcolm? / Was he not born of woman" (5.3.3–4).[25] It is therefore appropriate that Macbeth's final struggle to retain his throne and his life should entail two violent encounters, not one, and that the first of these—Macbeth's only act of slaughter directly depicted in the play—should be against Young Siward, who "only lived but till he was a man" (5.8.40). And the second of the encounters enacts the play's truest form of talionic punishment, for when Macduff announces that he "was from his mother's womb / Untimely ripped" (5.8.15–16), Macbeth's dream of self-creation returns as nightmare. Hearing Macduff's words, Macbeth says, "And be these juggling fiends no more believed / That palter with us in a double sense, / That keep the word of promise to our ear / And break it to our hope" (5.8.19–22). The broken hope of which he speaks is literally the hope ensuing from the witches' promise that no one born of woman will harm him. But at a more profound level, the hope broken here is existential. It is the hope for an existence "[w]hole as the marble, founded as the rock, / As broad and general as the casing air" (3.4.22–23), an existence exempt from "the lease of nature" and "time and mortal custom" (4.1.99–100)—an existence, as Macbeth slowly comes to realize, in which there must be no children.

V

Macbeth cannot step out of the river of blood because he does not understand that he cannot step out of the river of blood. This statement is not intended as paradox. When a young friend of mine became pregnant for the first time, I asked her what it felt like to be with child. Whenever the fetus moved, she said, she was made aware that part of herself was not part of her self. This amphibious condition, in which children are and are not part of their parents' being, in which parents love their children in their separateness even as they project upon them their own needs and desires, Macbeth cannot accept. The son he imagines, indeed, all people in the play younger than himself, exist primarily as threats to the integral self, the "single state of man" (1.3.141), that he desires and that he imagines is obtainable, even though his efforts to obtain it repeatedly fail. As James Calderwood says, "In no other play do the words 'do,' 'done,' and 'deed' appear so often or so centrally. . . . [Y]et if the play is about action, about what is done, it is also about not-action, what is undone." In each instance in which Macbeth expects "it" to be "done, when 'tis done," he discovers instead a form of incompletion. And he responds, as Calderwood says, by proceeding "to further acts that are themselves cursed with incompleteness."[26] "To be thus is nothing," Macbeth says, as he prepares for the murder of Banquo, "[b]ut to be safely thus" (3.1.49–50). "For mine own good," he says, as he prepares to visit the weird sisters, "[a]ll causes shall give way" (3.4.136–37).

As might be expected in a play centrally concerned with ambition, Macbeth gazes toward the past less frequently and less longingly than toward the future. But when he does turn his attention to the past, he seeks there the same completeness as he hopes to find in the future. In very nearly his final words in the play, he says, "I will try the last" (5.8.32), as if he still believes that a "last," other than the death that awaits him, a surcease that can catch entire success, is somehow obtainable. As with the last, so with the first. When Macbeth says, "I am in blood / Stepped in so far that, should I wade no more, / Returning were as tedious as go o'er" (3.4.137–39), he intimates the existence of two shores for the river he wades in, one to be reached by moving forward, the other by turning back. Whenever he looks back at that former shore, he envisions his existence there as having been perfect. "Had I but died an hour before this chance / I had lived a blessèd time" (2.3.93–94), he says, with unconscious irony, shortly after the murder of Duncan. And he envisions his return to the shore from which he had departed not as occurring within his present experience but as entirely annulling that experience. The examples he offers of "minster[ing] to a mind diseased" do not seek a healing encounter with his disease as a present and continuing reality but its complete eradication, even to the extent of eliminating its traces in memory. "Canst thou not," he asks the Doctor, "Pluck from the memory a rooted sorrow, / Raze out the written troubles of the brain, / And with some sweet oblivious antidote / Cleanse the stuffed bosom of that perilous stuff / Which weighs upon the heart" (5.3.42–47), only to learn to his further sorrow that the Doctor does not have this ability.

But if confession and repentance cannot restore radical innocence, what good are they? Why *should* Macbeth engage in the *amende honorable* if the social order to which he would be reconciling himself derives its validity not from morality but from power? Why *should* he engage in some religious form of confession, auricular or otherwise, if the existence of the life to come in which his repentance might be acknowledged and rewarded is at best uncertain? In the present cultural moment, oriented as it is toward the search for an individual and corporate ethos of forgiveness and regeneration, Macbeth's refusal to seek affirmative answers to these questions may seem to diminish his stature. But in the circumstances afforded him, might not accepting the burden of guilt and seeking reconciliation constitute a greater diminishment? In his exploration of the place of confession in the modern world, Peter Brooks says that "[w]hat is lacking [today] is a socially defined Sacred in terms of which to plead for true absolution," and he speculates about the sterility of "confessional discourse" in a world where "faith and grace are not viable concepts." Macbeth is far closer to a world where those concepts are viable and where a socially defined sacred is widely accepted than are we, and the pathos of his separation from that world is magnified accordingly. But so also is the significance of his intransigence. In his refusal to reconcile himself with the prevailing social and moral order, we may discern a nascent modernity, a foreshadowing of those figures— Stendahl's Julien Sorel, Dostoevsky's narrator in "Notes from the Underground," Faulkner's Joe Christmas, Camus's Mersault—for whom such refusal is an essential part of their identity.[27]

In psychological as well as cultural terms, Macbeth's intransigence possesses some degree of positive value. I do not imagine that Stanley Cavell had *Macbeth* in mind as depicting a desirable alternative way of living one's life when he said, in reference to *King Lear,* "what we need is not rebirth, or salvation, but the courage, or plain prudence, to see and to stop."[28] In looking back at an earlier existence imagined as "blessed," Macbeth exhibits a nostalgia parallel to Lear's when Lear imagines himself returning to infancy and setting his rest on Cordelia's kind nursery. But in rejecting repentance and social or religious reconciliation, Macbeth takes the first, necessary step toward disengagement from this fantasy and from Lear's related fantasy of literal rebirth. Among the various ways of describing Macbeth's tragic attractiveness, some emphasis should be given to his workmanlike quality, his willingness, with only intermittent interruptions, to live his life in a forward direction and in the terms afforded by his present circumstances. "They have tied me to a stake," he says. "I cannot fly, / But bearlike I must fight the course" (5.7.1–2), and bearlike he does. To anyone who has wasted some amount of his or her life pursuing the seductions of nostalgia, this willingness simply to soldier on must seem an advance in moral awareness. But it is, of course, perversely incomplete, for in rejecting nostalgia, Macbeth manages only to arrive at its polar opposite, a fantasy of an achievable future perfection, the be-all and end-all here, success, the last. A central concern in the remainder of Shakespeare's career is how (and whether) the polarities held rigidly apart in *King Lear* and *Macbeth,* nostalgia and denial, regeneration and resistance, can be fruitfully brought together. In the next play that we consider, *Antony and Cleopatra,* these polarities reconfigure in an attractive, erotically charged fashion, but one that nonetheless enacts yet another version of midlife resistance to generativity.

4
Cleopatra's Children

What role do children and allusions to children play in *Antony and Cleopatra?* Why does Shakespeare mention the existence of Cleopatra's children while at the same time leaving unmentioned their fate in the years following their mother's death? In most particulars regarding the children, Shakespeare follows Plutarch, his main source for *Antony and Cleopatra,* very closely. Octavius Caesar's speeches describing the Donations of Alexandria, at which Antony and Cleopatra had designated their sons, Alexander Helios and Ptolemy Philadelphus, "kings of kings" (3.6.13), derive directly from Plutarch, even to the extent of depicting the donations (in Agrippa's words) as the reason why the Roman citizens, "queasy with [Antony's] insolence already, / . . . their good thoughts call from him" (3.6.21–22). Similarly, Shakespeare follows Plutarch in having Cleopatra ask that Caesar "give [her] conquered Egypt for [her] son" (5.2.19) and in having Caesar threaten to put the "children / To that destruction which I'll guard them from" (5.2.130–31), should Cleopatra choose to follow Antony's example and commit suicide. But Shakespeare deviates in every instance in which Plutarch projects the fate of the children beyond the temporal limits of the play. He does not tell us that Caesarion, Cleopatra's son by Julius Caesar (by reputation) and the one for whom she requested "conquered Egypt," was assassinated upon Octavius's command; nor does he say that Cleopatra's three children fathered by Antony—Alexander, Ptolemy, and Alexander's twin sister, Cleopatra Selene—were "very honourably kept," to the extent of being raised by Antony's wife, Octavia, and, in the instance of Cleopatra Selene, of being matched in marriage to "a marvelous courteous and goodly prince," King Juba of Mauretania.[1]

These selective uses of Plutarch, in which attention is drawn to the existence of the children, but incompletely, exist alongside another set of references, not to children as real beings in the world but as elements in Cleopatra's (and occasionally Antony's) histrionic self-presentation. I am thinking of Cleopatra's climactic description of the asp as "my baby at my breast, / That sucks the nurse asleep" (5.2.309–10) and of Antony's claim, in deviance from the play's source, that he has his "pillow left unpressed in Rome, / Forborne the getting of a lawful race, / And by a gem of women" (3.13.107–9). I am thinking as well of the various references to childbirth, to abortion or miscarriage, and to the death of children that Cleopatra uses as a means of intensifying her expression of her emotions. "'Tis sweating labor," she says, as Antony prepares to leave for Rome, "To bear such idleness so near the heart / As Cleopatra this" (1.3.94–96). "Who's born that day / When I forget to send to Antony," she says after his departure, "Shall die a beggar"; "He shall have every day a several greeting, / Or I'll unpeople Egypt" (1.5.66–68, 80–81). "If it be so," she says, in response to Antony's "[c]oldhearted toward me?" after the encounter with Thidias, then "[t]he next Caesarion smite, / Till by degrees the memory of my womb, / Together with my brave Egyptians all, / By the discandying of this pelleted storm / Lie graveless till the flies and gnats of Nile / Have buried them for prey" (3.13.161, 165–70). And when she asks "Where art thou, Death?" after her capture by Proculeius, she pleads for it to "[c]ome, come, and take a queen / Worth many babes and beggars" (5.2.45–47).

When commenting on the role of children and references to children in the play, critics have tended to focus on one of these sets of references and to ignore the other. For an earlier generation of critics of a moralizing persuasion, Cleopatra's indifference to the future well-being of her children supported a view of her as an amoral sensualist, selfish and destructive. Romantically inclined commentators of the same era, eager to read the play, in G. Wilson Knight's words, as "a paradisal vision . . . of humanity's quest for love," instead emphasized the image of the baby at the breast, seeing in that imagined infant an embodiment of a "new reality" born from the "marriage of life and death." More recent commentators, weary of the push-me/pull-you of the quarrel between positive and negative assessments of the play's central characters, have argued that the play deliberately foregrounds the impossibility of arriving at a definitive judgment. But in this more recent criticism as well, the play's real and specular children tend to exist in isolation from one another. Thus Constance Brown Kuriyama argues, in an otherwise excellent interpretation, that "[d]eath, in a sense, is the progeny of Cleopatra's union with Antony," and "the asp, . . . the baby at her breast, the issue of their earthly love," without pausing to note that Antony and Cleopatra's love also had other, less metaphoric issue. And Janet Adelman, pursuing an argument that Cleopatra is a mother figure restoring Antony to heroic life "in the womblike receptive space of her female memory," remains silent about the similarities between Cleopatra's rhetoric of child-destruction and Lady Macbeth's, while claiming that "the baby cast violently away from Lady Macbeth's breast is restored to nurturance" in Cleopatra's death scene.[2]

I do not intend to revive the tradition of negative commentary regarding Antony and Cleopatra's attitude toward their parental responsibilities. But the argument I am developing regarding struggles over generativity requires that the play's real and specular children not be interpreted in isolation from one another. This is so because *Antony and Cleopatra* depicts a longer chronology of midlife experience than either *King Lear* or *Macbeth.* Like *King Lear* and *Macbeth, Antony and Cleopatra* depicts a midlife crisis; but, unlike the earlier plays, it does not itself *inhabit* that crisis. Shakespeare depicts Antony and Cleopatra not only struggling to evade a midlife loss of status and power but responding to that loss after it has occurred. Accompanying this change is a double shift in emphasis, from the inwardness of Lear's incestuous yearnings and Macbeth's oedipal murderousness to adult worldly and interpersonal concerns, and from a primarily male focus to a scrutiny of both male and female midlife behavior. In these changes, the two modes of reference to children intersect. *Antony and Cleopatra* is a tragedy with a difference, standing halfway between the darkness of *King Lear* and *Macbeth* and the (qualifiedly) affirmative vision of the romances. This difference manifests itself in the mixed status of the play's children, as the insistence on the reality of children of the romances mingles with the purely phantasmagorical representation accorded to them in *Macbeth.* Stopping short of the reconciliation between the generations depicted in the romances, *Antony and Cleopatra* nonetheless disengages from the intense struggle against generational succession depicted in

Macbeth. Understanding the nature and significance of this disengagement is the objective of this chapter.

I

Antony and Cleopatra may seem an unlikely play in which to look for evidence of a midlife crisis, or indeed of any psychologically oriented basis for interpretation. This is so for a variety of reasons, which I wish to consider before turning to the crisis that the play does depict. Among the several ways in which *Antony and Cleopatra* differs from the four preceding tragedies, none is more striking than its abandonment of the techniques of representation through which the earlier plays had allowed access to the states of mind of their protagonists. *Hamlet* is dominated by soliloquies, and *Othello, King Lear,* and *Macbeth* also provide ample opportunity for their central characters to reveal their internal conflicts and confusions. But *Antony and Cleopatra* lacks anything that can properly be called a soliloquy. In the instance of Cleopatra, it lacks even the opportunity for one, since she never appears on stage alone. And when Antony does appear alone, in 2.3, 4.12, and 4.14, the brief speeches that he delivers are soliloquies only in form, for they lack the internal orientation, the sense of rumination and reflection, that characterizes soliloquies in the earlier plays. As with the absence of soliloquies, so with the overall structure of the play, for this love tragedy is remarkable in containing no scene in which its two lovers appear on stage alone together. Antony and Cleopatra always appear in the company of subordinate characters, who often perform a quasi-choral function, commenting on the protagonists' speeches and actions either in anticipation of, during, or after their appearances. As Michael Neill notes, this structure too forestalls access to Antony's and Cleopatra's subjectivities, for it "serves to push the main action back into a perspective frame," thereby dividing the audience's attention between that action and the reactions it provokes in its observers.[3]

What *Antony and Cleopatra* offers in lieu of soliloquies is a performative conception of selfhood, a sense of the self as a site of continuous theatrical display. This is true to a remarkable degree for Cleopatra, but also for Antony and even for Octavius. When Octavia returns to Rome, rejected by Antony, she is greeted harshly by Octavius for having "stol'n upon us thus." "[Y]ou are come / A market maid to Rome," he says, "and have prevented / The ostentation of our love, which, left unshown, / Is often left unloved" (3.6.43, 51–54). This sense that identity derives from public display, rather than governs it, is pervasive throughout the play. The three main characters all view their greatness as validated and, in a sense, as created by the gaze of others. In the third of Antony's speeches delivered when he is alone on stage, he plans to commit suicide so that he may join Cleopatra, whom he believes to have died already. When he imagines himself and Cleopatra "hand in hand" "[w]here souls do couch on flowers," he does not envision himself alone with her, any more than he seeks opportunities to be alone with her while alive. He imagines instead that their "sprightly port [will] make the ghosts gaze," to the extent that "Dido and her Aeneas shall want troops, / And all the haunt be ours" (4.14.51–54). And when Cleopatra prepares for her own suicide, she thinks of it as replacing one form of self-display with another. If she allows herself to be carried in triumph back to Rome, "I shall see," she says, "[s]ome squeaking Cleopatra boy my greatness / I' the posture of a whore" (5.2.219–21). To forestall this humiliating possibility, she instead arranges what Michael Neill calls "the most self-consciously *performed,* the most elaborately gestural dying in all Shakespearean tragedy," a prolonged suicide in which "[e]ven its most intimate emotions seem tuned to the presence of an audience."[4]

This performative conception of selfhood makes it difficult to determine Antony's and Cleopatra's motives, or even to be confident that we are intended to think that motives exist. As Carol Cook says, speaking of Cleopatra, the play encourages us "to approach her less as a character, a psychology or personality, than as a figure for a certain kind of textual operation."[5] In the first half of the play, this anti-psychological orientation is encouraged as well by Antony and Cleopatra's behavior. Upon receiving the news of Fulvia's death, Antony says, "I must from this enchanting queen break off. / Ten thousand harms more than the ills I know / My idleness doth hatch" (1.2.135–37). But this attitude, with its implication of internal conflict, is the exception rather than the rule. Until the battle at Actium, Antony is more passive than active. In his opening speech, Caesar calls Antony "[o]ur great competitor" (1.4.3), in the sense of "partner," but with an overtone of "rival." If there is rivalry, though, it originates with Caesar, not with Antony, who seems content to continue indefinitely as one of the triple pillars of the world. All initiative in their struggle—the ouster of Lepidus, the arousal of Roman public opinion, the rapid crossing of the Aegean, and the taking of Toryne—originates with Caesar, not with Antony. A similar passivity is even more strikingly evident in Cleopatra, for the "idleness" that she bears "so near the heart" (1.3.95) as Antony prepares to leave dominates her behavior during his absence. When first seen after Antony's departure, she wishes that she "might sleep out this great gap of time / My Antony is away" (1.5.5–6). Failing this, she engages in sexual joking, creates erotic fantasies—"O happy horse, to bear the weight of Antony!" (1.5.22)—sends each day "twenty several messengers" (1.5.65), and hesitates between music, billiards, and fishing as possible pastimes. What she does not ever do is engage in purposeful activity.

Implicit in this passivity and idleness is a Lear-like understanding of status and role not as accident but as essence. If we ask why Antony and Cleopatra are so careless regarding the maintenance of their political power in the first half of the play, the answer seems to be that they do not truly believe that they can lose it. In 1.4, when the messenger brings the news to Octavius that Pompey "is beloved of those / That only have feared Caesar," Octavius says, "I should have known no less. / It hath been taught us from the primal state / That he which is was wished until he were; / And the ebbed man, ne'er loved till ne'er worth love, / Comes deared by being lacked" (1.4.37–38, 40–44). This view of power as contingent and uncertain dominates Octavius's behavior throughout the play, as can be seen in his constant watchfulness, his abstemiousness, and his relentless ambition. It can be seen as well in his bureaucratic organization of his regime, which allows him to exercise power by extension and to believe, in Enobarbus's words, that "being twenty times of better fortune, / He is twenty men to one" (4.2.4–5). For Antony and Cleopatra, by contrast, power is experienced as personal charisma. In Octavius's indictment of Antony's "lascivious wassails," he charges Antony with being willing "to sit / And keep the turn of tippling with a slave, / To reel the streets at noon, and stand the buffet / With knaves that smells of sweat" (1.4.57, 18–21). To Octavius, this behavior is intolerable because it ignores the need to manipulate and control "[t]his common body" (1.4.44) in the service of the acquisition and preservation of power. But for Antony and Cleopatra, the fact that they do not view these sorts of direct and unmediated encounters as threatening suggests that they do not view power itself as something that can either be acquired or lost. Here, as in Antony's tolerance of Enobarbus's mocking interruptions and Cleopatra's of Charmian's, a style of behavior implies a metaphysics of identity.[6]

This metaphysics bears an intuitive, if not empirically provable, relation to pre-midlife-crisis adult experience, for in its sudden onset of anxieties about mortality, the midlife crisis challenges the fantasy of omnipotence that William Hazlitt ascribed to youthfulness when he said that no young man believes that he will die. The play depicts Antony and Cleopatra's continued inhabitation of this fantasy in a variety of ways, most notably in its emphasis on the word *become.* Like *do, done*, and *deed* in *Macbeth, become* is a leitmotif in *Antony and Cleopatra.* The word and its cognates appear seventeen times in the play—twice as often as in any other play except *The Winter's Tale,* where it is also prominent. More striking than this frequency is the unusual way in which the word is used, for in only four instances does *become* carry its primary meaning of "to come into, or to bring into, being." In eleven instances, the word carries its secondary meaning of "to be suitable or flattering," while in the two remaining uses it hovers ambiguously between these meanings. Philo uses the word in its primary sense when he says that Antony's "captain's heart / . . . / . . . is become the bellows and the fan / To cool a gypsy's lust" (1.1.6, 9–10), as does Antony when he says that "[t]he present pleasure, / By revolution lowering, does become / The opposite of itself" (1.2.131–33). In almost all of the other uses, the word denotes the seemliness of a character's behavior—usually either Antony's or Cleopatra's—relative to a conception of his or her identity. We hear the word used in this way when Antony says, "Fie, wrangling queen! / Whom everything becomes, to chide, to laugh, / To weep" (1.1.50–52); when Cleopatra, imagining Antony as either "sad or merry," says, "[t]he violence of either thee becomes, / So does it no man else" (1.5.62–64); and when Enobarbus says of Cleopatra, "vilest things / Become themselves in her, that the holy priests / Bless her when she is riggish" (2.2.248–50).[7]

Emphasis on the secondary meaning of *become* combines with other unusual or paradoxical aspects of the play's depictions of temporality—

Enobarbus's statement in his River Cydnus speech regarding the effect of the fans on Cleopatra's cheeks, "what they undid did," is a good example (2.2.215)—to co-opt time as process, making it run backward, as it were, toward Antony and Cleopatra, rather than forward, toward the outcome of their actions.[8] And this co-optation links in turn with their view of power as personal to create a larger-than-life impression of Antony and Cleopatra, not only in their presence in the world but in their self-regard, as if they understood themselves as possessing a quasi-mythic, atemporal, and unchallengeable identity, a classical-world version of Macbeth's "single state of man." At first glance, this impression may seem to contradict the play's emphasis on the performative construction of the self. But in fact it simply alters the character of that construction, converting it from what one might expect, a dramatic action displaying a dynamic and evolving sense of identity, into something resembling a masque or pageant, in which Antony and Cleopatra enact an unvarying self-understanding. The nature of that self-understanding differs for the two characters. For Antony it is partial and episodic, the "great property" of his Roman identity as warrior and leader alternating with his belief that "[t]he nobleness of life / Is to do thus" (1.1.60, 38–39). For Cleopatra it is fluid and inclusive, the "cunning past man's thought" attributed to her by Antony, the "infinite variety" attributed to her by Enobarbus (1.2.152; 2.2.246). But for both characters, performative self-display is governed by a monumental self-regard, direct access to which we as audience and readers are not permitted to gain.[9]

II

The qualities of *Antony and Cleopatra* that I have just described so dominate the first half of the play that some commentators ascribe them to the play as a whole, in the form either of what Constance Brown Kuriyama terms "a static paradoxical equipoise of Rome and Egypt" or of an ascription to Antony and Cleopatra of an inexhaustible capacity for performance, Cleopatra's "infinite variety," as Katherine Eggert says, understood as allowing her to become "a space in which transformation occurs perpetually," her cloylessness as creating in Antony an insatiable appetite, such that "he is constantly unfinished in his desire, unstaled by any custom."[10] But these ascriptions treat a conditional aspect of Antony and Cleopatra's self-understanding as if it were an invariant truth. They overlook the way that in the second half of the play, in two crucial instances, for Antony immediately after the defeat at Actium, for Cleopatra immediately after the death of Antony, Shakespeare shifts artistic registers abruptly. "When we in our viciousness grow hard," Antony says, "the wise gods seel our eyes, / In our own filth drop our clear judgments, make us / Adore our errors, laugh at 's while we strut / To our confusion" (3.13.113–17); "No more but e'en a woman, and commanded / By such poor passion as the maid that milks / And does the meanest chares," says Cleopatra, when addressed by Iras as "Royal Egypt, Empress!" (4.15.78–80, 76). Here, in contrast to the performative self-display, idleness, and self-aggrandizing self-conceptions of the first half of the play, both characters engage in self-diminishment and self-rejection. Nor are these isolated acts of recrimination, without implication, for they signal a fundamental shift in Antony and Cleopatra's way of being in the world, from the inattention to consequence of the first three acts to the willfulness, defiance, denial, and regret of the last two.

Central to this shift for Antony are anxieties about age and aging of the sort typically found in a midlife crisis. The historical events depicted in the play, beginning with the death of Fulvia and concluding with Antony's and Cleopatra's suicides, occurred over a period of ten years, at the beginning of which Antony was approximately 42, Cleopatra 29, and Octavius 23, and at the end of which (of course) all three were ten years older.[11] Shakespeare compresses this ten-year period into a single continuous action, omitting both Antony's participation in the Parthian campaign and the eight years of his marriage to Octavia, during which he fathered two children. Along with this compression, Shakespeare exaggerates the age difference among the three characters, depicting Octavius throughout the play as if he were the 23-year-old of the beginning of the ten-year period and Antony and Cleopatra as if they were the 52-year-old and the 39-year-old of its end. Octavius is the "scarce-bearded Caesar," says Cleopatra (1.1.22); he "wears the rose / Of youth upon him," says Antony (3.13.20–21). Cleopatra is by her own description "wrinkled deep in time" (1.5.30); "[t]hough age from folly could not give me freedom," she says, "[i]t does from childishness" (1.3.57–58); in contrast to Octavius, she is the "blown rose," to be treated without ceremony by messengers who had formerly "kneeled unto the buds" (3.13.39–40). And Antony, also by his own description, has a "grizzled head" (3.13.17) on which "the white [hairs] / Reprove the brown for rashness, and they them / For fear and doting" (3.11.13–15).

Although emphasis on the difference in the characters' ages is continuous throughout the play, it is significantly *not* continuous in Antony's awareness. Cleopatra depicts Octavius as youthful and herself as comparatively advanced in years from the outset of the play, but Antony never comments on Octavius's age, on Cleopatra's, or on his own until after the defeat at Actium. At this point, his atemporal self-conception collapses, and there erupts into his consciousness an obsession with the disparity between his years and Octavius's, one that he exhibits in his abuse of the messenger Thidias and in the invective he directs at Cleopatra. Cleopatra's offer of her hand to Thidias to kiss, whatever her motive, echoes an offer she had earlier made to the messenger who brings her the news of Antony's marriage to Octavia. Before that messenger imparts his distressing news, Cleopatra says that if Antony is "well and free, / . . . there is gold, and here / My bluest veins to kiss—a hand that kings / Have lipped, and trembled kissing" (2.5.27–30). In offering her hand to Thidias, she forms a similar association, saying, "Your Caesar's father oft, / When he hath mused of taking kingdoms in, / Bestowed his lips on that unworthy place, / As it rained kisses" (3.13.83–86). In both instances, Cleopatra's offer of her hand, like her hopping forty paces in the public street and her wish (in Antony's words) to "wander through the streets and note / The qualities of people" (1.1.55–56), enacts her power charismatically, mingling erotic seductiveness with intimations of her queenly grandeur.

For Antony, by contrast, Cleopatra's offer of her hand provides evidence not of her continued possession of charisma but of the loss of his own. "Authority melts from me of late," he says, when the servants fail to respond immediately to his summons, and he replaces his earlier confidence in his charismatic power with an Octavius-like disapproval of Cleopatra's behavior as violating social and political hierarchy. "Have I my pillow left unpressed in Rome," he says, "to be abused / By one that looks on feeders?" "To let a fellow that will take rewards / And say 'God quit you!' be familiar with / My playfellow, your hand, this kingly seal / And plighter of high hearts!" "To flatter Caesar, would you mingle eyes / With one that ties his points?" (3.13. 91, 107–10, 125–28, 159–60). Accompanying this loss of confidence in his charismatic power is a lashing out against Octavius in the surrogate form of Thidias. Like Macbeth's indirect assault on Banquo's descendants in his slaughter of Macduff's wife and child, Antony's command that Thidias be whipped "[t]ill like a boy you see him cringe his face / And whine aloud for mercy" enacts displaced aggression against Octavius, specifically against the rose of youth he wears upon him (3.13.101–2). Similarly, Antony's earlier offer of individual combat seeks to re-center his authority within his physical being, the site of his charisma, while at the same time disparaging Caesar's exercise of power by extension, as if it were not fully adult and manly. "His coin, ships, legions, / May be a coward's, whose ministers would prevail / Under the service of a child as soon / As i' the command of Caesar," he says, and for that reason Caesar should "lay his gay caparisons apart / And answer me declined, sword against sword, / Ourselves alone" (3.13.22–28).[12]

The invective Antony directs at Cleopatra also enacts this midlife loss of identity and self-confidence. Like the disparity in the three main characters' ages, Cleopatra's sexual history is a continuous fact of the play, but not of Antony's consciousness. Cleopatra and Charmian refer to that history when Cleopatra asks, "Did I, Charmian, ever love Caesar so?" and Charmian jokingly replies, "O that brave Caesar!" (1.5.69–70); but until the encounter with Thidias, Antony never mentions it. In 1.1 and 1.3 he avoids responding directly to Cleopatra when she repeatedly draws attention to the distinction between Fulvia's status as wife and her own as mistress, and in 2.6 he slides aside from the opportunity to talk about Cleopatra's past provided by Pompey when Pompey says, disingenuously, "I have heard that Julius Caesar / Grew fat with feasting there" (2.6.64–65) and then refers to Apollodorus's having carried Cleopatra to Caesar wrapped in a mattress. But when Antony rounds on Cleopatra after the encounter with Thidias, her entire sexual history erupts into his consciousness. When it does, the food imagery so prominently associated with Cleopatra reverses its significance. When "[b]road-fronted Caesar / . . . wast here above the ground," Cleopatra says, "I was / A morsel for a monarch" (1.5.30–32). But in 3.13, Antony uses this morsel image with an opposite valuation, saying, "I found you as a morsel cold upon / Dead Caesar's trencher; nay, you were a fragment / Of Gnaeus Pompey's, besides what hotter hours, / Unregistered in vulgar fame, you have / Luxuriously picked out" (3.13.118–22). And with this reversal the impression created earlier of Cleopatra's cloylessness, wherein "she makes hungry / Where most she satisfies" (2.2.247–48) reverses itself as well, converting to an impression of Antony as experiencing satiation and sexual nausea.

In this abrupt deflation of Antony's claim that "[t]he nobleness of life / Is to do thus" (1.1.38–39), the play foregrounds the quality Jonathan Dollimore identifies when he says that Antony's "sexuality is informed by the very power relations which he, ambivalently, is prepared to sacrifice for sexual freedom."[13] A similar interdependence of sexuality and power is revealed in Cleopatra's behavior immediately subsequent to Antony's death. In the aftermath of the encounter with Thidias, Cleopatra subordinates her own sense of loss to Antony's, first helping Antony to recover his self-confidence and his trust in her, then saying, "It is my birthday. / I had thought t' have held it poor; but since my lord / Is Antony again, I will be Cleopatra" (3.13.188–90). In the following scenes, the impression that Cleopatra has not yet fully undergone an experience of loss parallel to Antony's is conveyed through her (ambiguously) self-preservative behavior—the surrender of her fleet during the second sea battle, her sending Mardian to tell Antony that she has killed herself, her refusal, "[l]est I be taken" (4.15.24), to come down out of her monument and join the dying Antony. But in her speech at the moment of Antony's death and the one immediately following, Cleopatra exhibits a diminishment of identity and charisma resembling Antony's. "O, withered is the garland of the war; / The soldier's pole is fallen," she says in the first speech, mingling in her grief recollection of Antony's military and his sexual abilities. "Young boys and girls / Are level now with men," she says, acknowledging in her reference to young boys the triumph of the scarce-bearded Caesar and in her reference to young girls the apparent passing of her own sexual allure and queenly authority (4.15.66–68).

Cleopatra's subsequent speech, the one beginning "[n]o more but e'en a woman" (4.15.78), expands on this sense of diminishment, in the process identifying the threats to her selfhood that her own journey into suicide must struggle to surmount. Accompanying Cleopatra's reference to herself as only a woman is an emphasis on the womanhood of Charmian and Iras, now her only companions. "O see, my women," she says in the first of the two speeches, "[t]he crown o' th' earth doth melt" (4.15.64–65), and in the second speech she uses the word *women* in reference to Charmian and Iras five more times (and *girls* once). This iteration underscores the interrelation of psychic and social loss. As Cleopatra, formerly endowed with sexual prowess, now sees herself reduced to a nugatory femininity, so her kingdom is here reduced to a minuscule and vulnerable community comprised only of females. And accompanying these reductions in selfhood and stature is a descent into a state of near despair. As Cleopatra begins to convince herself that suicide is "what's brave, what's noble," she envisions killing herself "after the high Roman fashion," as if the only meaning to be asserted through her death is an acquiescence to Octavius's triumph and to the ascendancy of Roman values (4.15.91–92). And twice in this speech as well, Cleopatra exposes to doubt the question of whether anything of value remains of Antony, now that he is dead. When she threatens to throw her scepter at the gods, "[t]o tell them that this world did equal theirs / Till they had stol'n our jewel," she locates Antony's value entirely in the past (4.15.82–83). And she implies a similar sense that Antony's bodily death destroys his meaning when she says, "This case of that huge spirit now is cold. / Ah, women, women! Come. We have no friend / But resolution, and the briefest end" (4.15.94–96).

III

The compressed, elliptical quality of these depictions of midlife loss performs a structural function, clearing space for an extended representation, first of Antony's, then of Cleopatra's, post-crisis behavior. For both characters, this behavior consists of a recovery, partial for Antony, more complete for Cleopatra, of the sense of self that had seemed lost in the time of crisis. A limitation of Erikson's original schema for adult development is its emphasis on a single aspect of midlife experience. Subsequent to the midlife polarity of generativity vs. stagnation, the only developmental polarity Erikson discusses is the final one of ego integrity vs. despair, as if the time between the beginning of middle age and the onset of old age were a flat plain, in which no developments of any particular significance beyond the choice (or refusal) of generativity could be expected to occur. Ego psychologists working in the Eriksonian tradition have sought to remedy this deficiency by subdividing the years of middle life into additional stages and by describing with more particularity the aftereffects of the midlife crisis. By and large I have found this body of work too specific to the conditions of modern American middle-class life to be of use in interpreting *Antony and Cleopatra.* But some of its more general insights are provocative. Bernice Neugarten, observing that the post-crisis middle years are characterized by an awareness that less time very likely remains to be lived than has already elapsed, argues that these years exhibit as well a "reversal in directionality," in which less attention is paid to planning for the future than to reassessment of the past, with the reassessment often taking the form of an explanatory or self-justifying narrative. And accompanying this reversal, Daniel Levinson argues, is at least a partial relinquishment of the fantasies of omnipotence attributable to adulthood in the pre-crisis years.[14]

Antony's behavior after his midlife collapse conforms to these observations, mixing together attempts to deny the reality of his loss, muted acknowledgments of its irreversibility, and nostalgic retrospection. In considering his behavior, it will be helpful to recall the elements of his personality—emotionality, generosity, trust, physicality, prowess as a warrior—that underpin his charismatic power and that make his attempted recovery of that power so affecting. In all instances, Antony's positive qualities stand in contrast to opposite qualities exhibited by Octavius. In commenting on Antony's speech in *Julius Caesar* beginning "O, pardon me, thou bleeding piece of earth, / That I am meek and gentle with these butchers!" (3.1.256–57), David Daniell observes that here, "[f]or the first time in the play, . . . violence is owned by the speaker."[15] A similar direct access to emotion, contrasting with Octavius's behavior, as in the earlier play with Brutus's and Cassius's, characterizes Antony in *Antony and Cleopatra.* Agrippa recalls Antony's emotionality when he says "[w]hen Antony found Julius Caesar dead, / He cried almost to roaring; and he wept / When at Philippi he found Brutus slain," and Enobarbus acknowledges the effect of those outbursts on himself when he replies, "What willingly he did confound he wailed, / Believe 't, till I wept too" (3.2.55–60). But Octavius, even when moved to tears by the news of Antony's death, will not allow his feelings to override his statecraft. When a messenger enters, Caesar interrupts his eulogy for Antony, saying, "I will tell you at some meeter season. / The business of this man looks out of him; / We'll hear him what he says" (5.1.49–51).

There is no evidence that a "meeter season" ever arrives for Octavius, either in this instance or in any other, and the overall effect of this austerity, as Pompey says early in the play, is that "Caesar gets money where / He loses hearts" (2.1.13–14). A similar contrast, also to Antony's advantage, can be seen in the other traits that Antony typically displays: in the contrast between his largesse and Caesar's grudging willingness to feast the army after Actium because "we have store to do 't, / And they have earned the waste" (4.1.16–17); in the trust Antony exhibits toward Cleopatra when he informs her of Caesar's shrewd offer, again after Actium, to "fill [her] wishes to the brim / With principalities" if she will "[t]o the boy Caesar send this grizzled head" (3.13.17–19); in the physicality Antony exhibits in his repeated touching of others, including subordinates, in contrast to Octavius, who almost never initiates any form of physical contact beyond a handshake, not even when his sister returns to Rome, alone and forlorn; in Antony's abilities as a warrior, acknowledged by Octavius himself in his recollection of Antony's endurance of physical privation after his defeat at Modena (1.4.57–72), this again in contrast to Octavius, who, as Antony complains, "at Philippi kept / His sword e'en like a dancer, while I struck / The lean and wrinkled Cassius, and 'twas I / That the mad Brutus ended. He alone / Dealt on lieutenantry, and no practice had / In the brave squares of war" (3.11.35–40).

The attractiveness of these qualities lends a positive emotional resonance to Antony's attempt to find "hope in 't yet" (3.13.179) after the defeat at Actium, a resonance enhanced, in a fashion only apparently paradoxical, by pervasive indications that the attempt is evanescent. In an almost schematic, step-by-step series of enactments, Antony not only reverts to the traits of personality that undergird his charisma but also revises other traits that in retrospect can be seen to have contributed to his downfall. The dilatoriness that prior to the battle at Actium had earned Cleopatra's rebuke, "[c]elerity is never more admired / Than by the negligent" (3.7.24–25), is replaced by eager anticipation, as shown in Antony's rejection, prior to the land battle, of Cleopatra's plea that he "[s]leep a little," and in his being armed and ready when a soldier enters and announces "[a] thousand sir, / Early though 't be, have on their riveted trim / And at the port expect you" (4.4.1, 21–23).[16] Equally important, the scene of the arming itself enacts a reversal of the earlier suggestions, voiced primarily but not exclusively by Roman observers, that Antony's infatuation with Cleopatra had effeminized him. In the most famous of those earlier suggestions, Cleopatra recalls the time when "[e]re the ninth hour, I drunk him to his bed, / Then put my tires and mantles on him, whilst / I wore his sword Phillipan" (2.5.21–23). But in the arming scene, not only is early morning debauchery replaced by an eagerness to arise "betimes," but the dressing motif itself is reversed, as Antony ascribes to Cleopatra the subordinate role of "armorer of my heart" (4.1.20, 7), and Cleopatra herself, who earlier had said "[a] charge we bear i' the war, / And as president of my kingdom will / Appear there for a man" (3.7.16–18), reveals that she is, in David Bevington's words, "[i]ronically, and charmingly too, . . . clumsily inexperienced" in the intricacies of dressing for warfare.[17]

Antony's success in the land battle and his encounter with Cleopatra immediately afterward continue the impression that he has recovered an imperiled identity, both military and sexual.[18] But the play never permits its audience—or Antony—to believe for long that this recovery is more than temporary. In preparing for the battle, Caesar instructs Agrippa (via a messenger) to "[p]lant those that have revolted in the van, / That Antony may seem to spend his fury / Upon himself" (4.6.9–11)—upon "himself," that is, understood in Octavian terms, as an identity inhering not in Antony's body but in the troops he commands. This is the form of self that Antony would need to continue to possess were he truly to be capable of contending with Octavius for dominance. Evidence of its disappearance is threaded throughout the scenes following the defeat at Actium, most obviously in Enobarbus's caustic comments about the "diminution in our captain's brain" (3.13.201) underlying Antony's call for individual combat and in his subsequent decision to leave Antony's service, but also in the mysterious scene of the departure of "the god Hercules, whom Antony loved" (4.3.21), and in such incidental details as Cleopatra's promise to give to Scarus "[a]n armor all of gold; it was a king's" (4.8.26–27), an armor only available because, as Canidius says, transferring his allegiance to Caesar, "[s]ix kings already / Show me the way of yielding" (3.10.34–35). In a similar fashion, despite his best efforts to the contrary, Antony's language betrays his awareness of the desperateness of his situation. It is "once more," not often, that he hopes to return from battle "[t]o kiss these lips"; "one other gaudy night," not many, that he plans to "mock the midnight bell"; "tomorrow," not later, that his weeping servants may perchance "serve another master"; only "tonight two hours," not longer, that he asks them to attend to his needs (3.13.176–77, 186–88; 4.2.28–29, 32).[19]

IV

With the defeat in the second sea battle, Antony's effort at self-recovery reaches its seeming conclusion, as he speaks of having arrived at "the very heart of loss" and as he imagines his "visible shape" dissolving, like a cloud that resembles a bear or lion or horse, but "even with a thought/. . . dislimns and makes it[self] indistinct/As water is in water" (4.12.29; 4.14.14, 9–11). Yet even here there occurs a further effort at recovery, as Antony, believing Cleopatra to have died, resolves to commit suicide, first by Eros's agency, then, after Eros instead dies by his own hand, by performing the act himself. In their deaths, presumed and actual, Antony says that Cleopatra and Eros "[h]ave by their brave instruction got upon me/A nobleness in record" (4.14.98–99). This concern with "record," with the place that a person achieves in history through his or her acts, extends a pattern established earlier by Enobarbus's claim that "he that can endure/To follow with allegiance a fall'n lord/. . ./. . . earns a place i' the story" (3.13.43–46); by his despairing insistence, after abandoning Antony, that "the world rank me in register/A master-leaver and a fugitive" (4.9.24–25); and by Antony's defiant vaunt, after the encounter with Thidias, that "I and my sword will earn our chronicle" (3.13.178). In the slow journey into death consequent upon his inefficient effort at self-slaughter, Antony makes a final attempt to achieve a nobleness in record, thereby affirming his identity in the fashion Bernice Neugarten describes as typical of the post-midlife-crisis middle years, not as an ongoing condition of existence but as a memorial reconstruction. "Not Caesar's valor hath o'erthrown Antony," he tells Cleopatra, "[b]ut Antony's hath triumphed on itself" (4.15.15–16). "The miserable change now at my end/Lament nor sorrow at," he says, "but please your thoughts/In feeding them with those my former fortunes, / Wherein I lived the greatest prince o' the world, / The noblest" (4.15.53–57).[20]

The significance of this effort at self-recovery through memorial reconstruction can best be understood in relation to the subsequent similar (but more successful) efforts at recovery on Cleopatra's part, both of Antony and of herself. Not surprisingly, classical and Early Modern representations of life as a series of stages are usually coded male. Although Jaques speaks of men *and* women in the prelude to his seven ages speech, he populates the five ages between an ungendered infancy and old age exclusively with males, with the middle part of life represented by the soldier and the justice. But as Peter Erickson observes, in *Antony and Cleopatra* Shakespeare reverses "the standard tragic ending, [in which] the woman dies first while the male protagonist is left to survey the damage for which he is in large part responsible. One measure of Cleopatra's stature is . . . [that] the woman survives to mourn the man." By reversing emphasis in this way, Shakespeare gives prominence to a specifically female form of midlife experience. Antony's death places Cleopatra in the circumstance of a midlife simulacrum of widowhood, and the developmental task she faces is to learn how to enact this role in a fashion that honors her attachment to Antony. On the one hand, there is the question of whether her identity is to continue to be defined by that relationship. Having been involved in two previous high-profile erotic relationships, why should she not conform to the stereotype, prominent in folklore and literature, of the lusty widow, and now seek a fourth? On the other hand, if she *is* to remain loyal to Antony, how is that loyalty best to be enacted?[21]

As Anne Barton has argued, the dramatic interest of the conclusion of *Antony and Cleopatra* consists in considerable measure in Cleopatra's rejection of the first of these options, through her affirmation—even, Barton argues, her final full discovery—of the authenticity of her affection for Antony.[22] It consists even more in the gradual expansion and deepening of her enactment of that discovery. If Cleopatra is to locate the meaning of her existence in the past, she needs to mourn the loss not only of Antony but of her own identity as queen and lover; but this she cannot do as long as she remains in the state of hopelessness to which she is reduced in the immediate aftermath of Antony's death. The final scene of the play consists of a three-part sequence of episodes by means of which a movement beyond this state is gradually achieved: first Cleopatra's account of her dream of "an emperor Antony" (5.2.75), in which she recovers Antony as a figure worthy of her grief; then her encounter with Octavius, in which she recovers some amount of her charismatic power, understood here again as seductiveness; and finally, her elaborately staged enactment of her suicide, in which she constructs a nobleness in record of her own.

The first of these episodes enacts Cleopatra's movement beyond despair through its use of the play's pervasive imagery of size and weight. At the beginning of the monument scene, just prior to Antony's arrival, Cleopatra says, "[o]ur size of sorrow, / Proportioned to our cause, must be / As great as that which makes it" (4.15.4–6), and when drawing Antony up into the monument, she associates her sadness with his weight when she says, "[h]ere's sport indeed! How heavy weighs my lord! / Our strength is all gone into heaviness, / That makes the weight" (4.15.33–35). The double implication of these speeches is that Cleopatra's greatness, as she understands it, obligates her to a corresponding magnitude of grief, and that Antony's weight—his dying physical being—can indeed be transformed into the "heaviness" of sorrow. Cleopatra's sense of loss in the immediate aftermath of Antony's death challenges both of these implications, with her sense of herself as "[n]o more but e'en a woman" providing no identity capable of enacting an appropriate size of sorrow, and with her observation that "[t]his case of that huge spirit now is cold" depicting Antony's body as merely physical, a material remnant of his existence that must immediately be buried, before further signs of its dissolution become evident (4.15.78, 94). And this challenge is intensified by the play's insistent naturalism, its refusal to provide any "context," in Janet Adelman's words, "which demands that we believe in the literal possibility of the afterlife; there is no evidence that either the Egyptians or the Romans in the play take the belief seriously." Hence if Antony's weight is to be transformed into something other than this cold case, subject to decay, it must be within the possibilities offered by this world, not those provided by belief in an otherworldly regeneration.[23]

Like Antony, the possibility that Cleopatra discovers is memorial reconstruction, the making of meaning through retrospection. When Cleopatra says at the beginning of the monument scene, "O Charmian, I will never go forth from hence" (4.15.1), it is not clear whether she has already begun to think of suicide or only hopes to find in the monument a desperate form of sanctuary. This equivocation continues in the question she poses at the end of the scene, "is it sin / To rush into the secret house of death," where she seems to be talking herself into a willingness to "do 't after the high Roman fashion," and again a scene later, when she sends an ambiguously worded message to Caesar, desiring instruction "[t]hat she preparedly may frame herself / To th' way she's forced to" (4.15.85–86, 92; 5.1.55–56). But in the encounter with Proculeius, as she is surprised and disarmed, her equivocation at least temporarily resolves itself. "This mortal house I'll ruin," she says, "[d]o Caesar what he can" (5.2.50–51). And following hard upon this commitment comes the dream that she recounts to Dolabella, in which Antony returns as a physical being, but with his size magnified hyperbolically. "His face was as the heavens," says Cleopatra, "and therein stuck / A sun and moon, which kept their course and lighted / The little O, the earth." "His legs bestrid the ocean; his reared arm / Crested the world; his voice was propertied / As all the tunèd spheres" (5.2.78–80, 81–83). The effect of this magnification, as the now-smitten Dolabella realizes, is to create an Antony of an amplitude sufficient to serve as the cause to which Cleopatra's size of sorrow can now be proportioned. "Hear me, good madam," he says, in the speech from which I once contemplated taking the title of this book, "[y]our loss is as yourself, great; and you bear it / As answering to the weight" (5.2.99–101).[24]

The cold case of Antony's body, reclaimed and transformed, provokes and justifies a corresponding heaviness of grief in Cleopatra. The episode with Octavius immediately following Cleopatra's account of her dream enacts a second reclamation, not of Antony but of Cleopatra herself, in her performative and seductive capacities. Discussion of this episode has often focused on the question of Cleopatra's motive in failing to provide a true account of her "money, plate, and jewels," as revealed by her treasurer, Seleucus (5.2.137). Is Cleopatra holding back more than half of her wealth because she has wavered in her resolution to commit suicide, and is she betrayed in her deception by Seleucus unawares? Or is Seleucus's "betrayal" a put-up job, arranged by Cleopatra beforehand, as part of an attempt to convince Caesar that she wishes to live? As in other instances where Cleopatra's motives are under scrutiny, definitive answers to these questions may be unattainable. But various details favor interpreting the episode as a deliberate ruse. It is clear, for example, that Cleopatra has prepared the means of her suicide before the scene begins, for after Caesar leaves, she sends Charmian to arrange for the delivery of the asp, saying, "I have spoke already, and it is provided; / Go put it to the haste" (5.2.195–96). Also, Plutarch ascribes to the encounter as a whole the effect that a ruse would be intended to achieve when he says that Cleopatra "suddenly altered her speech . . . as though she were afraid to die" and that Caesar persuaded himself "thereby that she had yet a desire to save her life." And Shakespeare strengthens the possibility that the episode with Seleucus is a deliberate contribution to this effect by not having Seleucus approach Caesar on his own initiative, "to seem a good servant," as he does in Plutarch, but by having Cleopatra herself call upon him to speak.[25]

More than these details of presentation, Cleopatra's overall demeanor makes it unlikely that she has wavered in her determination to commit suicide. The encounter with Octavius is arguably one of Cleopatra's greatest performances, second only to her suicide itself, for in it she recovers her seductive powers, and she does so in a difficult fashion, not by seeking a new relationship to replace the one with Antony, but by eschewing erotic purpose. If we ask whom Cleopatra resembles in this scene, the answer is not Cleopatra herself in any of her earlier self-enactments, but Octavia. Octavia's first appearance on stage begins with Antony saying, with unconscious irony, "[t]he world and my great office will sometimes / Divide me from your bosom." Octavia's reply, "[a]ll which time / Before the gods my knee shall bow my prayers / To them for you," associates kneeling with a willing female submission to Roman values (2.3.1–4). This association reemerges in Cleopatra's conversation with Proculeius, where she proposes to "kneel to [Octavius] with thanks" "[i]f he please / To give me conquered Egypt for my son," and again at the beginning of the scene with Octavius, when in fact Cleopatra does attempt to kneel (5.2.18–20; s.d. at 5.2.112). Throughout the encounter with Octavius what Proculeius calls Cleopatra's "sweet dependency" is evident as well in her language, as she twice calls Caesar "[m]y master and my lord," attributes to herself the "frailties which before / Have often shamed our sex," and describes herself as "one so meek" (5.2.26, 115, 190, 122–23, 161). And even her (pretended) rage at

Seleucus exemplifies this submissive self-presentation, since it is enacted within Caesar's observation and, as he twice intervenes, in apparent deference to his authority.[26]

The overall effect of this performance is to seduce an otherwise unseduceable man: by displaying an unerotic and submissive femininity, Cleopatra flatters Octavius into inattention, thereby securing the leisure she needs to commit suicide.[27] At a more fundamental level, the performance is also an act of self-recovery, for it co-opts Cleopatra's earlier fear that she had become "no more but e'en a woman," transforming that reductive conception of womanhood into one more of the many roles that comprise her infinite variety. In the suicide itself, this self-recovery continues, in a fashion that both echoes and amends Antony's earlier similar effort. As many commentators have observed, Antony's attempt to affirm his identity at the time of his death is bedeviled by the same antinomies that characterize his behavior earlier in the play. His sensual, erotic, and loving self is touchingly enacted in the monument scene in his calling for wine and for a final kiss, in his well-meaning if misinformed concern for Cleopatra's future well-being, and in his refusal to recriminate against her for the deception that led to his suicide. But as before, this self remains unintegrated with his Roman self of warrior and leader. When Antony attempts to achieve a final self-affirmation through retrospection, he must choose one of these identities, not both. The choice he makes—of describing himself as "a Roman by a Roman / Valiantly vanquished" (4.15.59–60)—continues the effort to reclaim his Roman identity begun when he commits suicide in the high Roman fashion, by falling on his sword. But as Michael Neill observes in an excellent discussion of the two suicide scenes, the botched nature of this attempt compromises Antony's later effort "to dress it in the language of heroic authenticity," making "his death seem less the resolution than the inevitable expression of the self-annihilating contradictions that have afflicted his problematic identity from the opening scene."[28]

By contrast, as Neill goes on to argue, Cleopatra's suicide "reverses the transformation suffered by the dying Anthony, becoming the act of supreme distinction at which Anthony can only gesture. . . . Where Anthony performed the ritual unmaking of his martial self as Eros removed his armour, Cleopatra enacts the formal reassumption of her regal identity as Iras invests her with robe, crown, and sceptre." Indeed, Cleopatra not only reclaims her regal identity, she expands upon it, incorporating into her self-conception elements of identity she has not hitherto possessed and revising other traits that she has in fact exhibited. Dismissing the need any longer either to fear or to enact the role of no more but e'en a woman, she says, "[m]y resolution's placed, and I have nothing/Of woman in me." Dismissing her former capriciousness, she says, "[n]ow from head to foot/I am marble-constant" (5.2.238–40). Wrinkled deep in time, she nonetheless reclaims, in Charmian's words, her identity as "[a] lass unparalleled" (5.2.316). Calling Antony "husband," she aggrandizes to herself the role of wife. Calling him "the curlèd Antony," she imagines him as he had been at the time of their meeting at the river Cydnus, when he was "barbered ten times o'er" (2.2.234), not as he had since become, when his grizzled head betokened his decline. Most of all, as Clare Kinney observes, she does not "slavishly imitate the 'high Roman fashion' of death," as she had intended, "but rather appropriates it and remakes it in her own image." Choosing the asp as her means of death and comparing "[t]he stroke of death" to "a lover's pinch,/Which hurts, and is desired," she reclaims her eroticism. Describing the asp as "my baby at my breast,/That sucks the nurse asleep," she adds yet another role to her steadily expanding self-conception: queen, wife, lass, lover, she is now also nurse or mother.[29]

V

Yet there remain those children. In his essay on *Antony and Cleopatra,* A. C. Bradley says that to deny the name of love to Antony and Cleopatra's relationship "is the madness of morality." To call into question Cleopatra's effort at heroic self-affirmation by directing attention to the fate of her children may seem, if not madness, at least an undue emphasis on family values. And it is true that in comparison to two of his sources other than Plutarch, the Countess of Pembroke's *Antonius* (a translation of Robert Garnier's *Marc Antoine*) and Samuel Daniel's *Cleopatra,* Shakespeare markedly lessens the prominence given to Cleopatra's children. In *Antonius* the children appear directly on stage, as they do not in *Antony and Cleopatra,* and in both works concern for the children's well-being is a prominent theme in Cleopatra's anguished deliberations over whether to commit suicide. But it is also true that Shakespeare had the freedom to omit mention of the children entirely, had he so wished. In other regards he softens the evidence provided by Plutarch of Antony's and Cleopatra's cruelty and despotism, most notably by omitting any mention of Antony's exercise of the power of decimation during the Parthian campaign, wherein he executed a tenth part of his army for a military failure, and by making only a highly veiled allusion (at 5.2.354–56) to Cleopatra's having watched while various poisons were administered to condemned men in prison, as a way of determining which were least painful in their effects. So the question is not whether we should suppress an awareness of Cleopatra's children but rather how awareness of their existence, as invited by Shakespeare, complicates (and enriches) the significance of Cleopatra's suicide.[30]

An approach to an answer to this question can be found in the cultural implications of Antony's and Cleopatra's efforts at self-recovery through memorial reconstruction. It has often been noted that the play's autumnal quality, its suffusion with nostalgia, reaches beyond the central characters' recollections of their own past identities into both the larger social order depicted in the play and the one within which it was written. As Michael Neill observes in the introduction to his edition of the play, "the Roman world is especially haunted by a sense of faded glories. . . . [T]he play is full of recollections of the colossic figures of late republican Rome, in whose vanished glamour the conniving politicians of the new age seek to deck their cause. . . . [And] it is Anthony above all, as the last survivor of a heroic age, whom the play bathes in a glow of admiring retrospection." Furthermore, as Jonathan Dollimore argues, this sense of Antony as an anachronistic survivor of an earlier age of heroic endeavor resonates against large-scale changes occurring in Shakespeare's own time, for "the professionalizing of warfare and the increasing efficiency of state armies" during this period meant that "there was considerably less scope for personal military initiative and military glory, [and] honour [was becoming] an informal personal code with an extremely attenuated social dimension." As with Antony, so with Cleopatra. Unlike Rome, the Egypt Cleopatra rules over is not depicted as especially haunted by a sense of past glories. But her own situation, like Antony's, does convey a larger meaning of this sort, insofar as her death and the termination of her queenship can be seen as encoding, and as coloring with nostalgia, the passing away of female sovereignty that had occurred with the death of Elizabeth and the accession of James.[31]

In *Antony and Cleopatra,* as in *Macbeth,* these larger cultural implications extend to the mortality crisis that Robert Watson argues was prevalent in Jacobean England. Commentators writing from a variety of perspectives have observed how both the structure and the meaning of *Antony and Cleopatra* require for their completion that Cleopatra die. For Anne Barton, reading the play as a love tragedy, "[o]nly if Cleopatra keeps faith with Antony now and dies can the flux of the play be stilled, and their love claim value." For Katherine Eggert, arguing the importance of the passing of Elizabeth's queenship to the development of "effeminized form" in Shakespeare's drama, "[n]ostalgia involves not only the inevitable historical consciousness of . . . knowing when and how Cleopatra dies, but also the recognition that her death is required so that we may remember her and revive her upon the stage." For Michael Neill, even the location of Cleopatra's suicide in her monument links the play to Jacobean anxieties about death as personal annihilation. Noting, like Greenblatt, Watson, and others, that "the anxieties attendant upon death and dying" were exacerbated by "the Protestant denial of purgatory," Neill argues (following Nigel Llewellyn) that one means Protestants used to assuage these anxieties was the construction of increasingly elaborate funerary monuments. "The more splendid [the tombs'] marble ornamentation, the richer their gilding and painting," he says, "the more eloquently these shrines of memory spoke of the longing for a species of immortality which . . . it might remain in the power of the living to confer." Hence in the site of Cleopatra's suicide, as in her depiction of herself as if she were now a funerary ornament, "marble-constant" (5.2.240), Neill argues that Shakespeare dramatizes both an awareness of and a defiance of "the undifferentiating power of death."[32]

This mixture of awareness and defiance at the cultural level is also present in the play at the level of psychology. Neill says that the play's "preoccupation with the fearful indistinction of death" is not articulated directly but is instead "characteristically displaced onto the self-abandon and dissolution of Anthony's sexual infatuation and the feminization of masculine identity which it entails." This observation, while valid, tells only part of the story, for the relation between loss of identity and fear of death also functions in the opposite direction. A cautionary observation offered by people who counsel suicidally inclined individuals is that suicide is a permanent solution to a temporary problem. Most counselors acknowledge that this advice is not universally applicable: some problems, a terminal illness, say, are not temporary. But the comment is true often enough to make it worthwhile to ask what local difficulty may be receiving hyperbolic expression at those times when a person's thoughts turn to death. Approaching *Antony and Cleopatra* in this fashion permits us to view the play's concern with death as multivalent, extending on the one hand toward a general Jacobean anxiety about personal annihilation and on the other toward the many local defeats, the grizzled head, the passing of the salad days, the military reversals, that make up Antony and Cleopatra's experience of the middle years. And it allows us to view the double suicide, Cleopatra's especially, as an effort to countermand this history of midlife decline by incorporating death itself, "that thing . . . / Which shackles accident and bolts up change" (5.2.5–6), into a memorial reconstruction ending not in defeat but in triumph.[33]

In this effort, *Antony and Cleopatra* joins with *King Lear* and *Macbeth* in turning aside from the hope that generational succession can serve as a palliative for the troubles of the middle years. As Joyce Green MacDonald observes, when Antony refuses "the value of the marriage of state with Octavius's sister, he refuses as well the authority of a precisely defined patriarchal 'family' as an authorizing model for the conduct of public life." And in glorifying their illicit liaison, Antony and Cleopatra evoke a further aspect of the play's pervasive nostalgia, preferring what Catherine Belsey calls "the medieval romance of adultery" over "the Renaissance romance of marriage." In these preferences, locating meaning in bodily pleasure, Antony and Cleopatra echo their preference for charismatic forms of political identity. But a significant difference in tone distinguishes *Antony and Cleopatra* from the two earlier tragedies. In an epigrammatic formulation, A. C. Bradley says of the conclusion of *Antony and Cleopatra,* "we are saddened by the very fact that the catastrophe saddens us so little; it pains us that we should feel so much triumph and pleasure." This paradoxical effect arises, at least in part, from the indirectness of Shakespeare's representation of the dynastic and familial consequences of Antony's and Cleopatra's suicides. Caesarion's unfortunate fate awaits him, but later, and offstage; no dead Cordelia, no slain son of Macduff, no slain Young Siward is present during Cleopatra's death scene to perturb what Constance Brown Kuriyama calls the play's "richly elaborated rendering of a basic human sexual fantasy"—the fantasy, that is, of *liebestod,* of an ecstatic intermingling of the desire for death and for erotic consummation. But because we know from the earlier parts of the play that Caesarion and the other children *do* exist, neither can we experience the *liebestod* fantasy entirely without reservation.[34]

The play's meta-dramatic quality, its emphasis on behavior as performance, contributes significantly to this effect of intense yet qualified empathy with Cleopatra's dying self-affirmation. A rhetorical analysis conducted by a pair of psychologists a number of years ago observed the prevalence in suicide notes of a pattern of narratorial splitting, wherein the note's author positions himself or herself simultaneously as writer, as agent and object of the impending suicide, and as observer of its effect on the intended recipient of the note.[35] Cleopatra's suicide exhibits a similar splitting, as she prepares the setting and her costume for maximum dramatic effect; says, "[m]ethinks I hear / Antony call; I see him rouse himself / To praise my noble act"; applies the asp to her breast; and then says, addressing the asp, "O, couldst thou speak, / That I might here thee call great Caesar ass / Unpolicied!" (5.2.283–85, 306–8). This performative self-awareness invites an interpretation of the meaning of the death scene—of its "truth"—as relative to the needs of its creator. The question is less whether Cleopatra has in fact triumphed over Caesar, as many critics have attempted to ascertain, than how her immortal longings function in the narrative she is constructing, as opposed to how Caesar's desire that she be eternal in his triumph functions in his. And this fictionalizing of the death scene, like Cleopatra's aggrandizement of the roles of wife, queen, lass, and nurse or mother, encourages the audience to respond in a similarly self-aware fashion. It allows the audience to experience the heady erotic pleasure of the *liebestod* fantasy as a truth of desire, without requiring that the fantasy be viewed as a guide for behavior in the world.

It should be evident that *Antony and Cleopatra*'s depiction of a post-midlife-crisis experience of temporality bears a direct relation to the play's liminal status, halfway between *King Lear* and *Macbeth* on the one hand and the late romances on the other. The corrosive power of Lear's rebirth fantasy and of Macbeth's fantasy of controlling the future lies in the literal-mindedness with which they are enacted. In both instances, the play's protagonist believes that he can reverse or eliminate the traumatic effects of life in time, specifically those related to the transfer of power, authority, and identity to a succeeding generation. Antony and Cleopatra accede to the impossibility of this belief, without, however, relinquishing the desire for a continuation of their identities in their own beings. Like the swan's down feather that stands upon the swell at full of tide, they stand poised between a sublimated investment in the future and a fictional reconstruction of the past. Choosing the second of these options over the first, they reconstitute themselves as icons of memory, a bridegroom in death, an autumn that grows the more by reaping, a lass unparalleled, a princess descended of so many royal kings. "Bid that welcome / Which comes to punish us," says Antony, "and we punish it, / Seeming to bear it lightly" (4.14.141–43). From this stance of simultaneous relinquishment and reacquisition of identity, it is but a short step to the late romances, where children reenter the scene in their own right, still at times the victims of parental rage or indifference, but at other times not. And it is a short step as well to a changed depiction of the parents themselves, once again primarily of the father, as he begins to soften his resistance to generativity and to explore how, if at all, he can enact redress for the harm caused by his past intransigence.

5
Hermione's Wrinkles

What should happen to Leontes in *The Winter's Tale* once he recognizes the folly of his ways? How should we as audience react to the prospect offered at the end of the play of a happy future life for Leontes, now reunited with Hermione, with Polixenes, and with Perdita, the soon-to-be-married daughter he had ordered exposed as an infant to almost certain death? For an earlier generation of critics, the answer to these questions is implicit within an interpretation of the play, in Kiernan Ryan's summary description, as "a timeless Christian, pagan or humanist tale of atonement and redemption." Viewed in these terms, Leontes' movement through the play exemplifies "the journey of the soul from sin and penitence to grace and salvation," and his final status as beneficent sovereign, husband, friend, and father is that journey's proper outcome. For more recent critics, though, and for some earlier ones as well, Leontes' final regeneration is troubling, first of all in the extent to which it can be said not to be complete. As Robert Grams Hunter observes, "Hermione's seeming death was not the only one to result from Leontes' crime. Antigonus, too, perished, . . . [and] more important is the memory of Mamillius," whose death must be glossed over or explained away by those critics who wish to argue for the thoroughness of the play's movement toward regeneration. There is considerable evidence, too, as B. J. Sokol observes, that in the final scene Leontes retains "his impatient leonine constitution, only partly tempered"; certainly his insistence that his newly reconciled wife greet Polixenes, the former object of his suspicion, is both unctuous and tactless. And the fact that Hermione speaks only to Perdita, not to Leontes, suggests that the conversation Leontes envisions when he says, "[l]ead us from hence, where we may leisurely / Each one demand and answer to his part / Performed in this wide gap of time since first / We were dissevered" (5.3.154–57), may not be entirely untroubled.[1]

In recent years as well, reservations about the completeness of Leontes' regeneration have expanded into discomfort with the play's underlying ideological assumptions. For feminist critics especially, the play's foregrounding of Leontes' struggle and growth has come to be seen as complicit with patriarchal assumptions about social priorities and values. While feminist critics often praise the prominence given to Paulina and to other female characters in bringing about Leontes' recovery, they recognize, as Janet Adelman says, that "the female agents of restoration turn out to have been good patriarchalists all along, working to permit the father's recovery of himself and of his heir." The overall dramatic action, Peter Erickson observes, consists "in the fashioning of a benign patriarchy." While the movement from jealousy to reconciliation entails "the recovery of a positive image of the feminine," that image "is congenial to patriarchal expectations" in that it "does not prevent Leontes from maintaining social control over female resources." Further, for some commentators, the discomfort occasioned by these insights has led to—or is occasioned by—a more wide-ranging dissatisfaction with the play's (and perhaps Shakespeare's) cultural preeminence. The time has come, says Abbe Blum, "to travel beyond the moral progress of a single protagonist or his victims." "We . . . collude in [the] process of associating child murder with mothers," says my colleague Frances Dolan, in commenting on *The Winter's Tale* in her study of Early Modern domestic crime, if we continue "valuing plays in which elite, murderous fathers, whose violence can be forgiven, are the protagonists."[2]

Whether one chooses to accede to the belief expressed in these quotations does not seem to me particularly amenable to debate. If reading *The Winter's Tale avec la lettre* seems an ethically suspect activity, then one will read it differently, or not at all. But it must be said that the life issues dramatized in Leontes' journey through the play will not therefore cease to be of importance. The imbalance in the sympathetic representation of male and female protagonists in past literature is a fact of history; but the existence of erring men and the need to consider whether they can be regenerated are also facts, both of history and of present experience. In a study of the place of forgiveness in *Measure for Measure,* Debora Shuger addresses this issue. Duke Vincentio's final pardon of Angelo, Lucio, and Barnardine, she argues, "conforms neither to literary conventions nor to those of fair play." Yet if our desire for poetic justice inclines us to want Angelo (in particular) to suffer the death to which he is initially condemned, what precisely is he to be executed *for?* The arguments Isabella advances on his behalf—that "[a] due sincerity governed his deeds, / Till he did look on me"; that Angelo's planned rape of her "did not o'ertake his bad intent"; that in her brother's execution (as she supposes) Claudio "had but justice, / In that he did the thing for which he died" (5.1.454–59)—may strike a modern audience as intolerably precisianist in their orientation. But as Shuger argues, they are in fact the opposite, for they are the sorts of arguments that would be considered in a court of law. More precisely, they are "considerations of equity," the body of guidelines developed over time to overcome the rigid formality of English common law by taking "into account all the collateral circumstances and mitigating factors relevant to a particular case."[3]

As with *Measure for Measure,* so with *The Winter's Tale.* Shuger's large objective is to explore two forms of intersection between religious belief and state authority in Shakespeare's time: the first Puritan, emphasizing, perhaps as a consequence of belief in predestination, the need for strict laws strictly enforced; the second latitudinarian, emphasizing the possibility of penitence and the potential for reform of sinners and criminals. Shuger argues that in *Measure for Measure* the first of these "political theologies" is embodied in Angelo, the second in Duke Vincentio. In *The Winter's Tale,* the two manifest themselves as states of mind inside Leontes himself: the first in his sense, shortly after awakening from his jealousy, that all his future holds is "shame perpetual," a daily ritual of tears shed at Hermione's and Mamillius's grave sites "[s]o long as nature / Will bear up with this exercise"; the second in the question he directs at the statue in the final scene, "[d]oes not the stone rebuke me / For being more stone than it?" and in the subsequent shift of his "remembrance" of his "evils" from fruitless repetition to purgation (3.2.238–41; 5.3.37–40). In the movement between these poles we may, if we wish, see a dimension of the play's continuing ethical relevance, as our own society continues to oscillate between the need to impose punishment and the desire to encourage regeneration.[4] And we may detect as well the relevance of the play to the concerns of this book, for in the death of Mamillius and the return of Perdita the issues of resistance to and acceptance of generativity emerge into prominence yet again. So the questions remain. What should happen to Leontes? And how should we as audience respond to what in fact does happen?

I

Consider first Leontes' jealousy. Throughout its duration, Shakespeare takes pains to emphasize the irrationality of Leontes' belief that Hermione has been unfaithful. A few commentators see in Polixenes' specification of the length of his visit—"Nine changes of the watery star hath been / The shepherd's note since we have left our throne / Without a burden" (1.2.1–3)—a plausible basis for Leontes' suspicion. As Nevill Coghill says, "For what other possible reason can Shakespeare have contrived the conversation so as to make [Polixenes] specify nine changes of the inconstant moon?" But that specification can as well be assigned an opposite implication, of Leontes' willingness to force his way *past* considerations of plausibility, since the fact that Hermione's pregnancy is near term means that her affair with Polixenes, if there were one, would have had to have begun practically at the moment when the two of them first met and to have gone undetected thereafter. In its larger career, Leontes' delusion exhibits a similar willingness, even eagerness. Operating by a paranoid (il)logic of "[a]ll's true that is mistrusted" (2.1.48), it expands to include anxiety about Mamillius's paternity—"Art thou my boy?" "Art thou my calf?" (1.2.120, 127)—even though illegitimacy in this instance would require Hermione to have had an affair with someone other than Polixenes. It finds in Camillo's flight a basis for believing not only that "Camillo was [Polixenes'] help in this, his pander" but that "[t]here is a plot against my life, my crown" (2.1.46–47). In Antigonus's inability to prevent Paulina's entry in 2.3, it finds grounds for calling Antigonus a "traitor, [who] hast set on thy wife to this" (2.3.131). And it culminates in an indictment against Hermione not only for adultery but for "conspiring with Camillo to take away the life of our sovereign lord the King" and for having counseled Polixenes and Camillo "for their better safety, to fly away by night" (3.2.15–21).[5]

This emphasis on an accelerating and expanding irrationality has combined with the suddenness of the onset of Leontes' delusion to convince many commentators, in David Schalkwyk's words, that "it is futile to search for a personal motivation for Leontes' . . . jealousy." Comparing the play to *Othello,* these critics see in the absence of an Iago, of an external provocation for Leontes' suspicions, an absence of motivation as such. But as Murray Schwartz observes in the first of two important psychoanalytic readings of the play, "what the[se] critics call lack of motivation is lack of rationalization. . . . *The Winter's Tale* . . . can be understood to dramatize not 'motiveless jealousy,' but jealousy whose motivation is embodied in the structure of linguistic and personal relationships acted out on the stage." As Stephen Orgel argues, Leontes' jealousy "is in fact realistic, far more true to human experience than Othello's super-rationalized passion." In its "lack of any external motivation," the jealousy seems "strikingly modern," for it provides "dramatic recognition of the compulsiveness of paranoid behaviour, and more generally, of the self-generating and autonomous nature of consciousness itself."[6]

Commentators following this line of interpretation have detected in Leontes' behavior a wide array of possible motives. In an early Freudian analysis, J. I. M. Stewart applies Freud's formula "I do not love him, she does" to *The Winter's Tale,* reading Leontes' jealousy as a protective screen concealing from himself the homosexual basis of his affection for Polixenes. C. L. Barber also applies a Freudian paradigm to the play, detecting in Leontes' jealousy a reenactment of an oedipal rivalry, with Hermione occupying the role of the mother (an association encouraged by her visible pregnancy) and Polixenes the role of the father, hated and feared for his ability to possess Hermione sexually. Beginning with Schwartz's two essays and continuing in a number of later (often feminist) commentaries, psychoanalytic interpretations have sought explanations of Leontes' behavior less in anxieties about sexual identity or in the Oedipus complex than in the earliest stage of infantile development, at the point, that is, where the (in this instance) male child becomes aware of the distinction between himself and the world. For Schwartz (and, as we saw in chapter 2, for Janet Adelman), this awareness takes the form of a discovery that "the maternity of the mother is not wholly benevolent," and the fear of maternal engulfment that this discovery produces leads in turn to a variety of defensive reactions: fantasies of an adult return to an unconflicted maternal nurturance, as in *King Lear,* fantasies of parthenogenesis, as in *Macbeth.*[7]

In *The Winter's Tale* these reactions first manifest themselves in Polixenes' description of his and Leontes' childhood as a timeless condition in which they "thought there was no more behind / But such a day tomorrow as today, / And to be boy eternal" (1.2.63–65). Schwartz argues that Polixenes' depiction of himself and Leontes as "twinned lambs," exchanging "innocence for innocence" (1.2.67, 69), is "rooted ontogenetically in the mother-child relationship," for it "preserves in masculine form a narcissistic and idealized version of the mother's dual unity with the son." Yet this fantasy of an integral childhood identity—of infantile omnipotence—contains within itself the seeds of its own destruction, for in "the myth of ideal masculine correspondence there lies a deeper set of fantasies in which the brothers are rivals for maternal love." Leontes' jealousy enacts the tension between these opposed fantasies. In his conviction that Hermione has been unfaithful with Polixenes, he replaces Polixenes' role as confirming mirror of his own imagined ideal childhood identity with that of sibling rival. And in his immediate turn to Mamillius and to an anxious need to reassure himself that his son's appearance "is a copy out of mine" (1.2.122), he seeks to reestablish in the present the lost mirror relationship. Further, Leontes adds to this effort a desire for parthenogenesis, for, as Janet Adelman observes, when he expresses anxiety about Mamillius's difference from himself, his concern is that Mamillius bears traces, not of an illegitimate father, but of Hermione herself. "I am glad you did not nurse him," he says. "Though he does bear some signs of me, yet you / Have too much blood in him" (2.1.57–59).[8]

These interpretations provide rich insights into the psychological dynamic at work in Leontes' jealousy. As Schwartz says, even Leontes' paranoia can be understood as an effort to retain the fantasy of infantile omnipotence, for in paranoia's attempt to make "the external world *nothing but* a confluence of symbols selected according to subjective and ambivalent wishes and fears" can be seen "a radical denial of separation, a perversion of the mutuality of the boyhood myth which shares with it a crucial element."[9] Yet in *The Winter's Tale,* as in the other plays we have examined (*King Lear* in particular), emphasis on early-formation theories of psychic development runs the risk of occluding the specifically adult aspects of Leontes' psychodrama. The pivot on which the action of *The Winter's Tale* turns is Mamillius's death. In a large sense, the central question posed for criticism of the play is why this death has to happen. Depicted as an outcome of Leontes' jealousy—"The Prince your son," a servant says, announcing the death, "with mere conceit and fear / Of the Queen's speed, is gone" (3.2.144–45)—Mamillius's death leads immediately to the termination of Leontes' paranoia. Along with Paulina's announcement that "[t]he Queen, the Queen, / The sweet'st, dear'st creature's dead" (3.2.200–201), it leads as well to Leontes' long subsequent effort at repentance. Yet this death, no more than Hermione's, is not a requirement of the play's plot, for Shakespeare, had he wished, could have revived Mamillius too. It is no more implausible for Mamillius to have survived for sixteen years in hiding than for Hermione to have done so. Why, then, did Shakespeare choose to leave this loss unrestored? Why did he choose to have the climactic event of the play consist of the revival, not of mother and son together, but of Hermione alone?

In seeking answers to these questions, it should not surprise us to find in *The Winter's Tale* yet another dramatization of a father's struggle over issues of generativity. A pair of important studies, approaching the play in markedly different ways, share this supposition. In a landmark exploration of skepticism and knowledge in the play, Stanley Cavell argues that we should be suspicious of Leontes' jealousy not only because it is empirically baseless but because it is psychologically derivative—in his view, derivative from a concern opposite to its manifest content. "We are by now so accustomed to understanding insistence or protestation . . . as modes of denial," he argues, "that we will at least consider that the *negation* of [the tale he constructs] is the object of Leontes' fear, namely the fear that he *is* the father." In a recent book, David Lee Miller draws on the work of the anthropologist Nancy Jay to arrive at a similar observation. Accepting Jay's argument that in early cultures "the function of blood sacrifice [of children] is to create patrilineal descent by substantiating fatherhood," Miller argues that this function is enacted in sublimated form in the Christian ritual of the Mass and that in Shakespeare's plays it is further sublimated into theatrical "witnessing." Shakespeare, he says, in an argument familiar from the work of C. L. Barber and others, understood "the commercial theater as a scene of public witnessing made possible by the dismantling of ritually based social technologies." In *The Winter's Tale* the object of this witnessing is the murderous logic of patrilineal patriarchy, which "begins to appear not as sacrificial ritual . . . but as the subjective basis of masculine identity." "Like God," he says, "and according to a similarly inscrutable logic, Leontes seems to require his own son's death in order to substantiate his fatherhood."[10]

Evidence in support of these claims can be found in Leontes' reaction to his inability to confine Mamillius inside the role of mirror of his own idealized childhood identity. Shortly after he claims to see in Mamillius's appearance "a copy out of mine" (1.2.122), Leontes says, "[l]ooking on the lines / Of my boy's face, methought I did recoil / Twenty-three years, and saw myself unbreeched, / In my green velvet coat, my dagger muzzled / Lest it should bite its master" (1.2.153–57). Leontes here depicts his identification with Mamillius in pre-sexual terms, imagining himself as "unbreeched," not yet old enough to wear male attire, his phallic dagger "muzzled," its potential for harm (which he significantly sees as directed at himself, not at another) not yet a matter of concern. In the slightly later conversation beginning "[g]o play, boy, play" (1.2.187), Leontes implies a similar identification, for of the three senses of "play" at work in the speech—childhood play, adulterous play, playing the role of cuckold—only the play Leontes ascribes to Mamillius is asexual. Yet these efforts to restrict Mamillius to an innocent mirror role fail, for as Graham Holderness observes, "[t]here is no innocent play at Leontes' court, not even for children." The one time we see Mamillius playing is at the beginning of 2.1, in the company of his mother and her waiting women. His play here involves, as Holderness says, "a very adult consciousness of sexual and courtly behavior," as Mamillius insists that he is no baby, makes knowing comments about fashions in female beauty, and professes "love" to one of the waiting women, another of whom responds with bawdy innuendo, teasingly telling Mamillius, who has just rejected her offer to be his "playfellow," that when the "fine new prince" is born, "you'd wanton with us, / If we would have you" (2.1.3, 17–19).[11]

Following this eroticized byplay, Mamillius engages in a conversation with his mother which, if innocent, nonetheless contains its own erotic overtones, as he responds to her invitation to "come sit down" and "[c]ome . . . give 't me in mine ear" by sitting close beside her and whispering his "sad tale" of "sprites and goblins" (2.1.25–32). It is to the observation of this encounter that Leontes enters. What Mamillius is whispering to his mother must of course remain unknown. But the meaning that their intimacy holds for Leontes, who has twice already fueled his paranoia by mention of whispering (1.2.216, 283), can be seen in his immediate reaction, as he insists that Mamillius be sequestered from Hermione, complains that "you / Have too much blood in him," and insinuates a gross sexual innuendo by saying, "let her sport herself / With that she's big with, for 'tis Polixenes / Has made thee swell thus" (2.1.59, 61–63). In forbidding any further contact between Mamillius and Hermione, Leontes ostensibly seeks to return his son to the pre-sexual state in which he sees his own (presumed) childhood innocence mirrored. But he can only succeed at this attempt by preventing the sexual maturation—in general terms, the development in time—whose precocious manifestation he has just observed. He thus inaugurates a classic tragic paradigm, for he ultimately obtains his wish in a form he did not anticipate, by bringing about the death of his son. As Cavell says, whereas Freud and Sophocles "look at the [oedipal] conflict as initiated by the son's wish to remove or replace the father, . . . in *The Winter's Tale* the conflict . . . seems primarily generated by the father's wish to replace or remove the son." "If the story of Oedipus is somewhere behind Leontes and Mamillius," Stephen Orgel wittily observes, "it is a version of the story in which Laius wins."[12]

II

A moment's reflection should lead us to see that this line of interpretation, while plausible, is nonetheless incomplete, for it leaves unexamined the question "why now?" Why, that is, should Leontes' struggle against the inevitability of his son's maturation erupt at this time and not earlier? From any rational point of view, awareness of this eventuality does not require as a trigger Mamillius's actual emergence into a state of precocious sexuality. As David Lee Miller observes, both Leontes and Polixenes express a "faintly belligerent" awareness of their sons' potential for development from the outset of the play. Leontes, he says, "generates a whole series of jocose nicknames that [either] magnify [Mamillius] beyond his years . . . or reduce him to the status of a morsel [of food]." When Leontes asks Polixenes, "Are you so fond of your young prince as we / Do seem to be of ours?" Polixenes responds with an expression of fatherly affection that betrays a similar doubleness, as he calls Florizel "[n]ow my sworn friend and then mine enemy, / My parasite, my soldier, statesman, all," and says that his son "makes a July's day short as December, / And with his varying childness cures in me / Thoughts that would thick my blood" (1.2.164–71). As Miller suggests, "[a]ll the elements so innocently present in Polixenes' speech—the hint of darkness in 'thoughts that would thick my blood,' the alternations from friend to enemy, July to December, child to statesman—have specific counterparts in Leontes' [characterizations] of Mamillius." Taken together, the two fathers' comments suggest "how volatile"—and how universally available to awareness—"the underlying tensions may be."[13]

If these tensions nonetheless require a specific impetus before gaining command of Leontes' consciousness, that impetus, I suggest, is less Mamillius's precociousness than the changed parental dynamic implicit in the birth of a second child. For what does it mean to use a child as a confirming mirror for a narcissistic fantasy if more than one mirror exists? In the study cited above, Stanley Cavell says that in "reading *The Winter's Tale,*" he "felt engulfed by economic terms." Tracing the interconnections between "two of the play's primary regions of ideas"—"telling," in the sense of counting and computation, and "breeding"—Cavell arrives finally at the claim that "Leontes wishes an evenness, or annihilation of debt, of owing, which would take place in a world without counting" and that "[w]hat specifically [Leontes] does not want to count is the other face of what he does not want to own, the time of breeding." If this is so, then the impending birth of a second child exacerbates these urgencies, for while, as Cavell says, all "counting implies multiplicity, differentiation," a second child literally *is* multiplicity. From the beginning of the play, when Camillo says that the affection between Leontes and Polixenes "cannot choose but branch now" and Polixenes says that "like a cipher, / Yet standing in rich place, I multiply / With one 'We thank you' many thousands more / That go before it" (1.1.24; 1.2.6–9), the language of the play foreshadows the impending increase in the number of Leontes and Hermione's offspring. But that expansion adds to Leontes' specular relation with Mamillius a second such mirroring, one which by its very repetitiveness problematizes the initial narcissistic bond. And it adds a further problematic possibility as well, of a mirror relationship, not between father and son, but between the children themselves.[14]

These considerations help to explain an otherwise puzzling aspect of the play: the expectation, prior to Perdita's birth, that the second child will be male. In the waiting woman's mention of "a fine new prince," in Leontes' brutal insinuation, "let her sport herself / With that she's big with," and in Paulina's question, "[a] boy?" when told that Hermione "is something before her time delivered" (2.1.17, 61–62; 2.2.25–26), we see this expectation expressed. For Leontes, the possibility that the second child will be male must summon into view a latent implication of Polixenes' Edenic fantasy, the one in which Polixenes says that he and Leontes, like twinned lambs, "knew not / The doctrine of ill-doing, nor dreamed / That any did" (1.2.69–71). For what looks like innocent twinship from within the experience of the brother-brother relationship from the point of view of the father may look like collusion, like a compact version of Freud's primal horde. The anticipated birth of a brother for Mamillius adumbrates the fatherly anxiety that Edmund plays upon in *King Lear,* when he includes in his fictitious letter from Edgar the statement, "If our father would sleep till I waked him, you should enjoy half his revenue forever and live the beloved of your brother" (1.2.53–55). By sequestering Mamillius from Hermione, and by believing the second child to be a bastard, Leontes seeks not only to restrict Mamillius to a pre-sexual identity but to constrain the twinning relationship itself, by preventing that relationship from "branching," from replicating itself in (and in the service of) the next generation.[15]

In the event, of course, the second child is not a son but "[a] daughter, and a goodly babe, / Lusty and like to live" (2.2.26–27). This development, while it can be assumed to alleviate the strand of Leontes' anxiety that I just described, provokes yet another, for the birth of a daughter as a second child is no less problematic for Leontes than is the birth of a son. When Paulina attempts to convince Leontes that Perdita is in fact his daughter, she appeals to the same sort of visible evidence as Leontes cited in seeing Mamillius as a copy of himself. "Behold, my lords," she says, "Although the print be little, the whole matter / And copy of the father—eye, nose, lip, / . . . / The pretty dimples of his chin and cheek, his smiles, / The very mold and frame of hand, nail, finger" (2.3.98–103). This effort fails, not only because by this point Leontes' paranoia is in full career, but because, as Lynda Boose observes, while "father and son are structurally homologous," father and daughter are not. In looking at a son, a father can see a copy of himself; in looking at a daughter, he must see difference as well as similarity. The core danger that the father confronts in the relationship with his daughter is therefore not the desire to forestall the development of a differentiated identity but the temptation to take advantage of the evident existing difference—the temptation, that is, toward incest. In *The Winter's Tale,* Boose argues (and in *Pericles* as well, where incest is overtly depicted), "[a]voidance, abandonment, and discarding of the daughter function . . . as inverted mirrors that reflect the father's flight from incest."[16]

Viewed in this way, Leontes' rejection of Perdita begins to look like a malign version of a positive ethical imperative. But looming behind that rejection is a less positive fatherly anxiety about incest, one rooted in the difference between the relationship of father and daughter and of brother and sister. In *The End of Kinship*, Marc Shell argues that throughout postclassical Western history the Christian cloistered orders embodied an ideal of egalitarian "universal siblinghood," in contrast to the hierarchical and patriarchal structures of episcopal and secular authority. He argues further, and convincingly, for the existence of a long tradition of representation in which this opposition is expressed metaphorically as a contrast between positively valued sibling incest on the one hand and negatively valued parental (almost always father-daughter) incest on the other. As I have argued in another context, even as late as the poetry of Shelley and the fiction of Faulkner we see this contrast at work. Shelley, for example, uses father-daughter incest in "The Cenci" as a metaphor for political and religious despotism and brother-sister incest in "Laon and Cythna" (the original, unexpurgated version of "The Revolt of Islam") as a metaphor for human perfectibility, even as an expression of egalitarian sexual relations, in which "free and equal man and woman greet / Domestic peace."[17]

At no point does Leontes envision an alliance between Mamillius and Perdita. But the shadowy presence of a fear of this possibility can be detected in his contrasting characterizations of the two children in the scene in which Paulina attempts to demonstrate that Perdita is in fact his daughter. Leontes' preferred way of responding to Perdita in this scene is to dehumanize her. In over a score of instances, he refers to the infant as "it," never as "she" or "her." When he does choose to humanize Perdita, in addition to calling her "bastard," he twice calls her "brat" (2.3.93, 163), as if even in her infancy he could see foreshadowed a childhood unruliness that itself would foreshadow both the sexual license he ascribes to Hermione and the forthrightness that he is encountering in Paulina.[18] When he inquires after Mamillius's health at the beginning of the scene, by comparison, he apparently believes that his stratagem of prohibiting contact with Hermione has succeeded, for he ascribes to his son not a precocious rebelliousness (nor, any longer, a precocious sexuality) but its opposite, a submissive internalization of his own conviction regarding Hermione's infidelity. "To see his nobleness!" he says. "Conceiving the dishonor of his mother, / He straight declined, drooped, took it deeply, / Fastened and fixed the shame on 't in himself" (2.3.12–15). The expulsion of Perdita, then, is overdetermined in its meanings. Protecting Leontes from the possibility of father-daughter incest, it also forestalls a contaminating contact, implicitly incestuous, potentially political, between Perdita and her brother. Like the sequestering of Mamillius itself, the expulsion serves the fantasy of an integral and unchallengeable selfhood, Macbeth's single state of man, "whole as the marble, founded as the rock, / As broad and general as the casing air" (3.4.22–23), reenacted in the domestic sphere.

III

The Winter's Tale is Shakespeare's only mature play in which he depicts a normative nuclear family: father, mother, multiple children. By the end of 3.2, Leontes, it appears, has succeeded in destroying this family completely. In bringing about the death of Mamillius and the supposed death of Hermione and in ordering the expulsion of Perdita, Leontes engages in behavior fully as harmful as that of any of the figures discussed in the previous chapters of this book. Yet here, in contrast to *King Lear, Macbeth,* and *Antony and Cleopatra,* the action of the play does not drive on toward the punishment and death of its protagonist but instead turns abruptly (and surprisingly) toward regeneration, a turn initiated by Leontes himself in his sudden realization that "Apollo's angry, and the heavens themselves / Do strike at my injustice" (3.2.146–47) and by the play as a whole in the shift of the setting from Sicily to Bohemia and from things dying to things newborn. By general consent, this turn in the action replaces the intense psychological realism of the first half of the play with a movement governed, in Alison Thorne's words, "more by the dictates of desire than by adhesion to any reality principle." "It is by now a critical commonplace," says Kiernan Ryan, commenting on all of the late romances, "to note . . . the violent simplifications of character and motive; the scandalous liberties taken with time and place; . . . the benign resolutions contrived in frank contempt of the laws of likelihood." And this sense that symbolism trumps psychology in these late plays often leads, in the instance of *The Winter's Tale,* to a view of Leontes' regeneration as a purely formal artifact, the outcome of a structural pattern of wish fulfillment unaccompanied by significant internal development.[19]

This view of *The Winter's Tale* and of the late romances in general seems to me only partially accurate. While the romances may depart from psychological realism as a style of representation, psychology remains the ground out of which their other styles of representation arise, and one task of the critic is to trace the connections between this ground and its reconfigurations. Equally important, as I suggested at the outset of this chapter, the disinclination to detect significant internal growth in Leontes' movement through the play should be seen as arising from ideological as well as interpretative considerations. For Catherine Belsey, to cite a striking example, a belief that in the present day "the Western family enclave . . . all too commonly conceals behind closed doors all kinds of subjugation and suffering" leads to an effort "to historicize an ideal which had come in the West to seem so inevitable that it passed for universal." And this effort leads in turn to an extended speculation, somewhat contrary to the evidence of the text, that the statue of Hermione at the end of *The Winter's Tale* may not be "a statue in our sense of the term, but an effigy, and the frame from which it 'descends' (5.3.99) . . . the marble and heraldry of a tomb." It is desirable for this to be so, Belsey argues, not only because of the "theatrical coup it would have been to show Hermione . . . coming down from her tomb" but because of the "comment the image would make on family values then or now: they survive after all, but only by a miracle, a resurrection, an impossibility, the effect of a supernatural intervention in the institution our own culture fervently longs to render inevitable and stable by attributing the family to natural causes."[20]

For Belsey, to denaturalize the nuclear family is to devalue it. From this perspective, the psychology at work in the first three acts of *The Winter's Tale,* which situates narcissism, nostalgia, and anger as the *fons et origo* of psychic life, comes to be seen as definitive and any effort to move away from that view toward an affirmation of the authenticity of romantic and familial love as meretricious. But is that psychology in fact definitive? The previous three chapters of this book and the previous two sections of this chapter provide repeated examples of the parent-child relationship serving as a vehicle for parental self-absorption and self-assertion. But if one believes, as I do, that human life is inherently social, then it follows that the impulse toward affiliation—call it love—cannot be understood as solely a screen for an underlying selfishness. In seeking theoretical support for this view, I have benefited from Theresa M. Krier's recent study of representations of maternity in classical, medieval, and Early Modern texts. It may be, as Derrida and Lacan claim, that absolute presence is impossible and that desire must therefore always fail of its object. But it does not follow, Krier argues, that "lack, loss, mourning, melancholy, and the past" entirely explain "the constitution of the [human] subject." Drawing on the theories of infantile development of Melanie Klein and David Winnicott and on the philosophical speculations of Luce Irigaray, Krier argues that what comes after mourning is equally important, for if birth is understood "less as an irreparable wound of separation" than as a necessary and desirable "claiming of distance," then the positive emotions of "praise, celebration, exultation, exaltation, [and] gratitude" gain authenticity in their own right, as "ways of greeting a demystified maternal."[21]

In adult developmental terms, a parallel to Krier's argument that "more than mourning work [is needed] to launch the nascent subject into action and invention, history and ethics" is a belief in the authenticity, even if never entirely uncompromised, of the generative impulse.[22] Yet Belsey's critique of family values should not be dismissed as merely short-sighted or cynical, for she is justified in refusing to view love as an absolute value. No less than other manifestations of human energy, love is enacted through, and constrained by, the agencies made available for its expression by a specific culture. An awareness of this dependency informs Shakespeare's representation of the immediate aftermath of Leontes' release from his jealousy. In its artificial and deceptive courtly rhetoric, its insistence on unequal gender relations, and its overweening faith in the power of reason, the Sicily of *The Winter's Tale* provides a cultural context within which Leontes' paranoid suspicions can grow and flourish. Throughout the first three acts of the play, Leontes' attempts to justify his suspicions exhibit the third of these characteristics in their reliance on "if-then" and "either-or" logic. In the scene culminating in his insistence that Camillo poison Polixenes, for example, Leontes asserts that Camillo is either dishonest, a coward, a negligent servant, or a fool, as if thereby exhausting the logical category of all possible explanations for Camillo's silence regarding Hermione's supposed infidelity (1.2.241–46). Similarly, in the extraordinary speech beginning "[i]s whispering nothing," Leontes responds to Camillo's resistance to his claim that "[m]y wife is slippery" with a reductive "if-then" construction, in which if "whispering, . . . leaning cheek to cheek, . . . meeting noses, . . . /[k]issing with inside lip" are nothing, then "the world and all that's in 't is nothing" (1.2.272, 283–85, 292).

If indifference to the laws of likelihood were in fact dominant in *The Winter's Tale,* then when the fever of Leontes' paranoia breaks, one might expect that the hold of the cultural suppositions enabling and supporting his behavior would also loosen. But in fact those suppositions—specifically undue faith in the power of reason—abide largely unchanged, preventing Leontes from transforming recognition of his folly into regeneration and recovery. The moment of breakthrough itself adumbrates the incompleteness of Leontes' alteration, both in his assumption that it is Apollo, the god of reason, who is angry and in his narcissistic reorientation of the news of Mamillius's death toward himself, when he says that "the heavens themselves / Do strike at my injustice" (3.2.146–47). In the remainder of the scene, this incompleteness manifests itself in Leontes' binary understanding of his situation. He first imagines an immediate rectification of the correctable effects of his jealousy, one in which any emotional engagement with the actuality of Mamillius's death remains absent. "I'll reconcile me to Polixenes," he says, "[n]ew woo my queen, recall the good Camillo" (3.2.155–56). But when Paulina enters with the news of Hermione's presumed death, this fantasy of rectification collapses, and Leontes shifts to its polar opposite, anticipating (as noted at the outset of this chapter) a future life of "shame perpetual," a daily ritual of tears shed "[s]o long as nature / Will bear up with this exercise" (3.2.238–41). Locked into a rationalistic either-or understanding of the relation of past behavior to future possibilities, Leontes enacts in miniature the tragic alternatives dramatized *in extenso* in *King Lear* and *Macbeth:* a fantasy of (nearly) entire regeneration on the one hand, a grim and unrelenting continuation in guilt on the other.[23]

The larger implications of this impasse can be seen if we reflect on Paulina's assumption of the role of penitential counselor. In the encounter leading up to the command that Polixenes be poisoned, Leontes says to Camillo, "I have trusted thee . . . / With all the nearest things to my heart, as well / My chamber councils, wherein, priestlike, thou / Hast cleansed my bosom. I from thee departed / The penitent reformed" (1.2.234–38). When Paulina accosts Leontes, defending Hermione's innocence and Perdita's legitimacy, she tries to arrogate this role to herself, saying, "I beseech you hear me, who professes / Myself your loyal servant, your physician, / Your most obedient counselor" (2.3.53–55). But as Paulina herself recognizes, a social reflex of Leontes' paranoia is a tyrannous understanding of male-female relationships. Hence her attempt to assume the role of counselor—a role that would have been unavailable to a woman in either the political or the religious culture of Shakespeare's age—is repeatedly opposed by Leontes. Drawing on a familiar array of ascriptions used in the Early Modern period to marginalize female unruliness, he accuses Paulina, "that audacious lady," of being "[a] mankind witch," "[a] most intelligencing bawd," a "Dame Partlet," a "crone," "[a] callet / Of boundless tongue," "[a] gross hag" (2.3.42, 68, 69, 76, 77, 91–92, 108). Externalizing the threat posed to his narcissistic self-understanding by Hermione's independent identity, he finds in Antigonus's inability to control Paulina evidence that Antigonus is "woman-tired, unroosted," a man whose wife "late hath beat her husband" (2.3.75, 92).

With the termination of his paranoia, Leontes' resistance to Paulina's assumption of the role of counselor also ends. When he says, "Go on, go on. / Thou canst not speak too much. I have deserved / All tongues to talk their bitterest" (3.2.214–16), he evinces a changed attitude, both personal and political, toward female autonomy. In psychological terms, as Krier argues, Paulina's freedom to speak angrily introduces into the play an altered valuation of female aggression, one present as well (by implication) in "Hermione's choice to let Leontes believe her dead." In broader cultural terms, Paulina's freedom to speak transforms the marginalizing identities earlier ascribed to her in a fashion analogous to the inversions of social hierarchy—the boy bishop, the lord of misrule—enacted on occasions of festive liberty.[24] Yet as long as the Sicilian frame of values remains basically intact, the extent of this transformation is limited, both for Leontes and for Paulina herself. Paulina's abrupt reversal of attitude, as she veers from "betake thee / To nothing but despair" to "[w]hat's gone and what's past help / Should be past grief—Do not receive affliction / At my petition" (3.2.209–10, 222–24), enacts the same binary understanding of life in time as did Leontes, in which the only imaginable alternatives for future behavior are either unending sorrow or amnesia. And while there is an undeniable element of emotional growth in Leontes' willingness to accept Paulina's anger, the eagerness with which he solicits it suggests the existence of yet another binary polarization. For as Schwartz observes, when Leontes "encourages [Paulina's] verbal punishment," he converts "his [earlier] sadistic intentions into their passive, masochistic counterpart."[25]

IV

As with the immediate aftermath of Leontes' jealousy, so with the subsequent sixteen years. If we ask what has changed in Leontes' relation to his sorrow between his exit in 3.2 and his reappearance in 5.1, the answer is not much. It is true, as Carol Neely observes, that Leontes has arrived at a fuller understanding of what he lost with the disappearance of Hermione. A striking fact about Leontes' jealousy, as Neely says, "is his divorce of sexuality from love"; so for him to speak of his wife as "the sweet'st companion" and to wish that he could "even now . . . [take] treasure from her lips" (5.1.11, 52–54) evinces "a new apprehension of Hermione . . . [as] peerless, sexual, and human."[26] But this shift in perception, promising as it is, occurs inside a larger set of negative continuities. When Time announces the sixteen-year gap in the action and the shift of the setting to Bohemia, he describes Leontes as "[t]h' effects of his fond jealousies so grieving/That he shuts up himself" (4.1.18–19). This sense of sterile self-enclosure pervades Leontes' reappearance in 5.1. When Cleomenes opens the scene by arguing that "you have done enough, and have performed/A saintlike sorrow," his language reveals the same rationalism as at the end of the trial scene. Saying that Leontes has "paid down/More penitence than done trespass" and should "forget [his] evil," he invokes a bookkeeping economy for the understanding of guilt, and he offers amnesia as its only release (5.1.1–5). Similarly, when Paulina speaks of Hermione as "she you killed," the anger of sixteen years earlier reappears unabated. And when Leontes speaks of Paulina's words as "bitter/Upon thy tongue," and begs her to "[s]ay so but seldom," he evinces the same masochistic abjection as before, tempered only by weariness at sixteen years of reminders of the loss he caused (5.1.15, 18–20).

As Stanley Cavell says in a gnomic formulation, "[t]he first move of revenge . . . seems easy to determine; the first move to set aside revenge, impossible."[27] For this impossibility to be overcome requires more than a willed effort on the part of Leontes and Paulina, more even than fulfillment of the prophecy that Perdita must be found. It requires that psychic and social transformations occur for which Perdita's return is both metonymy and provocation. It has lately become fashionable to emphasize the extent to which the antagonisms of the Sicilian scenes reappear when the action shifts to Bohemia. When Florizel responds to the Old Shepherd's promise to provide Perdita with a dowry that "will make/Her portion equal his" by saying "[o]ne being dead,/I shall have more than you can dream of yet" (4.4.385–88), he invokes (unwittingly in his father's presence) the specter of filial usurpation that had produced anxiety in both Polixenes and Leontes in the opening of the play. And Polixenes' angry reaction to Florizel's comment resembles Leontes' earlier behavior, for as Stephen Orgel says, Polixenes' "indignation . . . is malicious and sadistic, and the fury of his threats against Perdita and the old Shepherd recalls us to the courtly world of Leontes' rage." Similarly, the tendency in earlier criticism to downplay the reflexive elements of the play has recently come under challenge, as commentators have foregrounded the play's tendency, in the words of Graham Holderness, to turn back "on its own romance materials, criticizing their implausible dénouements as the creaking machinery of 'an old tale.'" Thus when Florizel and Perdita open the sheep-shearing scene by discussing the fictionality of her identity as Flora, they create awareness "not [of] the potentiality of theatre to enact transformations, but [of] the mechanisms by which such apparent transformations may be enacted." Overall, as William Morse observes, this metadramatic emphasis forestalls mystification of rural life as a "natural" alternative to the courtly settings of the play.[28]

These reminders of the play's artfulness, while useful, can be misleading if they diminish awareness of the ways in which the Bohemia of act 4 truly *is* different from the Sicily of the previous three acts and truly *does* provide the precondition for an "impossible" transformation. It will be well to remind ourselves of some of the more important contrasts between the two locales of the play, not only the broad-scale shift from winter to summer and from an indoor to an out-of-doors setting but the changes in social relations and individual attitudes as well. When the Old Shepherd discovers the infant Perdita, he assumes that her conception was the result of "some stair-work, some trunk-work, some behind-door-work" (3.3.72–73). But this assumption of illegitimacy leads to an outcome directly opposite to that of Leontes' similar assumption in the earlier acts, for the Old Shepherd's persistent designation for Perdita sixteen years later is "daughter," the Clown's is "sister," and Perdita herself is unaware that anyone other than the Old Shepherd is her blood father. Accompanying this relaxed and inclusive understanding of familial relationships are parallel changes in values and beliefs. The instinctive generosity seen in the Old Shepherd's insistence that Perdita, in her role as "mistress o' the feast," "bid / These unknown friends to welcome" (4.4.68, 64–65) and in the Clown's earlier offer of money to Autolycus in response to Autolycus's pretense that he has been robbed (4.3.76–77) contrasts sharply with the strained courtesy and underlying possessiveness of the Sicilian scenes. Similarly, the sexual grievances of the earlier scenes undergo transformation, as jealousy reappears briefly and harmlessly in the relationship between the Clown, Dorcas, and Mopsa, and bawdry, which inhabits Leontes' speech against his will, reemerges as the innocent (and unnoticed) accompaniment of festive mirth.[29]

The list of contrasts between the two locales could be extended to include (e.g.) Autolycus's role as a double of Leontes, transforming the conflicts and obsessions of the first three acts into their comic equivalents: parodying Leontes' obsession with sexual thievery in his own light-fingered behavior, parodying Leontes' fear that Polixenes and Hermione are merely playing the roles of friend and faithful wife in his continual shifting of identities, and recasting Leontes' paranoid delusions as the fantasies and fictions he uses to sell his wares in the sheep-shearing scene. Informing all of these contrasts is an overarching difference between two ways of experiencing life in time. When Time enters as chorus at the beginning of act 4, he locates himself outside the Sicilian frame of values, and indeed outside any specific cultural framework, saying, "it is in my power / To o'erthrow law and in one self-born hour / To plant and o'erwhelm custom" and describing himself as "[t]he same I am ere ancient'st order was / Or what is now received" (4.1.7–11). This sense that Time exists, as it were, outside time parallels a comprehensiveness Time ascribes to himself relative to issues of judgment. "I, that please some," he says, "try all, both joy and terror / Of good and bad, that makes and unfolds error" (4.1.1–2). In contrast to the linear understanding of temporal existence in the Sicilian scenes and its accompanying reliance on an oppositional logic of "if-then" and "either-or," Time here aligns himself with an inclusive logic of "both-and," in which he contains both joy and terror, good and bad, error and its disclosure.[30]

Time's disengagement of himself from any specific cultural frame of reference is the pivot on which the play moves from a Sicilian to a Bohemian experience of temporality. The experience of time in the Sicilian scenes is characterized not only by linearity but by anxiety. Polixenes' story of his and Leontes' Edenic childhood concludes in a maturation depicted as a fall from innocence, one whose furthest extension, as Marjorie Garber nicely observes, is the fear of mortality encoded in Mamillius's tale of "a man— . . . / Dwelt by a churchyard" (2.1.29–30).[31] In social terms, temporal anxiety pervades the opening discussion of whether Polixenes will prolong his visit. Because no time limit for the visit exists outside the desires of Polixenes and his hosts, the debate over staying or going becomes a game of masks and shadows, in which Polixenes' concern that he may have "stayed / To tire your royalty" cannot be allayed factually, only rhetorically, and the depth of his desire to leave can be gainsaid by Hermione's observation that he has used only "limber vows" in its support (1.2.14–15, 47). In Bohemia, by contrast, the sheep-shearing festival (prior to its disruption by Polixenes) is a relaxed social experience in large measure because its inception and duration derive from cultural sources independent of the desires of its participants. And to the larger Sicilian anxiety about mortality, the Bohemian world opposes a temporality keyed to the cycle of the seasons. It is no accident that as Perdita distributes her flowers, she says, "O Proserpina, / For the flow'rs now that, frighted, thou lett'st fall / From Dis's wagon!" (4.4.116–18). Apollo may reign over Sicily, but the presiding deity of Bohemia is Proserpina, whose yearly sojourn in Hades and return to earth enacts in mythical terms the yearly cycle of seasonal decline and renewal.

In the pattern of a circular journey made familiar by Northrop Frye, the fifth-act entry of Perdita and of the other Bohemian characters transports the reviving power of the Bohemian setting—what Frye calls "the green world"—into the sterile Sicilian court.[32] If this revival is to have more than symbolic significance, an existence elsewhere than in the experience of the play's spectators, it must influence the minds and emotions of the Sicilian characters, which is to say the mind and emotions of Leontes. It does so, I argue, through an abbreviated reenactment of the struggle over the nature of rebirth that we saw dramatized in *King Lear.* Based on his comment about having recoiled twenty-three years when looking on Mamillius's face (1.2.153–55), Leontes is around 30 years old in act 1. This means that he is 45 or thereabouts in act 5—an appropriate age for a midlife struggle in which the alternatives between which he oscillates are a Lear-like fantasy of literal rebirth and a turn toward generativity, toward a willingness to assist the transfer of power and identity to the succeeding generation.

The first of these alternatives enters the play obliquely, in the opening dialogue of act 5 in which Cleomenes and Dion urge Leontes to overcome his sorrow and to remarry. The two advisors argue the advisability of remarriage in dynastic and political terms, as a way of ensuring "remembrance / Of [Leontes'] most sovereign name" and of avoiding "[w]hat dangers by His Highness' fail of issue / May drop upon his kingdom" (5.1.25–28). Some commentators explore the scene directly in these terms, as an enactment of anxieties about succession prevalent in Shakespeare's time. But there is reason to prefer a different approach. *The Winter's Tale* is distinctive among Shakespeare's monarchical plays in its subordination of the political to the personal. In other plays depicting the lives of rulers, disruption in the life of the monarch produces disruption in the state, even, as in *Julius Caesar, King Lear,* and *Macbeth,* in nature or the cosmos. But in *The Winter's Tale,* no such consequences ensue. Leontes fantasizes retaliation against Polixenes, only to reject the idea, saying, "[t]he very thought of my revenges that way / Recoil upon me—in himself too mighty, / And in his parties, his alliance" (2.3.19–21). Hermione mentions that her father was the emperor of Russia, but not for political reasons, only to lament that he is dead and thus unable to "see / The flatness of my misery, yet with eyes / Of pity, not revenge" (3.2.121–23). And even "[t]he insistent theme [of] time," as Orgel says, is "removed from history and located within the family, time as defined by generations, by youth and age, by the relations between parents and children, and by the blood-brotherhood of male bonding."[33]

It should not surprise us, then, to find that under Paulina's agency the discussion of the possibility of remarriage shifts from its dynastic and political implications to its emotional significance. As she observes, "the tenor of [Apollo's] oracle" is that "Leontes shall not have an heir / Till his lost child be found." In any case, she argues, the concern over the absence of an heir is of no moment. "Care not for issue," she says, "[t]he crown will find an heir. Great Alexander / Left his to th' worthiest; so his successor / Was like to be the best" (5.1.38–40, 46–49). Rather than dynastic considerations, Paulina emphasizes the incomparability to Hermione of any possible second bride. If "one by one you wedded all the world," she says, "[o]r from the all that are took something good / To make a perfect woman, she you killed / Would be unparalleled" (5.1.13–16). The effect of this emphasis is double. On the one hand, as Theresa Krier suggests, Paulina's repeated reminders of Hermione's attractiveness help "Leontes move back toward the motility of desire."[34] On the other hand, in their insistence on the belatedness and second-hand status of any remarriage, they work to forestall the fantasy of entire self-renewal, the illusion that beginning over is the same as beginning for the first time. "No more such wives, therefore no wife," says Leontes. If given "the office / To choose you a queen," says Paulina, "[s]he shall not be so young / As was your former, but she shall be such / As, walked your first queen's ghost, it should take joy / To see her in your arms" (5.1.56, 77–80).

That Leontes needs to have the rebirth fantasy forestalled becomes evident when he encounters Florizel and Perdita. Anticipating Florizel's entry, Paulina echoes Polixenes' image of himself and Leontes as twinned lambs, displacing the image into the next generation. "Had our prince," she says, "[j]ewel of children, seen this hour, he had paired / Well with this lord. There was not full a month / Between their births" (5.1.115–18). Leontes' reaction is different. As I argued earlier, resistance to displacement of the twinning relationship into the succeeding generation is an element of Leontes' narcissism. It is therefore significant that when Florizel enters, Leontes invokes the twinship image not in reference to Mamillius but to himself. "Were I but twenty-one," he says, "Your father's image is so hit in you, / His very air, that I should call you brother, / As I did him" (5.1.126–29). In imagining the brother-brother relationship in this way, Leontes reveals that the fantasy of a self-regenerating return to the past is not dead in him. So also in his reaction to Perdita. When Florizel's ruse is revealed, he seeks an empathetic identification with his plight from Leontes, saying, "[b]eseech you, sir, / Remember since you owed no more to time / Than I do now . . . / Step forth mine advocate. At your request / My father will grant precious things as trifles." Instead he hears in response, "[w]ould he do so, I'd beg your precious mistress, / Which he counts but a trifle," a comment that not only reveals the fragility of Leontes' commitment to remaining unmarried but that encapsulates the interconnection, explored so extensively in *King Lear,* between incest and the dream of rebirth. As Paulina aptly says, "Sir, my liege, / Your eye has too much youth in 't" (5.1.218–25).

There is, of course, a significant difference between the incest motif as dramatized in *King Lear* and its recapitulation here: Leontes, unlike Lear, does not know that the young woman to whom he is attracted is his daughter. Even before this knowledge is revealed, Leontes exhibits an incipient readiness to move forward into generativity, as he twice compares Florizel and Perdita to his own lost children, saying, "[a]las, / I lost a couple that twixt heaven and earth / Might thus have stood begetting wonder" and "[w]hat might I have been, / Might I a son and daughter now have looked on, / Such goodly things as you" (5.1.131–33, 176–78). Hence when Perdita's true identity is revealed, the movement forward is effected without further internal conflict, as Leontes, "being ready to leap out of himself for joy of his found daughter," innocently "worries [her] with clipping her" (5.2.50–55). This movement is then broadened and expanded, first as the relaxed Bohemian understanding of familial relations enters Sicily in a comic register, when the Clown recalls how "the King's son took me by the hand and called me brother; and then the two kings called my father brother; and then the Prince my brother and the Princess my sister called my father father" (5.2.141–44); then as Polixenes and Leontes, accepting the betrothal of Florizel and Perdita, accept as well their children's status (in Paulina's words) as the "contracted / Heirs of your kingdoms" (5.3.5–6); and finally in the statue scene and the culminating reconciliation between Leontes and Hermione and reunion between Hermione and Perdita.

Various commentators have written knowledgeably about the ways in which the statue scene naturalizes both the story of Pygmalion and Galatea and Roman Catholic iconolatry, replacing the statue that magically comes to life in the Pygmalion tradition with Hermione's rationally explainable reappearance, and staging, as Julia Reinhard Lupton says, "the visual conditions of Catholic image worship, but only as canceled, with equal emphasis on both the act of staging and the fact of cancellation."[35] For purposes of the argument advanced here, the most important element of the scene's naturalism is the speech to which I allude in the title of this chapter, in which Leontes, looking at Hermione and supposing her a statue, says, "But yet, Paulina, / Hermione was not as much wrinkled, nothing / So agèd as this seems" (5.3.27–29). It is no exaggeration to say that in this comment the conflict explored in this book arrives at its fullest and most succinct moment of expression. When Cleopatra reports her dream of the emperor Antony, his legs bestriding the ocean, she enacts the reifying power of the human mind, the power wherein memories, even against our will, stabilize themselves, remaining unchanged as time advances. Leontes' shock at Hermione's appearance enacts this same power, revealing as it does the stasis at the heart of his sixteen years of grieving, the loss that his grief by its nature seeks to recover in its own form, without alteration.

Counterpoised against this memorial reification is the fact of Hermione's wrinkles. As Theresa Krier observes, in Hermione's initial appearance on stage, she enacts "forms of mobile desire, . . . a continually improvised choreography in which her literal, embodied movements figure forth her desire." In his jealousy, Leontes constrains this mobility, imposing a statuelike unchangeableness on Hermione. It is thus appropriate that the scene of reconciliation should culminate in Hermione's return to mobility, and, even more, in an acceptance of the mobility—the irreversibility—of time itself. In the sheep-shearing scene, Florizel expresses his affection for Perdita in images of movement depicted as repetition, saying, "[w]hen you speak, sweet, / I'd have you do it ever . . . / . . . / . . . When you do dance, I wish you / A wave o' the sea, that you might ever do / Nothing but that—move still, still so" (4.4.140–42). These images, while lovely, are only a way station on the path toward the final understanding of life in time depicted in the play, for to eternalize change as repetition defies the irreversibility of time no less than does reification of the past. The crisis of anagnorisis in *The Winter's Tale* is Leontes' response to Hermione's having aged. Its resolution is his response, "O, thus she stood, / Even with such life of majesty—warm life, / As now it coldly stands—when first I wooed her!" This speech anticipates Paulina's injunction, once Hermione is revealed to be alive, "[n]ay, present your hand. / When she was young you wooed her. Now in age / Is she become the suitor" (5.3.34–36, 107–9). Both speeches inaugurate a second courtship, devoted to Hermione not as an icon of memory but as her aging self. Both enact a truth no less true for its status as a truism—that renewal takes place inside of, not in defiance of, the onward movement of time.[36]

V

A word more. From Mamillius's mention of "sprites and goblins" through Antigonus's vision of Hermione as a "spirit[] o' the dead" walking again to Paulina's reference to Hermione as a "sainted spirit" that may "[a]gain possess her corpse," *The Winter's Tale* is haunted by ghosts and revenants (2.1.26; 3.3.15; 5.1.57–58). Yet the ghost that most haunts the play is nowhere mentioned in its conclusion. It is true that when Paulina mentions "our prince, / Jewel of children," Leontes begs her to be silent, saying "[h]e dies to me again when talked of" (5.1.115–16, 120). It is true as well, as noted above, that Leontes mourns the loss of both of his children in the scene in which he greets Florizel and Perdita. But in the aftermath of Hermione's revival, as he seeks to repair the loss of Antigonus by urging Paulina to marry Camillo and to repair the damage caused by his former suspicion by urging Hermione to greet Polixenes, Leontes nowhere mentions Mamillius. In this avoidance, commentators find cause for reservation about the extent of Leontes' rehabilitation. As Lynn Enterline observes, when Leontes looks upon Hermione, believing her to be a statue, he "still reads Hermione as a version of himself," for when he says, "[d]oes not the stone rebuke me / For being more stone than it" (5.3.37–38), "even [Hermione's] stoniness is not 'hers.'" So also with the final avoidance, for in "Leontes' accommodation to the death of his child," as Stephen Orgel observes, we see "a psychological strategy that . . . leaves the King, from a moral point of view, unpleasantly intact." Even in his earlier recovery from his paranoia, Orgel argues, "Leontes' ego remains resolutely unbruised. . . . The death of his son and wife, the loss of his daughter, are lessons to him—terrible lessons—but that is all they will be."[37]

While acknowledging the justice of these observations, I yet wonder whether we may not place a more positive construction on Leontes' final silence, one which interprets that silence as a somber acceptance of the irreversibility of time. I once asked an acquaintance whose son had committed suicide some years earlier whether she had sought help through counseling. She was kind in her response. She did not upbraid me for my ignorance. She merely said that her grief and her guilt could not be assuaged. I wish I could say to her now, a woman who herself later committed suicide, that perhaps we can at least continue on, unforgiven, unforgiving of ourselves, accepting in Hermione's silence her just censure, yet finding in her aging being a more authentic affiliation than can be found in any dream of lost Eden or future paradise. "Death is the mother of beauty, mystical," says Wallace Stevens in "Sunday Morning," "[w]ithin whose burning bosom we devise / Our earthly mothers waiting, sleeplessly." My acquaintance waited sleeplessly, but who waited for her? Can we not somehow find in that absence, as she could not, recourse from despair? Leontes' silence may indeed be avoidance, but it is difficult to imagine what he *could* say that would be adequate to the reality of his son's death. For some of our experiences, the pain we cause and the pain we suffer, amnesia may be our best hope. What we cannot bear, Nietzsche says, we must learn to forget.

EPILOGUE

Prospero's Anger

Anger *of* or anger *at?* Some thirty years ago, Joseph Summers published an essay entitled "The Anger of Prospero" in which he explored the first of these alternatives. Accepting the dominant interpretation of the time of *The Tempest* as centrally concerned with reconciliation and forgiveness, Summers argued that Prospero must relinquish his anger if "a comic vision, one that celebrates love and marriage and a new generation's assumption of power," is to prevail. Today, by comparison, one seldom comes across interpretations that place their emphasis where Summers placed his. Under the aegis of cultural materialist and feminist methodologies and ideological assumptions, critics have interpreted Prospero, at times quite harshly, as an embodiment of colonial and patriarchal tyranny. In his appropriation of the island despite Caliban's claim that "[t]his island's mine, by Sycorax my mother" (1.2.334), as in the apparent pleasure he takes in punishing Caliban, cultural materialist critics see encoded the treatment of indigenous peoples by their European conquerors. In the impending marriage of Ferdinand and Miranda, serving as it does Prospero's purpose of regaining his dukedom, feminist commentators see, in David Lindley's words, "no more than a mystification of patriarchal ideology, representing as romantic and spontaneous that which is controlled and determined by (male) political ends." And Prospero's anger itself, when it again becomes the focus of discussion, is interpreted either psychoanalytically, as a basically immutable part of his personality, deriving from childhood sources, or politically, as a manifestation of the unacknowledged guilt that his various forms of tyranny have induced in him.[1]

Readers who have persevered this far will not be surprised to learn that in these final pages I intend to return to the theme explored in Summers's essay. If we think of *The Tempest* in relation to the plays discussed in the previous chapters, it seems clear that here we witness a recapitulation and revision of attitudes and relationships that had earlier led to tragic consequences. In the play's emphasis on usurpation and on the relation between memory and forgiveness, as well as in its reliance on the language and structures of penitence, we see echoed elements in *Macbeth.* And as Ruth Nevo says, "[t]o live thus, father and daughter, alone and together, with no rival to challenge . . . what is this but the wishful fantasy of a Lear, who would sing like a bird in a cage with Cordelia."[2] Considered in this light, Prospero's relinquishment of his anger, however muted and qualified, must be understood as an important outcome of the intentional structure of the play. And this is true not only in his final recognition that "[t]he rarer action is / In virtue than in vengeance" (5.1.27–28) and in his consequent forgiveness of Alonzo and (grudgingly) of Sebastian and Antonio. It is true as well in the central relationship explored in this book, of parent to child. For however uncomfortable we may be made to feel by the gender politics of Miranda's betrothal to the "third man that e'er [she] saw, the first / That e'er [she] sighed for" (1.2.449–50), the fact remains that Prospero's role in encouraging her and Ferdinand's relationship is far more humanly positive than is Lear's disruption of Cordelia's impending marriage at the outset of *King Lear.* As Richard McCabe says, acknowledging the positive value of Prospero's relinquishment of control of his daughter's affections "is not to deny that her marriage serves his purposes but rather to recognize in those purposes a generosity of spirit unusual in one so powerful and so wronged."[3]

This positive dimension of Prospero's relationship to Miranda, and of his attitude toward her relationship to Ferdinand, can be seen not only in the overall movement of the play but in the *absence* of his anger where we might plausibly expect it to reveal itself. The anger is most prominently absent in 3.1, the scene in which, as David Lindley observes, Miranda "utterly subverts Prospero's attempted control by actually marrying the man she thinks he is opposed to, for a clandestine, but valid, marriage is what takes place in this scene."[4] The conscious reason for Prospero's lack of anger as he eavesdrops is of course that his opposition to the match is pretense, a matter of "this swift business/I must uneasy make, lest too light winning/Make the prize light" (1.2.454–56). But this conscious desire that Miranda and Ferdinand fall in love would not be sufficient to suppress anger over her overt rebelliousness, were not a deeper process, a willingness to release access to Miranda's sexuality to another man, at work in the scene.

The need for a parent to relinquish incestuous or quasi-incestuous control over a child's sexuality is a recurrent theme in Shakespeare's late plays—in *The Winter's Tale,* in *Pericles* (as I noted in my discussion of *The Winter's Tale*), and in *Cymbeline,* where the queen's intention to marry her son by a previous marriage to her husband's daughter by a previous marriage poses an analogue to incest that the action of the play as a whole is designed to overcome. *The Tempest* provides a more complete representation of the psychology at work in this relinquishment, in both parent and child, than can be found in any of the other of these plays. Within the limits imposed by the play's patriarchal assumptions, Prospero's interactions with Miranda can be construed as an education action whose goal is a loosening of the dyadic relationship that had existed during their previous twelve years on the island. In 1.2, in the initial encounter between Prospero and Miranda, Prospero says that "here/Have I, thy schoolmaster, made thee more profit/Than other princess' can" (1.2.172–74). Adding to that profit is the primary purpose of the encounter itself. When Miranda objects to the apparent destruction of the ship carrying Alonzo and his companions, saying "[h]ad I been any god of power, I would/Have sunk the sea within the earth or ere/It should the good ship so have swallowed" (1.2.10–12), she engages in a decorous form of adolescent rebellion, for the god of power who has caused the storm, she assumes, is her "dearest father" (1.2.1). Prospero's immediate response, "[b]e collected./No more amazement" (1.2.13–14), is not angry but placatory; and his fuller response, of having Miranda remove his magic robe "immediately dramatizes," as Summers says, "that he is to give his fifteen-year-old daughter the knowledge (and therefore the freedom) which will enable her to judge him—his past actions and present plans as a ruler and a brother as well as a father."[5]

In addition to exposing himself to his daughter's judgment, Prospero's removal of his robe serves the purpose of Miranda's ethical and, if one may so phrase the matter, her hermeneutical education. When

Miranda describes the ship as "[a] brave vessel, / Who had, no doubt, some noble creature in her, / Dashed all to pieces" (1.2.6–8), she exhibits simultaneously her youthful idealism—the same idealism that recurs at the end of the play, in her "O brave new world / That has such people in 't" (5.1.185–86)—and her assumption that no difference exists between the appearance she has witnessed and reality. The account Prospero gives of the sinking of the ship, of his loss of his dukedom, and of his and Miranda's journey to the island provides education in both of these regards, by announcing that the ship's inhabitants are actually safe, by revealing his own culpability in the usurpation, and by encouraging a complex interpretation of both the usurpation itself and the subsequent voyage. Miranda's receptivity to the lessons Prospero offers is delicately suggested by her reactions throughout the scene. When she asks "[w]hat foul play had we, that we came from thence? / Or blessèd was 't we did?" she exhibits an advance in interpretative sophistication over her initial comment about the brave vessel, an advance immediately supported and enriched by Prospero's response, "[b]oth, both my girl" (1.2.60–61), with its suggestion that their expulsion from Milan was a version of the fortunate fall. Similarly, when Miranda says "[g]ood wombs have borne bad sons" (1.2.120), she echoes Prospero's comment about Antonio, "my trust, / Like a good parent, did beget of him / A falsehood in its contrary as great / As my trust was" (1.2.93–96). And her subsequent questions, "[w]herefore did they not / That hour destroy us?" and "now I pray you, sir— / . . . your reason / For raising this sea-storm" (1.2.138–39, 176–78), enact a movement into a more analytical frame of mind than she had earlier exhibited.

The impression created by 1.2 that Miranda is successfully undergoing a compressed, schematic education action helps to explain Prospero's temperate and trusting behavior toward her in subsequent scenes, first in 3.1, then, after his acceptance of her and Ferdinand's love for one another, in the sequence beginning with his instruction to "retire into my cell / And there repose" (4.1.161–62). In 3.1, the temperateness of Prospero's reaction to Miranda's rebellion can be ascribed in part to the evidence she provides that she has learned the lessons he has taught her, not only in 1.2 but in their earlier time together on the island. At the outset of the scene, Miranda reverts to the rebelliousness of her opening speech by wishing that "the lightning had / Burnt up those logs that you are enjoined to pile," and by urging Ferdinand to "set [the log] down and rest you," saying that her father, "hard at study," is "safe for these three hours" (3.1.16–21). But she also shows that she has internalized Prospero's authority and his instruction, first when she says "O my father, / I have broke your hest to say so" and then when she says "I prattle / Something too wildly, and my father's precepts / I therein do forget" (3.1.36–37, 57–59). For this reason, as well as because "[i]t goes on, I see, / As my soul prompts it" (1.2.423–24), Prospero accepts with equanimity the larger rebellion, inaugurated by Miranda herself, of her and Ferdinand's marriage *per verba de praesenti*.

Yet as is so often observed, Prospero is not willing to allow the marriage to be consummated, absent "[a]ll sanctimonious ceremonies [which] may / With full and holy rite be ministered" (4.1.16–17). This anxiety on his part combines with two other qualities of the play to render remarkable his instruction to Ferdinand and Miranda to retire into his cell. The first is the evidence provided by Prospero's speech concluding "[b]e more abstemious, / Or else good night your vow" (4.1.53–54) that Ferdinand and Miranda have engaged in dalliance while Prospero's attention has been diverted by the instructions he has been giving to Ariel. The second is the fact that everywhere except in the episode of the retirement into the cell, Prospero either controls or watches over the play's events. Taken together, these considerations suggest that Prospero here engages in an extraordinary act of trust. Believing on the basis of his own experience that trust, like a good parent, can beget falsehood, watching Ferdinand and Miranda engage in dalliance, Prospero nonetheless puts to the test Ferdinand's claim that "the murkiest den, / The most opportune place, the strong'st suggestion / Our worser genius can, shall never melt / Mine honor into lust" (4.1.25–28). And in the event, the trust appears to be justified, for when Prospero reveals Ferdinand and Miranda to Alonzo, they are discovered playing chess, a game which, as Brian Loughrey and Neil Taylor observe, can "symbolize self-control, the exercise of intellect and the practice of art, as opposed to giving too much rein to dalliance."[6]

So have we arrived at last at a full-hearted and unequivocal transfer of power between the generations? Are the hesitations and confusions that bedeviled parents (particularly fathers) in the other plays that we have examined now resolved? I think not, or at least not entirely, and

I am supported in my skepticism not only by the contaminating factor, already mentioned, of Prospero's political motive for the marriage but by the evidence the play provides of a reluctance on his part to leave the island and the power he commands there. In a brilliant reading, Harry Berger Jr. explores the psychological bases of this reluctance. Interpreting Ariel's entrapment in the tree as an emblem of "Prospero's Milanese experience" in which he found "social and political circumstances . . . unduly burdensome," Berger argues that "the freeing of Ariel suggests that Prospero's exile had for him—whether or not he was aware of it—the character of a liberation." Similarly, he sees Prospero's "use of theatrical indirection" as "intimately connected with his habitual isolation, his aversion to social intercourse and consequent inexperience in dealing with others." And as not only Berger but others have argued, the values exhibited in these preferences reveal themselves in the play's curiously extended denouément, in which, as Berger says, "Prospero seems more unwilling to leave than ever. The closer he gets to leaving, the more Shakespeare shows him protracting and delaying the inevitable conclusion."[7]

This line of interpretation is further supported by the play's pervasive concern with aging, not only in Prospero's anticipated future "where / Every third thought shall be my grave" (5.1.314–15) but in his use of "agèd cramps" (4.1.262) as punishment for Caliban, Stephano, and Trinculo and in his alienating depiction of Sycorax as "with age and envy / . . . grown into a hoop" (1.2.259–60). The most overt moment of anger in the play comes when the wedding masque is interrupted by Prospero's recollection of "that foul conspiracy / Of the beast Caliban and his confederates / Against my life" (4.1.139–41). At one level, Prospero's anger upon recalling the conspiracy implies an attitude toward the condition of political watchfulness to which his resumption of his dukedom will oblige him. In larger terms, it signals a reluctant return to mortality itself, for whereas the pageant had depicted an Edenic condition of timelessness, "Spring come to you at the farthest / In the very end of harvest" (4.1.114–15), Prospero now speaks of "our little life / [As] rounded with a sleep" and of his "weakness," his "old brain," and his "infirmity" (4.1.157–60). The subsequent action continues this emphasis, as Prospero, breaking his staff and drowning his book, abandons the power his "rough magic" had given him to open graves and return the dead to life (5.1.48–50). And this association of Prospero's abandonment of his magic with an awareness of age and debility culminates in the epilogue, as Prospero, now ambiguously both himself as a character and the actor playing the role, says that "what strength I have 's mine own, / Which is most faint" and describes his "ending [as] despair / Unless I be relieved by prayer" (2–3, 15–16).[8]

In its concluding emphasis on Prospero's mortality, *The Tempest* evokes the fear of finitude that underlies the resistance to generativity, if not universally, at least ubiquitously in Western culture from Shakespeare's age to our own. Yet it does so while achieving, in Prospero's willing release of Miranda, a more modulated balance between the resistance and the desire to overcome the resistance than can be found anywhere else in Shakespeare. That this balance does not, and apparently cannot, tip further in the direction of overcoming the resistance merits a final reflection. Macbeth's aspiration to be whole as the marble, founded as the rock, characterizes not only human narcissism but human selflessness. We wish that we could be undivided not only in our self-regard but in our capacity to love, and we are as distressed by our inability to achieve a oneness of devotion as we are by our inability to achieve a oneness of self-enclosure. When Prospero says that every third thought will be of the grave, he does not tell us what the other two thoughts will be; but it is fair to assume that one will be of his duties in Milan and the other of Miranda, soon to be lost to Ferdinand, to Naples, and to time. Still, the old paradox remains true, for in releasing Miranda to another relationship and to her own future, Prospero thereby retains her, far more than Lear retains Cordelia, or Macbeth the son he never had and did not wish to have, or Cleopatra Caesarion, or Leonatus Mamillius. A third of one's thoughts journeying forth in love is not enough, because less than all is never enough. It may, however, suffice. For Prospero's sake, as for our own, let us hope so.

Notes

CHAPTER 1

1. Peter Laslett, *The World We Have Lost—Further Explored* (London: Methuen, 1983), p. 109. For the life expectancy data cited in this paragraph, see Roger Finlay, *Population and Metropolis: The Demography of London, 1580–1650* (Cambridge: Cambridge University Press, 1981), pp. 100 and 110, and Peter Laslett, *The World We Have Lost* (London: Methuen, 1965), p. 103. See also E. A. Wrigley et al., *English Population History from Family Reconstitution* (Cambridge: Cambridge University Press, 1997), pp. 280–93.

2. Samuel C. Chew, "'This Strange Eventful History,'" in *Joseph Quincy Adams Memorial Studies,* ed. James G. McManaway et al. (Washington, D.C.: The Folger Shakespeare Library, 1948), pp. 157–82. This essay appears in somewhat revised form as chapter 6 in Samuel C. Chew, *The Pilgrimage of Life* (New Haven: Yale University Press, 1962). For a discussion of the terms used for middle age in antiquity and the medieval and Early Modern eras, see Mary Dove, *The Perfect Age of Man's Life* (Cambridge: Cambridge University Press, 1986). Ovid's association of the stages of human life with the four seasons occurs in *Metamorphoses,* book 15, ll. 221–60 (lineation of the Arthur Golding translation). See also chapter 1, "The Ages of Life," in Philippe Ariès, *Centuries of Childhood: A Social History of Family Life,* trans. Robert Baldick (New York: Alfred A. Knopf, 1962); J. A. Burrow, *The Ages of Man: A Study in Medieval Writing and Thought* (Oxford: Clarendon Press, 1986); chapter 1, "Discourses of Aging and Their Uses in Early Modern England," in William Jeffrey Phelan, "The Vale of Years: Early Modern Aging, Gender, and Shakespearean Tragedy" (Ph.D. diss., University of California, Los Angeles, 1997); Elizabeth Sears, *The Ages of Man: Medieval Interpretations of the Life Cycle* (Princeton: Princeton University Press, 1986). Burrow provides a useful compendium of quotations from classical authors that describe life as a series of stages. Phelan does the same for authors of Early Modern medical treatises and also provides a chart comparing their varying chronological demarcations of the different ages. Sears discusses primarily medieval visual representations.

3. David Bevington, ed., *The Complete Works of Shakespeare,* 4th ed. (New York: HarperCollins, 1992). Unless otherwise noted, all citations of Shakespeare's plays are to this edition.

4. C. L. Barber, *Shakespeare's Festive Comedy: A Study of Dramatic Form and its Relation to Social Custom* (1959; reprint, Cleveland: Meridian, 1963), p. 15.

5. Chew, "History," pp. 170–71, 173; Dove, *Perfect Age,* p. 7. For a discussion of the way in which Jaques' melancholy affects his presentation of the seven ages, see Alan T. Bradford, "Jaques' Distortion of the Seven Ages Paradigm," *Shakespeare Quarterly* 27 (1976): 171–76.

6. Lawrence S. Wrightsman, *Adult Personality Development,* vol. 1: *Theories and Concepts* (Thousand Oaks, Calif.: Sage Publications, 1994), p. 2; Erik H. Erikson, *Childhood and Society.* 2nd ed. revised and enlarged (New York: W. W. Norton, 1963), p. 267.

7. Simon Biggs, *The Mature Imagination: Dynamics of Identity in Midlife and Beyond* (Buckingham, England: Open University Press, 1999), p. 28; Daniel J. Levinson et al., *The Seasons of a Man's Life* (New York: Alfred A. Knopf, 1978), p. 57; George E. Vaillant, *The Wisdom of the Ego* (Cambridge, Mass.: Harvard University Press, 1993), pp. 150–52; John Kotre, *Outliving the Self: Generativity and the Interpretation of Lives* (Baltimore: Johns Hopkins University Press, 1984), pp. 16–18. See also Dan P. McAdams and Regina L. Logan, "What Is Generativity?" in *The Generative Society: Caring for Future Generations,* ed. Ed de St. Aubin et al. (Washington, D.C.: American Psychological Association, 2004), pp. 15–31.

8. Kathleen Woodward, *Aging and Its Discontents: Freud and Other Fictions* (Bloomington: Indiana University Press, 1991), p. 20; Wrightsman, *Adult Personality Development,* pp. 70 and 81; Baine B. Alexander et al., "Generativity in Cultural Context: The Self, Death, and Immortality as Experienced by Older American Women," *Ageing and Society* 11 (1991): 417–42 (the quoted phrase appears on p. 417); Ruthellen Josselson, *Finding Herself: Pathways to Identity Development in Women* (San Francisco: Jossey-Bass, 1987) (quoted in Wrightsman, p. 140); Biggs, *Mature Imagination,* pp. 87, 56, 59.

9. Levinson, *Seasons,* p. ix; Alexander et al., "Generativity in Cultural Context," pp. 421, 425, 437, 438; Biggs, *Mature Imagination,* pp. 26, 33, 34.

10. Ariès, *Centuries of Childhood,* pp. 30–31. See also Creighton Gilbert, "When Did a Man in the Renaissance Grow Old?" *Studies in the Renaissance* 14 (1967): 7–32. Phelan, "The Vale of Tears," cites a number of instances in which old age is said to begin at 50 or even 40. Defining chronological boundaries for the depictions of middle age in Shakespeare's plays is complicated by his tendency to depict age less as a condition of the calendar than of his characters' consciousness and of a play's themes. Juliet's marriage at 13 underscores the theme of impetuosity in *Romeo and Juliet,* but as Peter Laslett observes, it is *not* characteristic of marriage practices in Shakespeare's England, where young women tended to marry, as they do now, in their early 20s (*World We Have Lost—Further Explored,* pp. 81–84). And both Cleopatra's "wrinkled deep in time" and Antony's "this grizzled head" (1.5.30; 3.13.17)

tell us more about their experiences of political and emotional loss than about their chronological ages.

11. Ariès, *Centuries of Childhood,* pp. 24, 20, 22, 26. Elizabeth Sears observes that "[e]ach scheme [of the ages of man] described an ideal life. No one ever died before seventy, no matter what life expectancy might have been in society at large" (*Ages of Man,* p. 6). Several of Ariès's assertions regarding the nature of childhood in the pre-modern world have been called into question. See, e.g., Barbara Hanawalt, "The Child in the Middle Ages and the Renaissance," in *Beyond the Century of the Child: Cultural History and Developmental Psychology,* ed. Willem Koops and Michael Zuckerman (Philadelphia: University of Pennsylvania Press, 2003), pp. 21–42.

12. Susan Dwyer Amussen, *An Ordered Society: Gender and Class in Early Modern England* (Oxford: Basil Blackwell, 1988), p. 7; F. H. Mares, ed., *Much Ado About Nothing* (Cambridge: Cambridge University Press, 2003), p. 31.

13. Catherine Belsey, "Richard Levin and In-different Reading," *New Literary History* 21 (1990): 449–56 (the quoted phrase appears on p. 452); Stephen Greenblatt, "Psychoanalysis and Renaissance Culture," in *Literary Theory/Renaissance Texts,* ed. Patricia Parker and David Quint (Baltimore: Johns Hopkins University Press, 1986), pp. 210–24 (pp. 215, 217); Jacob Burckhardt, *The Civilization of the Renaissance in Italy,* trans. Samuel G. C. Middlemore (New York: Harper and Brothers, 1929), p. 28. For the phrase "salutary anxiety," see Stephen Greenblatt, *Shakespearean Negotiations: The Circulation of Social Energy in Renaissance England* (Berkeley: University of California Press, 1988), p. 135. The literature discussing the relationship between psychoanalysis and New Historicism/cultural materialism is large and varied. For an excellent overview, with many useful citations, see Carla Mazzio and Douglas Trevor, "Dreams of History: An Introduction," in *Historicism, Psychoanalysis, and Early Modern Culture,* ed. Carla Mazzio and Douglas Trevor (London: Routledge, 2000), pp. 1–18. Catherine Belsey's essay is a response to Richard Levin's sharp-tongued but insightful "Unthinkable Thoughts in the New Historicizing of English Renaissance Drama," *New Literary History* 21 (1990): 443–47.

14. Jonathan Goldberg, "Shakespearean Inscriptions: The Voicing of Power," in *Shakespeare and the Question of Theory,* ed. Patricia Parker and Geoffrey Hartman (London: Methuen, 1985), p 118; Robert N. Watson, *The Rest is Silence: Death as Annihilation in the English Renaissance* (Berkeley: University of California Press, 1994), pp. 326 (n. 5), 4, 2. For historians who emphasize continuities in social and psychic life, see, e.g., David Aers, "Reflections on Current Histories of the Subject," *Literature & History,* 2nd series, 2 (1991): 20–34; David Cressy, *Birth, Marriage, and Death: Ritual, Religion, and the Life Cycle in Tudor and Stuart England* (Oxford: Oxford University Press, 1997); Ralph A. Houlbrooke, *The English Family: 1450–1700* (London: Longman, 1984); Linda A. Pollock, *Forgotten Children: Parent-Child Relations from 1500 to 1900* (Cambridge: Cambridge University Press, 1983). See also Katherine Eisaman Maus, *Inwardness and Theater in the English Renaissance* (Chicago: University of Chicago Press, 1996).

15. C. L. Barber and Richard P. Wheeler, *The Whole Journey: Shakespeare's Power*

of Development (Berkeley: University of California Press, 1986), p. xvii. Barber and Wheeler's book is a psychoanalytically oriented study emphasizing, among other matters, the importance to Shakespeare's artistic development of the Protestant rejection of worship of the Holy Family and of Mary as a virgin mother. I find compelling *The Whole Journey*'s argument that in his tragedies Shakespeare depicts the disastrous consequences of "the search for equivalents of the Holy Family of Christianity in the human family" (p. 1) and that "the roots in infancy from which identity grows . . . and which religion taps for its forms of worship, become, in tragic situations, the source of impossible, destructive, and self-destructive demands" (p. 21). But I am not convinced that medieval Catholicism's worship of the Holy Family was any more efficacious in meeting these demands than is Shakespearean tragedy. Both religious worship and tragic drama seem to me to address psychic conflicts that at their core are unresolvable.

16. Margaret Morganroth Gullette, *Declining to Decline: Cultural Combat and the Politics of the Midlife* (Charlottesville: University Press of Virginia, 1997), pp. 3, 6, 14. See also Margaret Morganroth Gullette, *Aged by Culture* (Chicago: University of Chicago Press, 2004).

17. Gail Sheehy, *Understanding Men's Passages: Discovering the New Map of Men's Lives* (New York: Random House, 1998), pp. 10, 23.

CHAPTER 2

1. Bevington's *Complete Works of Shakespeare,* cited here, conflates the quarto and folio editions of *King Lear.* Differences between the two versions will be noted where relevant. The most recent Arden edition of *King Lear* marks differences between the two versions in an easily accessible fashion, but I have not used it as my citation text because it differs from other contemporary editions in an important instance of scene division, incorporating the scenes usually marked as 2.3 and 2.4 into a single long 2.2. See R. A. Foakes, ed., *King Lear.* The Arden Shakespeare, 3rd series (Walton-on-Thames: Thomas Nelson and Sons, 1997).

2. Jeffrey Stern, "*King Lear:* The Transference of the Kingdom," *Shakespeare Quarterly* 41 (1990): 299–308. For a discussion of Lear's preference for Burgundy as Cordelia's husband, see Harry V. Jaffa, "The Limits of Politics: *King Lear,* Act I, Scene I," in Allan Bloom with Harry V. Jaffa, *Shakespeare's Politics* (New York: Basic Books, 1964), pp. 113–45 (cited in Stern). For a counterargument, favoring France as Lear's choice, see Ralph Berry, "Lear's System," *Shakespeare Quarterly* 35 (1984): 421–29.

3. Janet Adelman, *Suffocating Mothers: Fantasies of Maternal Origin in Shakespeare's Plays, "Hamlet" to "The Tempest"* (London: Routledge, 1992), pp. 102, 117.

4. Ibid., pp. 110, 109.

5. Coppélia Kahn, "The Absent Mother in *King Lear,*" in *Rewriting the Renaissance: The Discourses of Sexual Difference in Early Modern Europe,* ed. Margaret W.

Ferguson, Maureen Quilligan, and Nancy Vickers (Chicago: University of Chicago Press, 1986), p. 39. For extended discussions of the opening scene as an aborted wedding ceremony, see Lynda Boose, "The Father and the Bride in Shakespeare," *PMLA* 97 (1982): 325–47, and Barber and Wheeler, *The Whole Journey,* pp. 282–97.

6. Jacques Derrida, *Of Grammatology,* trans. Gayatri Chakravorty Spivak (Baltimore: Johns Hopkins University Press, 1976), p. 155.

7. Stanley Cavell, "The Avoidance of Love," in *Must We Mean What We Say: A Book of Essays* (1969; reprint, Cambridge: Cambridge University Press, 1976), pp. 286, 299. For a representative humanist reading acknowledging the presence of incestuous elements in the play while arguing against their persistence into the later stages of the play, see Paul A. Jorgensen, *Lear's Self-Discovery* (Berkeley: University of California Press, 1967), pp. 128–35. See also David Bevington, *Shakespeare: The Seven Ages of Human Experience,* 2nd ed. (Oxford: Blackwell, 2005), pp. 197–98. Valuable correctives to the tendency to downplay the importance of incestuous impulses in Lear's attitude toward Cordelia can be found in Barber and Wheeler, *The Whole Journey;* Boose, "The Father and the Bride"; and William N. Chaplin, "Form and Psychoanalysis in *King Lear,*" *Literature and Psychology* 19 (1969): 31–44.

8. Biggs, *Mature Imagination,* pp. 55, 64. Lear's investment in the fantasy of literal rebirth helps to explain his giving away the "power, / Preeminence, and all the large effects / That troop with majesty" while retaining "[t]he name and all th' addition to a king" (1.1.130–31, 136). He is retaining not only a past but a fantasized future identity. In displacing developmental issues chronologically, *King Lear* resembles both *Hamlet* and *Othello*—*Hamlet* in delaying adolescent issues until Hamlet is 30 years old, *Othello* in delaying Othello's first experience of romantic love until middle age. I am indebted to the anonymous reader at LSU Press for this observation.

9. The referent for the Fool's "wild fire" and "old lecher" is ultimately revealed to be Gloucester, who enters at this point carrying a torch, and whom the Fool calls "a walking fire" (3.4.113). Depending on the timing of Gloucester's entrance, though, the referent can first seem to be Lear, the only old man on stage when the Fool begins speaking.

10. Combining Lear's "sulphurous pit" comments with his immediately subsequent response to Gloucester's request to kiss his hand—"Let me wipe it first; it smells of mortality" (4.6.133)—Adelman argues that in this scene Lear traces "his mortality to its source" and that "his origin in and vulnerability to the sulphurous pit . . . is what Lear smells out in the storm" (*Suffocating Mothers,* p. 113). The smell Lear wishes to wipe away can be interpreted with equal plausibility as sexual in origin, as if he were first imagining an incestuous sexual encounter, then seeking to eliminate its physical traces. The point, though, is not to force a choice between Lear's infantile and his incestuous fantasies but to recognize the importance of each to an interpretation of the play. The sulphurous pit is the site not only of parturition but of intercourse, and one source of its odors is the glands of Bartholen.

11. G. Wilson Knight, *The Wheel of Fire: Interpretations of Shakespearean Tragedy*

with Three New Essays (1930; reprint, London: Methuen, 1965), p. 198; Michael Holahan, "'Look, her lips': Softness of Voice, Construction of Character in *King Lear*," *Shakespeare Quarterly* 48 (1997): 414, n. 22; Maynard Mack, *"King Lear" in Our Time* (Berkeley: University of California Press, 1965), pp. 100, 117. In saying that Cordelia teaches Lear familial love, Holahan summarizes Elder Olsen's argument in *Tragedy and the Theory of Drama* (Detroit: Wayne State University Press, 1961), pp. 207–9. What human benefit accrues from this lesson having been learned by a man who himself immediately dies is a question Holahan does not explore.

12. Jorgensen, *Lear's Self-Discovery,* p. 82; Boose, "The Father and the Bride," p. 335; Adelman, *Suffocating Mothers,* pp. 119–20.

13. Kathleen McLuskie, "The Patriarchal Bard: Feminist Criticism and Shakespeare: *King Lear* and *Measure for Measure,*" in *Political Shakespeare: New Essays in Cultural Materialism,* ed. Jonathan Dollimore and Alan Sinfield (Manchester, England: Manchester University Press, 1985), pp. 102, 106, 97, 102. McLuskie's reading of *Lear* as unequivocally enforcing a patriarchal ideology relies on (1) an untheorized notion of authorial intentionality and (2) a limited sense of the ways in which the play can be (and has been) interpreted in the theater. Acknowledging that "the text contains possibilities for subverting [its misogynist] meanings" (p. 103), McLuskie accords the palm of authorial intention only to the misogyny, never to the subversion. Similarly, she argues that "in the theater . . . the tragic power of the play endorses its [misogynistic] ideological position at every stage" (p. 100), unaware, apparently, of the strong tradition, reaching back to the 1960s and beyond, of counter-hegemonic productions. For a discussion of Peter Brooks's and Herbert Blau's productions of this sort, negative in its assessment of their value, see Mack, *"King Lear" in Our Time,* pp. 29–41. For a defense of McLuskie's essay from criticisms leveled by Carol Neely and Lynda Boose, see Jonathan Dollimore, "Shakespeare, Cultural Materialism, Feminism, and Marxist Humanism," *New Literary History* 21 (1990): 471–91, especially pp. 472–75.

14. Kiernan Ryan, "*King Lear:* A Retrospect, 1980–2000," *Shakespeare Survey* 55 (2002): 8; Adelman, *Suffocating Mothers,* p. 126; Ann Thompson, "Are There Any Women in *King Lear*?" in *The Matter of Difference: Materialist Feminist Criticism of Shakespeare,* ed. Valerie Wayne (Ithaca: Cornell University Press, 1991), p. 126 (cited in Ryan, "*King Lear,*" p. 7, n. 37); Adelman, *Suffocating Mothers,* pp. 124, 125, 126.

15. See, e.g., Jonathan Dollimore's description of cultural materialist reading practices: "Cultural materialism does not, like much established literary criticism, attempt to mystify its perspective as the natural, obvious or right interpretation of an allegedly given textual fact." Instead, it recognizes that "culture is made continuously and [that] Shakespeare's text is reconstructed, reappraised, reassigned all the time through diverse institutions in specific contexts." (Jonathan Dollimore, "Preface," in *Political Shakespeare: New Essays in Cultural Materialism,* ed. Jonathan Dollimore and Alan Sinfield [Manchester, England: Manchester University Press, 1985], p. viii). See also Faith Nostbakken, "Cultural Materialism," in *Encyclopedia of Con-*

temporary Literary Theory: Approaches, Scholars, Terms, gen. ed. and comp. Irena R. Makaryk (1993; reprint, Toronto: University of Toronto Press, 1997), pp. 21–25.

16. Janet Bottoms, "'Look on her, look': The Apotheosis of Cordelia," *Shakespeare Survey* 55 (2002): 108, 111–12 (p. 112). The embedded quotation is from Sally Mitchell, "Sentiment and Suffering: Women's Recreational Reading in the 1860s," *Victorian Studies* 21 (1977): 32.

17. Harry Berger Jr., "The Lear Family Romance," in *Making Trifles of Terrors: Redistributing Complicities in Shakespeare,* ed. (with an intro.) Peter Erickson (Stanford: Stanford University Press, 1997), pp. 26, 27. See also in the same work "Text Against Performance: The Gloucester Family Romance," pp. 50–69.

18. Ibid., pp. 42, 43.

19. Ibid., pp. 44–45, 45, 46. An interpretation of Cordelia similar to Berger's underlies Jane Smiley's depiction of Caroline Cook, the youngest of the three daughters of Larry Cook, the Lear figure in *A Thousand Acres,* Smiley's novel based on the Lear-Gloucester story (Jane Smiley, *A Thousand Acres* [New York: Random House: Columbine, 1991]). Adelman acknowledges the force of Berger's argument (as presented in an earlier essay version), but objects that "he can construct this case only by overlooking the extent to which the play—rather than Cordelia herself—sanctifies her" (*Suffocating Mothers,* p. 309, n. 54). In rejoinder, I observe (1) that the only place that this sanctification occurs, outside Cordelia's self-presentations and Lear's responses, is in the Gentleman's comments in 4.3; and (2) that the Gentleman, no less than Cordelia and Lear, should be interpreted as a character expressing a point of view, not as an editorial commentator. Also, 4.3 appears only in quarto, not in folio, so that in folio no foreshadowing characterization is provided for Cordelia; she simply appears on stage unannounced in 4.4. Noting this change, and entertaining the hypothesis that "Folio *Lear* represents Shakespeare's own revisions of Quarto *Lear,*" Adelman argues that the cut was made because Shakespeare had come to believe "that he could trust the audience to see Cordelia as a redemptive presence without it" (*Suffocating Mothers,* p. 306, n. 43). This argument rests on a *petitio principi,* since it assumes that Shakespeare intended Cordelia so to be perceived. A more convincing interpretation, consistent with a number of other changes between quarto and folio, such as the elimination of the music and the Doctor in 4.7, is that Shakespeare revised toward an increased naturalism, in which Cordelia's "saintliness" (*vide* Berger) can be seen to be a role she assumes, not an attribute she is assigned.

20. The charge can, however, be answered through appeal to a distinction between cultural and personal repression. Universalist, trans-historical conceptions of Shakespeare's genius are—or should be—passé. However extensive the reach of his imagination, it was limited to the possibilities for representation available within the social, cultural, intellectual, and material conditions of Early Modern England. But it is a far step from acknowledging Shakespeare's imbrication in Early Modern systems of belief to claiming that he is an advocate for any one of those systems. Ar-

guably, Shakespeare's deepest affiliation was not to any particular Early Modern ideology but to drama as an art form, and therefore to the passive ventriloquism in which, as Coleridge claims, no character's speech is ever out of character. This passivity itself has political implications, an emerging awareness of which can perhaps be inferred from Shakespeare's turn toward tragedy in the middle phase of his career. But to say this is not to say that Shakespeare invests any of the disasters he depicts with personal (as opposed to generic and cultural) authority. To depict Cordelia and Desdemona and Ophelia and Lear dying and not, in Yeats's phrase, "break up their lines to weep"—*this,* and not approval or disapproval of the political structures partly responsible for the deaths themselves, is Shakespeare's deepest ideological commitment.

21. In an early challenge to Christian humanist readings, Barbara Everett makes a similar observation: "That Lear should be forced, by the evil of two of his daughters, to kneel and plead ironically . . . is terrible, and the moral impact of the moment is great; but that Lear should choose, because of the goodness of his third daughter, to kneel and confess . . . has also something of the terrible in it, and the impact is not, perhaps, what could be called precisely a 'moral' one." Barbara Everett, "The New *King Lear,*" *Critical Quarterly* 2 (1960): 334–35.

22. Alexander Leggatt, *King Lear,* Twayne's New Critical Introductions to Shakespeare (Boston: G. K. Hall & Co., 1988), p. 85; Barber and Wheeler, *The Whole Journey,* p. 290; Leggatt, *King Lear,* p. 87. Cf. S. L. Goldberg, *An Essay on "King Lear"* (Cambridge: Cambridge University Press, 1974), p. 143: "[I]t is significant and worth insisting on that even in the reconciliation scene [Cordelia] has to see Lear as merely a victim, and he see in her, even now, only the possibility of '*forgetting* and forgiving'" (emphasis Goldberg's).

23. Adelman, *Suffocating Mothers,* pp. 127, 122. As Berger mordantly notes, Lear's claim that "[h]e that parts us shall bring a brand from heaven"(5.3.22) "embraces friend and foe indifferently, and by no means excludes France" (*Making Trifles of Terrors,* p. 47). In "The Vale of Years," Phelan provides a detailed account of the sexual overtones of Lear's speeches in 4.7 subsequent to his awakening, when he encounters the blinded Gloucester (pp. 346–52). He also links Lear's crown of weeds and flowers to the custom (abandoned by Shakespeare's time but mentioned by Spenser and depicted in works of visual art) of adorning bride and bridegroom with floral crowns, calling it an "ersatz betrothal crown" (p. 348).

24. Adelman, *Suffocating Mothers,* p. 121; Alan Dundes, "'To Love My Father All': A Psychoanalytic Study of the Folktale Sources of *King Lear,*" *Southern Folklore Quarterly* 40 (1976): 359. The word *court* appears in the play only one other time, in the Fool's reference to flattery as "court holy water in a dry house" (3.2.10).

25. Regan alludes to this possibility when, in attempting to wheedle information out of Oswald regarding her sister's relations with Edmund, she says, "I know you are of her bosom" (4.5.28). Humanist commentators tend to interpret Lear's fantasy of his and Cordelia's activities in prison as a purifying transformation of the forms of behavior prevalent at Goneril's and Regan's courts. In John Danby's words, Lear

and Cordelia's "strategy [of mutual forgiveness] will be a cunning superior to the foxship of the machiavels." (John F. Danby, *Shakespeare's Doctrine of Nature: A Study of "King Lear"* [London: Faber and Faber, 1949], p. 195.)

26. Lear's "sing like birds i' the cage" may also contain a reminiscence of his conversation with Poor Tom, who at one point says "[t]he foul fiend haunts Poor Tom in the voice of a nightingale" (3.6.29).

27. Barber and Wheeler, *The Whole Journey,* p. 290; Adelman, *Suffocating Mothers,* p. 126; Foakes, The Arden *King Lear,* 3rd series, pp. 84–85; Thomas Clayton, "'Is this the promis'd end?': Revision in the Role of the King," in *The Division of the Kingdoms: Shakespeare's Two Versions of "King Lear,"* ed. Gary Taylor and Michael Warren (Oxford: Clarendon Press, 1983), p. 122; A. C. Bradley, *Shakespearean Tragedy: Lectures on "Hamlet," "Othello," "King Lear," and "Macbeth"* (1905; reprint, New York: St. Martin's Press, 1960), p. 291; Judah Stampfer, "The Catharsis of *King Lear,*" *Shakespeare Survey* 13 (1960): 1–10 (the quoted phrase appears on p. 10). For a provocative deconstructive reading exploring how "our evaluations of the play are unfixed," see Stephen Booth, *"King Lear," "Macbeth," Indefinition, and Tragedy* (New Haven: Yale University Press, 1983) (the quoted phrase appears on p. 56). See also Derek Peat, "'And that's true too': *King Lear* and the Tension of Uncertainty," *Shakespeare Survey* 33 (1980): 43–53.

28. I am reminded here of Nicodemus's question to Jesus, "How can a man be born when he is old? Can he enter a second time into his mother's womb, and be born?" (The Gospel According to St. John 3:4).

29. Berger, *Making Trifles of Terrors,* pp. 48–49; John Keats, "On Sitting Down to Read *King Lear* Once Again," in *John Keats: Selected Poems and Letters,* ed. Douglas Bush (Cambridge: Houghton Mifflin, 1959), pp. 132–33; Everett, "The New *King Lear,*" p. 335.

30. Adelman, *Suffocating Mothers,* p. 305, n. 40; A. D. Nuttall, *Why Does Tragedy Give Pleasure?* (1996; reprint, Oxford: Clarendon Press, 2001), pp. 98–101.

31. Booth, *"King Lear," "Macbeth," Indefinition, and Tragedy,* p. 13.

32. William H. Matchett, "Some Dramatic Techniques in *King Lear,*" in *Shakespeare: The Theatrical Dimension,* ed. Philip C. McGuire and David A. Samuelson (New York: AMS Press, 1979), p. 203. Lear's "Pray you, undo this button. Thank you, sir" extends a pattern of empathetic social awareness initiated in the storm scene, when he says to the Fool, "How dost my boy? Art cold?/I am cold myself"(3.2.68–69) and later speaks of the "[p]oor naked wretches, wheresoe'er you are,/That bide the pelting of this pitiless storm" (3.4.28–29). See J. K. Walton, "Lear's Last Speech," *Shakespeare Survey* 13 (1960): 11–19.

33. Cavell, *Must We Mean What We Say,* p. 309.

34. Bradley, *Shakespearean Tragedy,* p. 247. The Gloucester subplot repeats Lear's struggle over generational issues with a difference, by gendering the relationship between parent and child. The primary issue raised in the subplot is not the fantasy of renewal through incest but the fear of being supplanted by a child identical in gender. I regret that I did not become aware of Maureen Quilligan's *Incest and*

Agency in Elizabeth's England (Philadelphia: University of Pennsylvania Press, 2005) until my manuscript was in page proof. Here I will say only that Quilligan's understanding of the relationship between incest and female agency in *King Lear* runs counter to my own.

CHAPTER 3

1. Helen Gardner, "The Tragedy of Damnation," in *Elizabethan Drama: Modern Essays in Criticism,* ed. Ralph J. Kaufmann (New York: Oxford University Press, 1961), p. 322; James L. Calderwood, *If It Were Done: "Macbeth" and Tragic Action* (Amherst: University of Massachusetts Press, 1986), p. 22; Paul Jorgensen, *Our Naked Frailties: Sensational Art and Meaning in "Macbeth"* (Berkeley: University of California Press, 1971), p. 212; A. P. Rossiter, *Angel with Horns and Other Shakespeare Lectures* (New York: Theatre Arts Books, 1961), p. 228. Gardner's essay originally appeared as "Milton's 'Satan' and the Theme of Damnation in Elizabethan Tragedy," *Essays and Studies* 1 (1948): 46–66.

2. Wilbur Sanders, *The Dramatist and the Received Idea: Studies in the Plays of Marlowe and Shakespeare* (Cambridge: Cambridge University Press, 1968), p. 282.

3. Roy Walker, *The Time is Free: A Study of "Macbeth"* (London: Andrew Dakers Ltd., 1949), p. 36; G. R. Elliott, *Dramatic Providence in "Macbeth": A Study of Shakespeare's Tragic Theme of Humanity and Grace* (Princeton: Princeton University Press, 1958), p. 223.

4. Peter Brooks, *Troubling Confessions: Speaking Guilt in Law and Literature* (Chicago: University of Chicago Press, 2000), p. 159; J. A. Sharpe, "'Last Dying Speeches': Religion, Ideology, and Public Execution in Seventeenth-Century England," *Past and Present* 107 (May 1985): 158–59, quoting Mervyn James, *English Politics and the Concept of Honour, 1485–1642. Past and Present,* Supplement No. 3 (Oxford: Past and Present Society, 1978), p. 44; Michel Foucault, *Discipline and Punish: The Birth of the Prison,* trans. Alan Sheridan (New York: Pantheon Books, 1977), pp. 47–48. See also Lacey Baldwin Smith, "English History Trials and Confessions in the Sixteenth Century," *Journal of the History of Ideas* 15 (1954): 471–98.

5. David Norbrook, "*Macbeth* and the Politics of Historiography," in *Politics of Discourse: The Literature and History of Seventeenth-Century England,* ed. Kevin Sharpe and Steven N. Zwicker (Berkeley: University of California Press, 1987), p. 78; Kenneth Muir, ed., "Introduction," in *Macbeth,* The Arden Shakespeare (1951; reprint, London: Routledge, 1995), pp. xliv–xlv; Berger, *Making Trifles of Terrors,* pp. 72–74, 78.

6. A. R. Braunmuller, ed., *Macbeth,* The New Cambridge Shakespeare (Cambridge: Cambridge University Press, 1997), p. 16; William C. Carroll, ed., *William Shakespeare, "Macbeth": Texts and Contexts* (New York: Bedford/St. Martin's, 1999), p. 5. For a good discussion of the ambiguities surrounding monarchical succession as depicted in *Macbeth,* see Michael Hawkins, "History, Politics, and *Macbeth,*" in

Focus on "Macbeth," ed. John Russell Brown (London: Routledge and Kegan Paul, 1982), pp. 155–88. See also Alan Sinfield, "*Macbeth:* History, Ideology, and Intellectuals," *Critical Quarterly* 28 (1986): 63–77, and Michael Echeruo, "Tanistry, the 'Due of Birth' and Macbeth's Sin," *Shakespeare Quarterly* 23 (1972): 444–50. As William C. Carroll notes, the four monarchies depicted or alluded to in the play—Duncan's, Macbeth's, Edward the Confessor's, and Malcolm's—variously represent kingship as "elected or inherited, unnatural or holy, legitimate or tyrannical" (*"Macbeth": Texts and Contexts,* p. 6).

7. "Hail" is used as a greeting only three times: here at the end of the play, in the witches' opening salutations to Macbeth and Banquo (1.3.48–50, 62–64, 69), and in subsequent references to those initial salutations (1.5.8; 3.1.61). Like the echoes of Duncan's favors toward Macbeth in Malcolm's promise of rewards to his followers, the linked opening and closing "hails" suggest a continuation of what A. R. Braunmuller calls "the cycle of trust and betrayal" (Braunmuller, *Macbeth,* p. 238, n.). Macbeth's rejection of the Roman option of noble suicide is consistent with *Macbeth*'s ambiguous generic identity, halfway between the English history plays, where suicide is not an option, and the Roman plays, where it often is.

8. Stephen Greenblatt, *Hamlet in Purgatory* (Princeton: Princeton University Press, 2001), pp. 19, 23, 32.

9. Greenblatt's *Hamlet in Purgatory* is part of a widespread recent reconsideration of the emotional effects of changes in religious practice occurring during the English Reformation, the literature of which is vast and often contentious. For studies emphasizing the traumatic effects (and the incompleteness) of the move away from Catholic belief and ritual, see (e.g.) Eamon Duffy, *The Stripping of the Altars: Traditional Religion in England c. 1400–c. 1580* (New Haven: Yale University Press, 1992), and Christopher Haigh, *English Reformations: Religion, Politics, and Society under the Tudors* (Oxford: Clarendon Press, 1993). For a strongly worded rejoinder, emphasizing the emotional and spiritual benefits of the shift to Protestantism, as well as the benefits to Shakespeare of his having inherited "a vast, vigorous and open Protestant English literature of many kinds," see David Daniell, "Shakespeare and the Protestant Mind," *Shakespeare Survey* 54 (2001): 1–12 (the quoted phrase appears on p. 8). See also Debora K. Shuger, "Subversive Faiths and Suffering Subjects: Shakespeare and Christianity," in *Religion, Literature, and Politics in Post-Reformation England, 1540–1688,* ed. Donna B. Hamilton and Richard Strier (Cambridge: Cambridge University Press, 1996), pp. 46–69 (cited in Daniell).

10. Geoffrey Rowell, "The Anglican Tradition: From the Reformation to the Oxford Movement," in *Confession and Absolution,* ed. Martin Dudley and Geoffrey Rowell (London: SPCK, 1990), p. 91; Thomas N. Tentler, *Sin and Confession on the Eve of the Reformation* (Princeton: Princeton University Press, 1977), pp. 349, 360. Tentler's book provides an excellent overview of the topic named in its title.

11. Martin Luther, *De Servo Arbitrio,* quoted in Jean Delumeau, *Sin and Fear: The Emergence of a Western Guilt Culture, 13th–18th Centuries,* trans. Eric Nicholson

(New York: St. Martin's Press, 1990), p. 493; C. S. Lewis, *English Literature in the Sixteenth Century Excluding Drama,* The Oxford History of English Literature, vol. 3 (Oxford: Clarendon Press, 1954), p. 33.

12. Lewis, *English Literature in the Sixteenth Century,* p. 34; Brooks, *Troubling Confessions,* p. 91. On diary-writing as a Protestant—more specifically, Puritan—"substitute for the confessional," see William Haller, *The Rise of Puritanism* (New York: Columbia University Press, 1938), pp. 95–98.

13. It is not often observed that this naturalizing tendency begins with the initial encounter between the witches and Macbeth and Banquo. In Holinshed's *Chronicles,* Duncan awards the title of Thane of Cawdor to Macbeth *after* the encounter with the witches, so that the witches' hailing of Macbeth first by this title, then by the title of king, unambiguously comprises *two* predictions. But Shakespeare reverses the sequence, having Duncan announce the transfer of the title at the end of 1.2, prior to the encounter. Because Macbeth and Banquo are unaware of Duncan's action, they assume that the witches are making two predictions—in Duncan's words, "[m]y noble partner / You greet with . . . great prediction / Of noble having *and* of royal hope" (1.3.54–56; italics mine)—when in fact only the comment that Macbeth "shalt be king hereafter" has that status. The witches' silent equivocation—their failure to correct Duncan's mistaken assumption—leads in turn to Macbeth's mistaken belief that his accession to the title of Thane of Cawdor confirms their prophetic power (see 1.3.116–30 and 1.5.1–3). (For the relevant passage in Holinshed's *Chronicles,* see Carroll, *Texts and Contexts,* pp. 141–42.)

14. As G. R. Elliott observes, Lady Macbeth's practice of writing on a piece of paper "while in a most fast sleep" (5.1.7) can be seen as a form of confession, one resembling, I add, the Puritan practice of diary-writing mentioned in n. 12. As Elliott also notes, Lady Macbeth's broken speech in the immediately subsequent sleepwalking scene suggests the inadequacy of merely private and written confession: "[H]er heart yearns for *oral* confession; the dire words she writes and reads in secret clamor to be spoken aloud" (Elliott, *Dramatic Providence in "Macbeth,"* p. 184).

15. Tentler, *Sin and Confession,* pp. 82, 83, 85, 100. The now-familiar confessional box, which ensures that the confessor and the confessant will not look directly at one another, is a post-Trentine invention. Pre-Reformation confessions were typically heard in an open space inside the church, with the priest seated and the penitent kneeling in front of or beside him. See Tentler, *Sin and Confession,* p. 82, and Jeremy Tambling, *Confession: Sexuality, Sin, the Subject* (Manchester, England: Manchester University Press, 1990), pp. 66–73. In a chapter heading in *Troubling Confessions,* Peter Brooks quotes as an epigram Freud's claim for the greater methodological sophistication of psychoanalysis: "In Confession [sic] the sinner tells what he knows; in analysis the neurotic has to tell more" (p. 113).

16. Berger, *Making Trifles of Terrors,* p. xiii.

17. Watson, *The Rest is Silence,* pp. 2, 4, 5, 6–7. The relationship between generativity and the desire for immortality is a recurrent topic of discussion in present-day studies of generativity. For a psychologically and philosophically informed explora-

tion of this relationship, see Jerome C. Wakefield, "Immortality and the Externalization of the Self: Plato's Unrecognized Theory of Generativity," in *Generativity and Adult Development: How and Why We Care for the Next Generation,* ed. Dan P. McAdams and Ed de St. Aubin (Washington, D.C.: American Psychological Association, 1998), pp. 133–74. See also Kotre, *Outliving the Self.*

18. Watson, *The Rest is Silence,* pp. 44, 109–10, 120; Karl F. Zender, "Isabella's Choice," *Philological Quarterly* 73 (1994): 88; Watson, *The Rest is Silence,* p. 120. Foucault's discussion of "biopower" (which he claims was an eighteenth-century invention) can be found in Michel Foucault, *The History of Sexuality,* vol. 1 (New York: Pantheon, 1978), pp. 138–45.

19. Robert N. Watson, *Shakespeare and the Hazards of Ambition* (Cambridge, Mass.: Harvard University Press, 1984), p. 2; Sigmund Freud, *Collected Papers,* trans. Joan Riviere et al., vol. 4 (London: Hogarth Press, 1934), p. 330 (cited in Watson, *Hazards,* p. 296, n. 35). The argument that Lady Macbeth seeks a literal disruption of her menstrual cycle was first advanced by Jennijoy La Belle in "'A Strange Infirmity': Lady Macbeth's Amenorrhea," *Shakespeare Quarterly* 31 (1980): 381–86. See also Alice Fox, "Obstetrics and Gynecology in *Macbeth,*" *Shakespeare Studies* 12 (1979): 127–41. Fox provides ample evidence of the ubiquity of birth imagery in *Macbeth,* in particular imagery of miscarriage and of difficult deliveries. Her attempt to infer from this imagery a prior history for Macbeth and Lady Macbeth is less successful.

20. Watson, *The Rest is Silence,* pp. 140, 144. Cf. Watson, *Hazards:* "With the loss of his wife, Macbeth's hopes for diurnal or generational renewal disappear" (p. 112). Other expressions of the view that Macbeth and Lady Macbeth's barrenness is punishment can be found in (e.g.) Carroll, *Texts and Contexts,* p. 17, and Jorgensen, *Our Naked Frailties,* pp. 153–54.

21. Calderwood, *If It Were Done,* p. 90; Adelman, *Suffocating Mothers,* p. 139; David Willbern, "Phantasmagoric *Macbeth,*" *ELR* 16 (1986): 523.

22. Calderwood, *If It Were Done,* pp. 42–45. See also Dennis Biggins, "Sexuality, Witchcraft, and Violence in *Macbeth,*" *Shakespeare Studies* 8 (1975): 255–77. Lady Macbeth's cry of "My husband!" is the only time that she uses the word. See Carolyn Asp, "'Be bloody, bold and resolute': Tragic Action and Sexual Stereotyping in *Macbeth,*" *Studies in Philology* 78 (1981): 153–69. In the rapidity and intensity of its exchanges, the "harrowing aftertalk" itself has a coital rhythm, an effect well conveyed by Nigel Williamson and Janet Lapotaire in the BBC production of the play.

23. Calderwood, *If It Were Done,* pp. 45–46. When Macbeth describes the scene of the murder, he says, "Here lay Duncan, / His silver skin laced with his golden blood / And his gashed stabs looked like a breach in nature / For ruin's wasteful entrance" (2.3.113–16). The ambiguity of Macbeth's phrasing allows "ruin's wasteful entrance" to be read as moving in two directions: *into* Duncan's body through the act of murder, and *out* of his body into the world, as a monstrous parturition. In "Obstetrics and Gynecology in *Macbeth,*" Alice Fox emphasizes the presence in Macbeth's speech of "images evocative of the gory sights of difficult births" (p. 135).

In "Phantasmagoric *Macbeth*," David Willbern traces a pattern of associations that in his view allow the murder of Duncan itself to be read as "symbolic infanticide" (p. 524).

24. In *Shakespeare's Wordplay* (London: Methuen, 1957), M. M. Mahood observes that "*Firstlings* can mean 'firstborn young' as well as 'the first results of anything, or first-fruits'" (p. 135; cited in Biggins, "Sexuality, Witchcraft, and Violence in *Macbeth*," p. 277). So in contrast to the "son of mine succeeding" referred to at 3.1.65, Macbeth's firstborn here is an act of child-slaughter. When Macbeth enters the scene, he expresses a willingness to have "the treasure / Of nature's germens tumble all together, / Even till destruction sicken," if this is what is needed to compel the witches to "answer me / To what I ask you." But this fantasy of a universal onanism leads instead to a reaffirmation of fecundity, in the apparition of a crowned child holding a tree "[t]hat rises like the issue of a king" and in the show of the eight kings (4.1.58–60, 87).

25. Macbeth's obsession with the youthfulness of his opponent leads a few lines later to his addressing the servant who brings the news of the arrival of Malcolm's army as "[t]hou lily-livered boy" (5.3.15).

26. Calderwood, *If It Were Done*, pp. 33, 40. See also Stephen Booth, *"King Lear," "Macbeth," Indefinition, and Tragedy*, pp. 93–94. In "Phantasmagoric *Macbeth*" David Willbern observes that Macbeth's mental makeup lacks the "mediating ground where things *may be:* instead, things *are* and *are not.* There is no place for fantasy, no interim for the provisional play of wish and deed." Compelled to enact his fantasies," Willbern says, "[Macbeth] must be and do" (pp. 532, 534).

27. Brooks, *Troubling Confessions*, pp. 168, 49. In the contemporary world, the polarity of the relation between the dominant social order and the individual has reversed itself, with emphasis now falling more on the need of the social order to reparate individuals and groups harmed by past policies than on the need of offending individuals to reconcile themselves with society: hence the emergence of South Africa's Truth and Reconciliation Commission and of various efforts to seek or to offer monetary recompense to the descendants of victimized groups: Jews and others killed during the holocaust, Japanese interned during World War II, African Americans enslaved in the United States prior to the Civil War. For a discussion of some of the moral and ethical implications of these efforts, see Julia Kristeva, "Forgiveness: An Interview," and Peter Brooks et al., "Responses to 'Forgiveness: An Interview,'" *PMLA* 117 (2002): 278–95 and 296–323.

28. Cavell, "The Avoidance of Love," in *Must We Mean What We Say*, p. 309.

CHAPTER 4

1. The quotations from Plutarch are from T. J. B. Spencer, ed., *Shakespeare's Plutarch* (London: Penguin, 1964), pp. 285, 294. For an excellent account of the Donations of Alexandria and of Cleopatra's life generally, see Michael Grant, *Cleopatra* (London: Weidenfeld and Nicolson, 1972). Grant says that Alexander Helios and

Ptolemy Philadelphus were "given" to Cleopatra Selene and King Juba; he speculates that "they, too, went to Mauretania, and lived a cautious life that evoked no perilous memories" (p. 231).

2. G. Wilson Knight, *The Imperial Theme: Further Interpretations of Shakespeare's Tragedies Including the Roman Plays* (1931; reprint, London: Methuen, 1954), pp. 227, 262; Constance Brown Kuriyama, "'The Mother of the World': A Psychoanalytic Interpretation of Shakespeare's *Antony and Cleopatra*," *ELR* 7 (1977): 330. Adelman, *Suffocating Mothers*, pp. 184, 191. For a summary of the negative appraisal of Cleopatra based on her indifference to the fate of children, see Willard Farnham, *Shakespeare's Tragic Frontier: The World of His Final Tragedies* (Berkeley: University of California Press, 1950), pp. 194–203. For a representative moralizing interpretation, see Franklin Dickey, *Not Wisely But Too Well: Shakespeare's Love Tragedies* (San Marino: Huntington Library, 1957), pp. 144–202.

3. Michael Neill, "Introduction," in *Anthony and Cleopatra*, ed. Michael Neill, The Oxford Shakespeare (Oxford: Oxford University Press, 1994), p. 89. Because the folio occasionally uses "Anth" and "Antho" as speech-prefixes, Neill has chosen to spell "Antony" with an "h," both in this edition and in his *Issues of Death*, cited in n. 28 below.

4. Neill, "Introduction," *Anthony and Cleopatra*, p. 78.

5. Carol Cook, "The Fatal Cleopatra," in *Shakespearean Tragedy and Gender*, ed. Shirley Nelson Garner and Madelon Sprengnether (Bloomington: Indiana University Press, 1996), p. 253. As Anne Barton observes, the difficulty readers face in assessing attitudes and motives is exacerbated by the contradictory epithets directed at Antony and Cleopatra throughout the play. Antony is called "the triple pillar of the world," "a mine of bounty," "the demi-Atlas of this earth," *and* "a strumpet's fool," "the abstract of all faults that all men follow," "a doting mallard"—without, however, a certain basis ever being provided for preferring the one set of appellations over the other. The effect is to suggest that "the same quality . . . [can] become a virtue or a vice depending on the position of the viewer." Anne Barton, "'Nature's piece 'gainst fancy': The Divided Catastrophe in *Antony and Cleopatra*," in *Essays, Mainly Shakespearean* (Cambridge: Cambridge University Press, 1994), pp. 127–28, 130. For a similar argument, see Janet Adelman, *The Common Liar: An Essay on "Antony and Cleopatra"* (New Haven: Yale University Press, 1973), pp. 15–39.

6. Enobarbus expresses Antony and Cleopatra's charismatic conception of power perfectly when he describes Cleopatra as having hopped forty paces through the public street. "Having lost her breath," he says, "she spoke and panted, / That she did make defect perfection, / And, breathless, power breathe forth" (2.2.240–42). The modern understanding of charisma as a form of power originates with the sociologist Max Weber, who distinguished between charismatic, traditional, and legal sources of political authority. See Max Weber, *Max Weber on Charisma and Institution Building: Selected Papers*, ed. S. N. Eisenstadt (Chicago: University of Chicago Press, 1968). *Antony and Cleopatra*'s emphasis on charisma gains significance when viewed in relation to Queen Elizabeth's and King James's uses of ritualized self-

display as a means of instilling respect for monarchical authority. Cf. the references to "charisma" in the index to Stephen Greenblatt, *Shakespearean Negotiations: The Circulation of Social Energy in Renaissance England* (Berkeley: University of California Press, 1988).

7. The two ambiguous uses are Cleopatra's "Look, prithee, Charmian, / How this Herculean Roman does become / The carriage of his chafe" (1.3.83–85) and Caesar's instruction to Thidias, "Observe how Antony becomes his flaw, / And what thou think'st his very action speaks / In every power that moves" (3.12.34–36). For commentary on the play's distinctive uses of "become," see Cook, "The Fatal Cleopatra," pp. 255–56, and Susan Snyder, "Patterns of Motion in *Antony and Cleopatra*," *Shakespeare Survey* 33 (1980): 113–22 (especially pp. 115–16 and 118–19).

8. Images of a temporal process as oscillating, hesitating, or paradoxically reversing its direction occur frequently in the play. "This common body," says Octavius, "[l]ike to a vagabond flag upon the stream, / Goes to and back, lackeying the varying tide / To rot itself with motion" (1.4.44–47). Octavia's conflicting emotions as she says goodbye to her brother, Antony says, are like "the swan's down feather, / That stands upon the swell at full of tide, / And neither way inclines" (3.2.48–50). "Other women cloy / The appetites they feed," says Enobarbus, but Cleopatra "makes hungry / Where most she satisfies" (2.2.246–48). Cf. Peter Berek, "Doing and Undoing: The Value of Action in *Antony and Cleopatra*," *Shakespeare Quarterly* 32 (1981): 295–304.

9. As suggested above, Antony's alternation between his Roman and his Egyptian identities occasionally offers evidence of internal conflict. But as A. C. Bradley says, in this play Shakespeare basically eschews "his matchless power of depicting an inward struggle. . . . Antony breaks away from Cleopatra without any strenuous conflict. No serious doubt of his return is permitted to agitate us. . . . [A]nd not a line portrays any inward struggle preceding [the return itself]." A. C. Bradley, *Oxford Lectures on Poetry* (1909; reprint, New York: St. Martin's Press, 1965), pp. 286–87. With only momentary exceptions, Antony inhabits his contradictory identities sequentially rather than simultaneously, thereby creating the impression that each, although partial, is also absolute.

10. Kuriyama, "'The Mother of the World,'" p. 327; Cook, "The Fatal Cleopatra," p. 252; Katherine Eggert, *Showing Like a Queen: Female Authority and Literary Experiment in Spenser, Shakespeare, and Milton* (Philadelphia: University of Pennsylvania Press, 2000), p. 144. A contrasting strand of recent criticism emphasizes the fragility of identity in the play, in particular of Antony's sense of his masculinity. See (e.g.) Jonathan Gil Harris, "'Narcissus in thy face': Roman Desire and the Difference it Fakes in *Antony and Cleopatra*," *Shakespeare Quarterly* 45 (1994): 408–25; Laura Levine, *Men in Women's Clothing: Anti-Theatricality and Effeminization, 1579–1642*, Cambridge Studies in Renaissance Literature and Culture 5 (Cambridge: Cambridge University Press, 1994), pp. 44–72; Cynthia Marshall, "Man of Steel Done Got the Blues: Melancholic Subversion of Presence in *Antony and Cleopatra*," *Shakespeare Quarterly* 44 (1993): 385–408.

11. For helpful chronologies, see Grant, *Cleopatra,* pp. 283–85, and Eleanor Goltz Huzar, *Mark Antony: A Biography* (Minneapolis: University of Minnesota Press, 1978), pp. 258–61. For an interpretation of Antony (but not Cleopatra) as undergoing a midlife crisis, see Bevington, *Shakespeare: The Seven Ages,* pp. 173–81.

12. Commentators offering psychoanalytic interpretations of *Antony and Cleopatra* have emphasized the oedipal rivalry between Antony and Octavius, at times interpreting Antony as the oedipal father whom Octavius must strive to overthrow, at other times inverting the age difference between the two, reading Antony as the rebellious child and Octavius as the embodiment of a repressive Roman "law of the father." See (e.g.) Adelman, *Suffocating Mothers,* pp. 180–81, and Kuriyama, "'The Mother of the World,'" pp. 334–35. The servants' failure to respond to Antony's command, although momentary, resembles a similar instance in *King Lear.* In the scene before Gloucester's house, Lear notices Oswald and says, "This is a slave, whose easy-borrowed pride / Dwells in the fickle grace of her he follows. / Out, varlet, from my sight!" (2.4.186–88). Some thirty lines later, casting about for an example of how absurd it would be for him to accede to Regan's request that he return and live with Goneril "till the expiration of your month," Lear says, "Return with her? / Persuade me rather to be slave and sumpter / To this detested groom" (2.4.203, 216–18). The detested groom is Oswald, who has not moved.

13. Jonathan Dollimore, *Radical Tragedy: Religion, Ideology, and Power in the Drama of Shakespeare and His Contemporaries,* 3rd ed. (London: Palgrave, 2004), p. 217.

14. Bernice L. Neugarten, "The Awareness of Middle Age," in *Middle Age and Aging,* ed. Bernice L. Neugarten (Chicago: University of Chicago Press, 1968), p. 97; Levinson et al., *Seasons of a Man's Life,* especially pp. 278–304. See also David A. Karp, "A Decade of Reminders: Changing Age Consciousness Between Fifty and Sixty Years Old," *The Gerontologist* 28 (1988): 727–38.

15. David Daniell, ed., *Julius Caesar,* The Arden Shakespeare (Watson-on-Thames: Thomas Nelson and Sons Ltd., 1998), p. 71.

16. Antony expresses his eagerness to begin the battle when he says "[t]o business that we love we rise betimes / And go to 't with delight"; he associates his eagerness with denial of aging when he says, "[t]his morning, like the spirit of a youth / That means to be of note, begins betimes" (4.4.20–21, 26–27). Evidence of Antony's having replaced dilatoriness with celerity also occurs after the battle, when he says, "[t]omorrow, / Before the sun shall see 's, we'll spill the blood / That has today escaped" (4.8.2–4). In the next scene, a sentry in Caesar's camp says, "they say we shall embattle / By the second hour i' the morn" (4.9.3–4).

17. David Bevington, ed., *Antony and Cleopatra,* The New Cambridge Shakespeare (Cambridge: Cambridge University Press, 1990), p. 202.

18. The mode of the land battle enacts the contrast between Octavius's "lieutenantry" and Antony's delight in "the brave squares of war," as Antony tells his troops, "[y]ou that will fight, / Follow me close. I'll bring you to 't," and Octavius tells his subordinate, "[g]o forth, Agrippa, and begin the fight" (4.4.34–35; 4.6.1). When Antony returns from the battle, the reversal of the earlier signs of effemi-

nization continues, as he assumes command over the motif of hand-kissing that had so offended him when Cleopatra had exercised control over it herself. Entering with Scarus and encountering Cleopatra as she also enters, Antony says, "[b]ehold this man; / Commend unto his lips thy favoring hand.— / Kiss it, my warrior" (4.8.22–24).

19. Even in the exhilaration of the aftermath of the land battle, Antony's language betrays the reality of his situation. "You have shown all Hectors" (4.8.7) he says to his troops, a foreboding comparison, given Hector's fate.

20. The writing of life stories has recently gained popularity as a form of group therapy, particularly among the elderly. For an overview of the theoretical underpinnings of this development, see chapter 1, "Language, Narrative, Self, and Adult Development," in Ruth E. Ray, *Beyond Nostalgia: Aging and Life Story Writing* (Charlottesville: University Press of Virginia, 2000), pp. 18–32. Ray follows Margaret Morganroth Gullette in viewing "the conventional scripts for age [as] essentially decline narratives"; in seeing these narratives as cultural, not biological, in origin; and in arguing that therapists should "promote counternarratives that overturn . . . ageist assumptions" (p. 29). Cf. Gullette, *Declining to Decline* and *Aged by Culture.*

21. Peter Erickson, *Patriarchal Structures in Shakespeare's Drama* (Berkeley: University of California Press, 1985), pp. 124–25. Some feminist commentators, while welcoming the prominence given to Cleopatra at the end of the play, nonetheless see the play's emphasis on relational issues as continuing a tradition of representation in which Cleopatra is marginalized as a political figure. For accounts of the ways in which Cleopatra has been imagined and reimagined throughout history, see Mary Hamer, *Signs of Cleopatra: History, Politics, Representations* (London: Routledge, 1993), and Lucy Hughes-Hallett, *Cleopatra: Histories, Dreams, and Distortions* (New York: Harper & Row, 1990). For the folklore motif of the lusty widow, see Stith Thompson, *Motif-Index of Folk-Literature,* revised and enlarged edition (Bloomington: Indiana University Press, 1957), entry T230ff. (A literary example of the motif, written shortly before *Antony and Cleopatra,* is George Chapman's play, *The Widow's Tears.*) For an interesting attempt to apply life-cycle theory to women's experiences in the Early Modern period, focused primarily on midlife sexuality, see Lois W. Banner, *In Full Flower: Aging Women, Power, and Sexuality* (New York: Alfred A. Knopf, 1992), pp. 164–231. Banner notes Jaques' reliance on male examples in the seven ages speech.

22. Barton, "'Nature's piece 'gainst fancy,'" passim.

23. Adelman, *The Common Liar,* p. 166. The fictive quality of Antony's and Cleopatra's references to the afterlife can be seen in the way in which those references conform to the shape of their desires. The afterlife Antony imagines as he prepares for suicide, "[w]here souls do couch on flowers" (4.14.50), rewrites Virgil's *Aeneid* in a fashion consistent with the meaning he wishes his own relationship with Cleopatra to have, converting Dido from the woman Aeneas abandons in the service of Roman values into Aeneas's otherworldly lover. And when Cleopatra prepares for her suicide, she imagines her reunion with Antony not in an otherworldly paradise

but in this world, at the place where their love affair began. "I am again for Cydnus," she says, "[t]o meet Mark Antony" (5.2.228–29).

24. My emphasis on the psychological utility of Cleopatra's dream should not be taken to mean that I find unimportant the question of its truth value. For an eloquent meditation on this question, see Adelman, *The Common Liar,* pp. 102–68 (especially pp. 157–68). My own belief that there is a form of truth in Cleopatra's dream is personal in origin. Late in his life, a friend of mine who suffered from multiple sclerosis told me that whenever he appeared as a character in his dreams, his body was always whole and sound. What power of mind impels such images and ensures their longevity? As Cleopatra says, "[n]ature wants stuff / To vie strange forms with fancy." But our idealized images either of others or of ourselves—our Antonys—are "nature's piece 'gainst fancy, / Condemning shadows quite" (5.2.96–99).

25. Spencer, ed., *Shakespeare's Plutarch,* pp. 287, 289. In Plutarch, Seleucus is said to be present "by chance" (p. 287), but in the play his presence appears to be intentional. When Cleopatra asks him to speak, she says, "Where's Seleucus?" (5.2.139) as if she expects him to be present. For a thorough discussion of the episode, see Brents Stirling, "Cleopatra's Scene with Seleucus: Plutarch, Daniel, and Shakespeare," *Shakespeare Quarterly* 15 (1964): 299–311.

26. Shakespeare's association of female kneeling with compliance to Roman values should remind us of *Julius Caesar,* where the contrast between Portia's attempt to kneel to Brutus, forestalled by Brutus, and Calpurnia's similar attempt, unopposed by Caesar, enacts the difference between Brutus's temperamental republicanism and Caesar's authoritarian tendencies. See *Julius Caesar,* 2.1 and 2.2.

27. My colleague Richard A. Levin and I agree in interpreting Cleopatra's encounter with Octavius as an effort at seduction, but we differ in our interpretation of its method and goal. Whereas I believe that Cleopatra de-eroticizes her seductiveness, in order to appeal to Octavius's asceticism, Professor Levin interprets her effort as directly sexual, in both performance and intended outcome. See Richard A. Levin, *Shakespeare's Secret Schemers: The Study of an Early Modern Dramatic Device* (Newark: University of Delaware Press, 2001), pp. 94–108.

28. Michael Neill, *Issues of Death: Mortality and Identity in English Renaissance Tragedy* (Oxford: Clarendon Press, 1997), pp. 320, 318. The seriocomic elements of the episode of Cleopatra and her attendants hoisting Antony up into her monument also compromise his final effort at heroic self-affirmation. See the discussion of "the ironies of visual hierarchy" in this scene in David Bevington, *Action is Eloquence: Shakespeare's Language of Gesture* (Cambridge, Mass.: Harvard University Press, 1984), p. 107. My summary of the sensual, erotic, and loving qualities exhibited by Antony in the monument scene is taken from Bradley, *Oxford Lectures in Poetry,* p. 298.

29. Neill, *Issues of Death,* pp. 321, 323; Clare Kinney, "The Queen's Two Bodies and the Divided Emperor: Some Problems of Identity in *Antony and Cleopatra,*" in *The Renaissance Englishwoman in Print: Counterbalancing the Canon,* ed. Anne M. Haselkorn and Betty S. Travitsky (Amherst: University of Massachusetts Press, 1990), p. 185.

30. For Antony's exercise of the power of decimation and Cleopatra's observation of the effects of poison, see Spencer, ed., *Shakespeare's Plutarch,* pp. 226 and 267. In Samuel Daniel's *Cleopatra,* Cleopatra attempts to save Caesarion by sending him away to India, but she is betrayed by his tutor, Rodon. See Samuel Daniel, *The Complete Works in Verse and Prose of Samuel Daniel,* ed. Alexander B. Grosart, vol. 2 (1885; reprint, New York: Russell & Russell, 1963). For the Countess of Pembroke's *Antonius,* I have consulted Mary Sidney Herbert, *The Collected Works of Mary Sidney Herbert, Countess of Pembroke,* ed. Margaret P. Hannay, Noel J. Kinnamon, and Michael G. Brennan, vol. 1 (Oxford: Clarendon Press, 1998).

31. Neill, ed., *Anthony and Cleopatra,* p. 95; Dollimore, *Radical Tragedy,* p. 205. There is a long history of parallels being drawn between Shakespeare's Cleopatra and Elizabeth I. Recent efforts include Elizabeth A. Brown, "'Companion Me with My Mistress': Cleopatra, Elizabeth I, and Their Waiting Women," in *Maids and Mistresses, Cousins and Queens: Women's Alliances in Early Modern England,* ed. Susan Frye and Karen Robertson (Oxford: Oxford University Press, 1999), pp. 131–45; Eggert, *Showing Like a Queen,* pp. 131–68; Theodora A. Jankowski, *Women in Power in the Early Modern Drama* (Urbana: University of Illinois Press, 1992), pp. 147–63. Antony's complaint that at Philippi Octavius "kept / His sword e'en like a dancer" (3.11.35–36) echoes objections by characters in other of Shakespeare's plays to the newfangled style of fighting with rapier rather than with broadsword. See (e.g.) Leonato's angry comments about Claudio's "nice fence" and "foining fence" in *Much Ado About Nothing* (5.1.75, 84) and Mercutio's mockery of Tybalt in *Romeo and Juliet* as "[t]he very butcher of a silk button, a duellist, a duellist" (2.4.23–24). For relevant background, see Joan Ozark Holmer, "'Draw if You Be Men': Saviolo's Significance for *Romeo and Juliet,*" *Shakespeare Quarterly* 45 (1994): 163–89.

32. Barton, "'Nature's piece 'gainst fancy,'" p. 131; Eggert, *Showing Like a Queen,* pp. 13, 133; Neill, *Issues of Death,* pp. 38, 40–41, 46. Neill's citation of Nigel Llewellyn is to *The Art of Death: Visual Culture in the English Death Ritual* (London: Reaktion Books in association with the Victoria and Albert Museum, 1991).

33. Neill, *Issues of Death,* pp. 314–15.

34. Joyce Green MacDonald, *Women and Race in Early Modern Texts* (Cambridge: Cambridge University Press, 2002), p. 66; Catherine Belsey, *Shakespeare and the Loss of Eden: The Construction of Family Values in Early Modern Culture* (London: Macmillan, 1999), p. 19; Bradley, *Oxford Lectures on Poetry,* p. 304; Kuriyama, "'The Mother of the World,'" p. 328. For a discussion of the play's references to children in relation to its images of "sex without generation" and "generation without sex," see Gabriel Egan, *Green Shakespeare: From Ecopolitics to Ecocriticism,* Accents on Shakespeare (London: Routledge, 2006), pp. 108–21. I am indebted to an anonymous reader at LSU Press for calling my attention to this book.

35. I read this study in my early days as an assistant professor, in conjunction with a course I was teaching, but my efforts to track down the citation (or even to recall the name of the course) have unfortunately proven unsuccessful. For an ex-

cellent meditation on the psychology of suicide, see A. Alvarez, *The Savage God: A Study of Suicide* (London: Weidenfeld and Nicolson, 1971).

CHAPTER 5

1. Kiernan Ryan, "Introduction," in *Shakespeare: The Last Plays,* ed. Kiernan Ryan (London: Longman, 1999), pp. 6, 11; Robert Grams Hunter, *Shakespeare and the Comedy of Forgiveness* (New York: Columbia University Press, 1965), pp. 201–2; B. J. Sokol, *Art and Illusion in "The Winter's Tale"* (Manchester: Manchester University. Press, 1994), p. 53.

2. Adelman, *Suffocating Mothers,* p. 235; Erickson, *Patriarchal Structures,* pp. 148, 160, 163; Abbe Blum, "'Strike all that look upon with mar[b]le': Monumentalizing Women in Shakespeare's Plays," in *The Renaissance Englishwoman in Print: Counterbalancing the Canon,* ed. Anne M. Haselkorn and Betty S. Travitsky (Amherst: University of Massachusetts Press, 1990), p. 113; Frances E. Dolan, *Dangerous Familiars: Representations of Domestic Crime in England, 1550–1700* (Ithaca: Cornell University Press, 1994), p. 169.

3. Debora K. Shuger, *Political Theologies in Shakespeare's England: The Sacred and the State in "Measure for Measure"* (Houndmills: Palgrave, 2001), pp. 132, 101.

4. A former colleague of mine was fond of saying that the long-projected tenth campus of the University of California was in fact the maximum security prison at Pelican Bay, this because in his view the economic resources used to build the prison—a consequence of a three strikes law—could have been used instead to build the campus. For an extended application of the concept of equity to *The Winter's Tale,* see Constance Jordan, *Shakespeare's Monarchies: Ruler and Subject in the Romances* (Ithaca: Cornell University Press, 1997), pp. 104–46.

5. Nevill Coghill, "Six Points of Stage-craft in *The Winter's Tale,*" *Shakespeare Survey* 11 (1958): 33. In a brilliantly mischievous reading, Howard Felperin asks "on what authority do we assume . . . that Hermione is in fact innocent of Leontes's suspicions in the opening act?" and argues that "Leontes's jealous and destructive passion is not quite so flimsy and fanciful . . . as is often casually assumed." Felperin's purpose is not to call into question Hermione's innocence, which he seems actually to accept, but to explore "the inescapable mediacy of language, the radical difference between presence and reference, and the ultimate subjectivity of all interpretation." See "'Tongue-tied, Our Queen?' The Deconstruction of Presence in *The Winter's Tale,*" in Howard Felperin, *The Uses of the Canon: Elizabethan Literature and Contemporary Theory* (Oxford: Oxford University Press, 1990), pp. 37, 41, 54.

6. David Schalkwyk, "'A Lady's "Verily" Is as Potent as a Lord's': Women, Word, and Witchcraft in *The Winter's Tale,*" *ELR* 22 (1992): 248; Murray M. Schwartz, "Leontes' Jealousy in *The Winter's Tale,*" *American Imago* 30 (1973): 251; Stephen Orgel, "Introduction," in *William Shakespeare: "The Winter's Tale,"* ed. Stephen Orgel, The Oxford Shakespeare (Oxford: Oxford University Press, 1996), p. 19. Schwartz's sec-

ond essay on *The Winter's Tale,* developing further the argument of "Leontes' Jealousy," is "*The Winter's Tale:* Loss and Transformation," *American Imago* 32 (1975): 145–99.

7. J. I. M. Stewart, *Character and Motive in Shakespeare: Some Recent Appraisals Examined* (London: Longmans, Green and Co., 1949), pp. 30–37; C. L. Barber, "'Thou That Beget'st Him That Did Thee Beget': Transformation in 'Pericles' and 'The Winter's Tale,'" *Shakespeare Survey* 22 (1969): 59–67. Other psychoanalytic interpretations, often feminist in emphasis, include Adelman, *Suffocating Mothers,* pp. 220–38; Coppélia Kahn, *Man's Estate: Masculine Identity in Shakespeare* (Berkeley: University of California Press, 1981), pp. 214–19; Carol Thomas Neely, *Broken Nuptials in Shakespeare's Plays* (Urbana: University of Illinois Press, 1993), pp. 191–209; and Nevo, *Shakespeare's Other Language,* pp. 95–119. For a recent reading exploring homoeroticism in the play, see Nora Johnson, "Ganymedes and Kings: Staging Male Homosexual Desire in *The Winter's Tale,*" *Shakespeare Studies* 26 (1998): 187–217. The quoted phrase is from Schwartz, "Leontes' Jealousy," p. 253.

8. Schwartz, "Leontes' Jealousy," pp. 256, 261–62; Adelman, *Suffocating Mothers,* p. 225. For an insightful interpretation of Leontes' jealousy, and of the play as a whole, in relation to Early Modern birthing and nursing practices, see Gail Kern Paster, *The Body Embarrassed: Drama and the Disciplines of Shame in Early Modern England* (Ithaca: Cornell University Press, 1993), pp. 260–80.

9. Schwartz, "Leontes' Jealousy," p. 262.

10. Stanley Cavell, "Recounting Gains, Showing Losses: Reading *The Winter's Tale,*" in *Disowning Knowledge in Seven Plays of Shakespeare* (Cambridge: Cambridge University Press, 2003), p. 195; David Lee Miller, *Dreams of the Burning Child: Sacrificial Sons and the Father's Witness* (Ithaca: Cornell University Press, 2003), pp.104, 97, 96, 95. For Nancy Jay's work on blood sacrifice, see Nancy Jay, *Throughout Your Generations Forever: Sacrifice, Religion, and Paternity* (Chicago: University of Chicago Press, 1992).

11. Graham Holderness, "*The Winter's Tale:* Country into Court," in *Shakespeare Out of Court: Dramatizations of Court Society,* ed. Graham Holderness, Nick Potter, and John Turner (New York: St. Martin's Press, 1990), pp. 203, 201. For the custom of breeching, see Susan Snyder, "Mamillius and Gender Polarization in *The Winter's Tale,*" *Shakespeare Quarterly* 50 (1999): 1–8.

12. Cavell, "Recounting Gains, Showing Losses," p. 199; Orgel, "Introduction," in *William Shakespeare: "The Winter's Tale,"* p. 34. Cavell notes the connection between Mamillius's whispering and Leontes' earlier uses of the word (p. 194). In *Suffocating Mothers,* Janet Adelman observes that when Leontes says "let her sport herself/With that she's big with," he "imagines the unborn baby he would disown as the mother's illicit sexual partner" (p. 225). I take this extraordinary fantasy to be a further effort on Leontes' part to protect Mamillius and, by extension, himself from the contamination of sexuality. If Hermione must necessarily "sport" in an oedipal scenario, then let her do so with someone who "does [not] bear some signs of me" (2.1.58).

13. Miller, *Dreams of the Burning Child,* p. 93. Compare Nevo, *Shakespeare's Other Language:* "On the face of it, Polixenes is describing childish games . . . but can we ignore the subversive connotations of 'enemy,' of 'parasite,' above all of the strange inversion of July and December? . . . . Thoughts that would thick the blood are indeed soothed, stilled, by the charm of a child but the child is also a threat, a supplanter, a usurper" (pp. 107–8).

14. Cavell, "Recounting Gains, Showing Losses," pp. 199, 211, 208. In *Art and Illusion in "The Winter's Tale,"* pp. 42–49, Sokol argues for the pertinence to an understanding of Leontes' jealousy of the "couvade syndrome," a term used to designate aberrant physical and psychological reactions manifested by expectant fathers. Sokol provides evidence of references to these reactions in the literature of Shakespeare's age. He also cites a study indicating that the reactions are more "complex and ambivalent . . . at a time of subsequent fatherhood" than during a first pregnancy (p. 47). An alteration Shakespeare made in his primary source, Robert Greene's *Pandosto: The Triumph of Time,* is relevant here. In Greene's novella, Bellaria (the character antecedent to Hermione) does not discover that she is pregnant until after Pandosto has become jealous and she has been consigned to prison. Arranging the events of the story in this sequence encourages an interpretation of Pandosto's jealousy as entirely sexual in origin. Shakespeare's decision to move the pregnancy forward in time invites the more complex, if less commonsensical, interpretation proposed by Sokol.

15. Editors of *The Winter's Tale* often annotate the waiting woman's "fine new prince" by observing that in Shakespeare's time the word *prince* could refer to either sex. While true, the annotation rationalizes the text unnecessarily, by anticipating knowledge that neither the characters nor the audience possess at this point in the play. Had the child in fact proven to be male, would editors find it necessary to observe that "fine new prince" could mean "fine new princess"?

16. Lynda E. Boose, "The Father's House and the Daughter in It: The Structures of Western Culture's Daughter-Father Relationship," in *Daughters and Fathers,* ed. Lynda E. Boose and Betty S. Flowers (Baltimore: Johns Hopkins University Press, 1989), pp. 21, 31. In "Bastards and Broadsides in *The Winter's Tale*" (*Renaissance Drama* 30 [1999–2001]: 43–71), Aaron Kitch argues that images and metaphors of printing in Paulina's speech and elsewhere provide "an important perspective from which to evaluate the central but paradoxical structure of paternity and its anxieties" (p. 44). "[B]oth the press and paternity," he argues, "are legitimating structures (of texts and children, respectively) whose weak link is the reproducibility of that structure through the production of multiple copies" (pp. 51–52). Whereas Kitch emphasizes the threat to paternal identity posed by a second child that is a bastard, I argue that any second birth, whether legitimate or illegitimate, is a potential source of fatherly anxiety.

17. Marc Shell, *The End of Kinship: "Measure for Measure," Incest, and the Ideal of Universal Siblinghood* (Stanford: Stanford University Press, 1988); Karl F. Zender, chapter 1, "The Politics of Incest," in *Faulkner and the Politics of Reading* (Baton

Rouge: Louisiana State University Press, 2002), pp. 1–31. I have reused a few sentences and phrases from "The Politics of Incest" in this paragraph. For the quotation from "Laon and Cythna," see Percy Bysshe Shelley, *The Complete Poetical Works of Percy Bysshe Shelley,* ed. Neville Rogers, 4 vols. (Oxford: Clarendon Press, 1975), vol. 2 , canto 2, stanza 37, ll. 995–96. For a wide-ranging and historically informed discussion of depictions of sibling incest in Elizabethan, Jacobean, and Restoration drama, see the entries in the index under "Incestuous relationships; Siblings" in Richard A. McCabe, *Incest, Drama, and Nature's Law, 1550–1700* (Cambridge: Cambridge University Press, 1993).

18. Fawnia, the Perdita character in Greene's *Pandosto,* is referred to as "brat" several times, not only by Pandosto but by Porrus, her shepherd foster-father, and by Fawnia herself.

19. Alison Thorne, "Introduction," in *Shakespeare's Romances,* ed. Alison Thorne, New Casebooks (London: Palgrave, 2003), p. 6; Ryan, "Introduction," in *Shakespeare: The Last Plays,* pp. 4–5. For an insightful discussion of the decreased emphasis on consistency of characterization in the late romances, see Anne Barton, "Leontes and the Spider: Language and Speaker in Shakespeare's Last Plays," in *Essays: Mainly Shakespearean,* pp. 161–81.

20. Belsey, *Shakespeare and the Loss of Eden,* pp. 22, 111–12, 120.

21. Theresa M. Krier, *Birth Passages: Maternity and Nostalgia, Antiquity to Shakespeare* (Ithaca: Cornell University Press, 2001), pp. xiv, 5–7.

22. Ibid., p. x.

23. In "Metacriticism and Materiality: The Case of Shakespeare's *The Winter's Tale,*" *ELH* 58 (1991): 283–304, William R. Morse interprets Leontes' characterization as a critique of the "analytico-referential discourse" that in the Early Modern period was supplanting "an old discourse of analogies" (pp. 287, 286). "Leontes' madness," he says (and, I would add, Leontes' immediate response to its cessation), "is best understood in the context of [the emergent] rationalist ideology. Because the basis of the rationalist project is a thoroughgoing hypostatization of primal reality, a transformation of mutable nature into conceptual field, change or flux is not merely inaccessible to reason, but fundamentally antipathetic to it" (p. 290). My view of the place of Apollo in *The Winter's Tale* agrees with that of Howard Felperin in "'Tongue-tied, Our Queen?'" in *The Uses of the Canon.* Noting the absence of a direct representation of the god (in contrast to the theophanies depicted in *Pericles* and *Cymbeline*), Felperin calls Apollo a "*deus absconditus,*" one whose authority is "disturbingly difficult to verify or validate" (p. 42). For a contrary reading, in which Apollo is said to preside over the entire movement toward reconciliation, see David M. Bergeron, "The Apollo Mission in *The Winter's Tale,*" in *"The Winter's Tale": Critical Essays,* ed. Maurice Hunt (New York: Garland, 1995), pp. 361–79.

24. Krier, *Birth Passages,* p. 246. For a Bakhtinian analysis of Paulina as an embodiment of festive liberty disrupting the "decorous, claustrophobic world of the royal bedchamber," see Anthony Gash, "Shakespeare, Carnival, and the Sacred: *The Winter's Tale* and *Measure for Measure,*" in *Shakespeare and Carnival: After Bakhtin,*

ed. Ronald Knowles (New York: St. Martin's Press, 1998), pp. 177–210 (the quoted phrase appears on p. 189).

25. Schwartz, "*The Winter's Tale:* Loss and Transformation," p. 155. As is often observed, Shakespeare reverses the settings of Robert Greene's *Pandosto,* making Leontes the king not of Bohemia but of Sicily. In "*The Winter's Tale* and the Religious Politics of Europe," in Thorne, ed., *Shakespeare's Romances,* pp. 171–204, James Ellison argues that a primary purpose for this change is to align the religious identities of the two settings—Sicily Catholic, Bohemia Protestant—with the play's overall movement toward a reconciliation of conflicting religious beliefs, a reconciliation of the sort James I was pursuing through his proposals for dynastic marriages across doctrinal lines. This is an intriguing suggestion, but as far as penitential counseling is concerned, the alignment of Sicily with Catholicism is inexact. Prior to the onset of his paranoia, Leontes can avail himself of Camillo's services in what looks very much like the Catholic practice of auricular confession. But with Paulina, the situation is reversed. Paulina's name alludes to St. Paul, whose writings were particularly attractive to Protestant theologians, and her inability to offer guilt-alleviating counsel echoes the difficulties posed for Protestant reformers by their rejection of the sacrament of confession. Not until the statue scene, when the two settings are conjoined, is Paulina able to use a Catholic-inflected language of worship and redemption. For a similar argument regarding Paulina's behavior prior to the final scene, see Martine Van Elk, "'Our praises are our wages': Courtly Exchange, Social Mobility, and Female Speech in *The Winter's Tale,*" *Philological Quarterly* 79 (2000): 429–57.

26. Neely, *Broken Nuptials,* pp. 193, 204–5.

27. Cavell, "Recounting Gains, Showing Losses," p. 220.

28. Orgel, "Introduction," in *William Shakespeare: "The Winter's Tale,"* p. 50; Holderness, "*The Winter's Tale:* Country into Court," pp. 234–35, 226; Morse, "Metacriticism and Materiality," p. 298. While still in disguise, Polixenes reveals a fear of debility in his response to Florizel's "[o]ne being dead," asking "[i]s not your father grown incapable / Of reasonable affairs? Is he not stupid / With age and altering rheums? Can he speak? Hear? / Know man from man?" (4.4.387, 399–402).

29. When Leontes accuses Hermione of infidelity, he says, "I'll not call [thee] a creature of thy place, / Lest barbarism, making me the precedent, / Should a like language use to all degrees / And mannerly distinguishment leave out / Betwixt the prince and beggar" (2.1.84–88). The parallel Leontes establishes here between social and linguistic hierarchy helps to explain the clotted quality of much of his speech, as "low" phrases—"sluiced in 's absence," "his pond fished by his next neighbor," "[m]y wife's a hobbyhorse" (1.2.194, 195, 275)—erupt from beneath a repressiveness he misunderstands as decorum. For discussions of the obscurity of Leontes' language, see Stephen Orgel, "The Poetics of Incomprehensibility," *Shakespeare Quarterly* 42 (1991): 431–37, and (responding to Orgel), David Laird, "Competing Discourses in *The Winter's Tale,*" *Connotations* 4 (1994–95): 25–43.

30. Cf. Schwartz, "*The Winter's Tale*: Loss and Transformation": "Time is *in-*

clusive ('joy *and* terror,' 'good *and* bad,' 'makes *and* unfolds'), in sharp contrast to the exclusive priorities of the play's earlier action" (pp. 162–63). For my summary of Autolycus's parodic qualities, I am indebted to Neely, *Broken Nuptials,* pp. 203–4. Good discussions of the theme of time and of the role of Time can be found in Inga-Stina Ewbank, "The Triumph of Time in *The Winter's Tale,*" *Review of English Studies* 5, no. 2 (1964): 83–100, and Michael D. Bristol, "In Search of the Bear: Spatiotemporal Form and the Heterogeneity of Economies in *The Winter's Tale,*" *Shakespeare Quarterly* 42 (1991): 145–67.

31. Marjorie Garber, *Shakespeare After All* (New York: Pantheon Books, 2004), p. 830.

32. Northrop Frye, "The Argument of Comedy," in *Shakespeare: Modern Essays in Criticism,* ed. Leonard Dean (New York: Oxford University Press, 1967), pp. 79–89.

33. Orgel, "Introduction," in *William Shakespeare: "The Winter's Tale,"* p. 17. For a discussion in political terms of Dion and Cleomenes' advice that Leontes have an heir, see Stuart M. Kurland, "'We need no more of your advice': Political Realism in *The Winter's Tale,*" *Studies in English Literature: 1500–1900* 31 (1991): 365–86. For a wide-ranging discussion of *The Winter's Tale* in relation to political and legal debates current in Shakespeare's time, see Jordan, *Shakespeare's Monarchies,* pp. 107–46.

34. Krier, *Birth Passages,* p. 244.

35. Julia Reinhard Lupton, *Afterlives of the Saints: Hagiography, Typology, and Renaissance Literature* (Stanford: Stanford University Press, 1996), p. 216. See also Ruth Vanita, "Mariological Memory in *The Winter's Tale* and *Henry VIII,*" *Studies in English Literature: 1500–1900* 40 (2000): 311–37. Good discussions of Shakespeare's reuse of the Pygmalion story can be found in Leonard Barkan, "'Living Sculptures': Ovid, Michelangelo, and *The Winter's Tale,*" *ELH* 48 (1981): 639–67 ; and Lynn Enterline, "'You speak a language that I understand not': The Rhetoric of Animation in *The Winter's Tale,*" *Shakespeare Quarterly* 48 (1997): 17–44.

36. Krier, *Birth Passages,* p. 238. On Leontes' "reliving of [his] time of wooing," see Sokol, *Art and Illusion,* p. 40.

37. Enterline, "'You speak a language that I understand not,'" p. 42; Orgel, "Introduction" in *William Shakespeare: "The Winter's Tale,"* p. 35.

EPILOGUE

1. Joseph H. Summers, "The Anger of Prospero," *Michigan Quarterly Review* 12 (1973): 131; David Lindley, "Introduction," in *The Tempest,* ed. David Lindley, The New Cambridge Shakespeare (Cambridge: Cambridge University Press, 2002), p. 67. Summers's essay can also be found in Joseph H. Summers, *Dreams of Love and Power: On Shakespeare's Plays* (Oxford: Clarendon Press, 1984). The body of cultural materialist and feminist critiques of *The Tempest* is vast. See (e.g.) Paul Brown, "'This Thing of Darkness I Acknowledge Mine': *The Tempest* and the Discourse of Colonialism," in *Shakespeare: New Essays in Cultural Materialism,* ed. Jonathan Dol-

limore and Alan Sinfield (Manchester: Manchester University Press, 1985), pp. 48–71; Kim F. Hall, *Things of Darkness: Economies of Race and Gender in Early Modern England* (Ithaca: Cornell University Press, 1995), pp. 141–53; and Ann Thompson, "'Miranda, Where's Your Sister?' Reading Shakespeare's *Tempest*," in *Feminist Criticism: Theory and Practice*, ed. Susan Sellers (London: Harvester Wheatsheaf, 1991), pp. 45–56. For a psychoanalytic interpretation emphasizing the incompleteness of Prospero's resolution of oedipal conflicts, see Coppélia Kahn, "The Providential Tempest and the Shakespearean Family," in *Representing Shakespeare: New Psychoanalytic Essays*, ed. Murray M. Schwartz and Coppélia Kahn (Baltimore: Johns Hopkins University Press, 1980), pp. 217–43 (especially pp. 236–40).

2. Nevo, *Shakespeare's Other Language*, pp. 133–34. For the relationship between *The Tempest* and *Macbeth*, see Paul A. Cantor, "Shakespeare's *The Tempest:* The Wise Man as Hero," *Shakespeare Quarterly* 31 (1980): 64–75, and Michael Neill, "Remembrance and Revenge: *Hamlet, Macbeth*, and *The Tempest*," in *Jonson and Shakespeare*, ed. Ian Donaldson (London: Macmillan, 1983), pp. 35–56.

3. McCabe, *Incest, Drama, and Nature's Law*, p. 189.

4. Lindley, "Introduction," in *The Tempest*, p. 72. For a discussion of how the exchange between Miranda and Ferdinand constitutes a "legally binding union," see Lindley's note on 3.1.91–92, p. 162. See also the discussion of a similar scene in *As You Like It* in Agnes Latham, ed., *As You Like It*, The Arden Shakespeare (1967; reprint, London: Routledge, 1993), appendix B.

5. Summers, "The Anger of Prospero," p. 140. For a contrary interpretation, emphasizing Prospero's "repetitive verbal harshness" toward Miranda as a reflex of "an anger not of the present time and place," see B. J. Sokol, "*The Tempest:* 'All Torment, Trouble, Wonder, and Amazement': A Kleinian Reading," in *The Undiscover'd Country: New Essays on Psychoanalysis and Shakespeare*, ed. B. J. Sokol (London: Free Association Books, 1993), pp. 179–216 (the quoted phrases appear on pp. 188 and 189). For a discussion of the theme of education in *The Tempest*, see Frank Kermode, ed., *The Tempest*, The Arden Shakespeare (1954; reprint, London: Routledge, 1994), pp. xliii–xlvii.

6. Bryan Loughrey and Neil Taylor, "Ferdinand and Miranda at Chess," *Shakespeare Survey* 35 (1982): 114. For a similar view of the significance of the scene, see Gary Schmidgall, "The Discovery at Chess in *The Tempest*," *English Language Notes* 23, no. 4 (1986): 11–16. Even here, though, Prospero may be called upon to exercise restraint in the face of his daughter's and Ferdinand's behavior, for their joking exchange regarding playing false and wrangling combines with the frequent depictions in the romance tradition of chess as a sexual metaphor to suggest that dalliance may again be occurring. For a strong argument in support of this possibility, see William Poole, "False Play: Shakespeare and Chess," *Shakespeare Quarterly* 55 (2004): 50–70.

7. Harry Berger Jr., "Miraculous Harp: A Reading of Shakespeare's *Tempest*," *Shakespeare Studies* 5 (1970): 253–83 (the quoted phrases appear on pp. 257, 258, 269, and 277). See also Curt Breight, "'Treason doth never prosper': *The Tempest* and the

Discourse of Treason," *Shakespeare Quarterly* 41 (1990): 1–28, and Lindley, "Introduction," in *The Tempest,* pp. 79–80. Breight interprets the extension of the play beyond the revelation of Miranda and Ferdinand together in the cell in political terms, as an "orchestrated parade of the tortured and humiliated lower-class conspirators as a grim object lesson for Prospero's upper-class enemies" (p. 20). Psychoanalytically oriented commentators interpret Prospero's "[t]his thing of darkness I / Acknowledge mine" (5.1.278–79) as an acknowledgment of Caliban-like qualities in himself, including the incestuous temptations that he has managed to overcome.

8. Berger says that the mood of the epilogue "is in sharp contrast to the theatrical *carpe diem* of the previous scene. The first impression is of drained energy; literally of collapsed spirits" ("Miraculous Harp," p. 277). For the role of the epilogue in undermining any supposition that Prospero leaves the island in possession of a stable identity, see Nora Johnson, "Body and Spirit, Stage and Sexuality in *The Tempest,*" *ELH* 64 (1997): 683–701.

Bibliography

Adelman, Janet. *The Common Liar: An Essay on "Antony and Cleopatra."* New Haven: Yale University Press, 1973.

——. *Suffocating Mothers: Fantasies of Maternal Origin in Shakespeare's Plays "Hamlet" to "The Tempest."* London: Routledge, 1992.

Aers, David. "Reflections on Current Histories of the Subject." *Literature & History,* 2nd series, 2 (1991): 20–34.

Alexander, Baine B., et al. "Generativity in Cultural Context: The Self, Death, and Immortality as Experienced by Older American Women." *Ageing and Society* 11 (1991): 417–42.

Amussen, Susan Dwyer. *An Ordered Society: Gender and Class in Early Modern England.* Oxford: Basil Blackwell, 1988.

Ariès, Philippe. *Centuries of Childhood: A Social History of Family Life.* Trans. Robert Baldick. New York: Alfred A. Knopf, 1962.

Asp, Carolyn. "'Be bloody, bold, and resolute': Tragic Action and Sexual Stereotyping in *Macbeth.*" *Studies in Philology* 78 (1981): 153–69.

Banner, Lois W. *In Full Flower: Aging Women, Power, and Sexuality.* New York: Alfred A. Knopf, 1992.

Barber, C. L. *Shakespeare's Festive Comedy: A Study of Dramatic Form and Its Relation to Social Custom.* 1959. Reprint, Cleveland: Meridian, 1963.

——. "'Thou That Beget'st Him That Did Thee Beget': Transformation in 'Pericles' and 'The Winter's Tale.'" *Shakespeare Survey* 22 (1969): 59–67.

Barber, C. L., and Richard P. Wheeler. *The Whole Journey: Shakespeare's Power of Development.* Berkeley: University of California Press, 1986.

Barkan, Leonard. "'Living Sculptures': Ovid, Michelangelo, and *The Winter's Tale.*" *ELH* 48 (1981): 639–67.

Barton, Anne. "Leontes and the Spider: Language and Speaker in Shakespeare's Last Plays." In *Essays, Mainly Shakespearean.* Cambridge: Cambridge University Press, 1994.

——. "'Nature's piece 'gainst fancy': The Divided Catastrophe in *Antony and Cleopatra*." In *Essays, Mainly Shakespearean*. Cambridge: Cambridge University Press, 1994.

Belsey, Catherine. "Richard Levin and In-different Reading." *New Literary History* 21 (1990): 449–56.

——. *Shakespeare and the Loss of Eden: The Construction of Family Values in Early Modern Culture*. London: Macmillan, 1999.

Berek, Peter. "Doing and Undoing: The Value of Action in *Antony and Cleopatra*." *Shakespeare Quarterly* 32 (1981): 295–304.

Berger, Harry, Jr. *Making Trifles of Terrors: Redistributing Complicities in Shakespeare*. Ed. (with an intro.) Peter Erickson. Stanford: Stanford University Press, 1997.

——. "Miraculous Harp: A Reading of Shakespeare's *Tempest*." *Shakespeare Studies* 5 (1970): 253–83.

Bergeron, David M. "The Apollo Mission in *The Winter's Tale*." In *"The Winter's Tale": Critical Essays*. Ed. Maurice Hunt. New York: Garland, 1995.

Berry, Ralph. "Lear's System." *Shakespeare Quarterly* 35 (1984): 421–29.

Bevington, David. *Action is Eloquence: Shakespeare's Language of Gesture*. Cambridge, Mass.: Harvard University Press, 1984.

——. *Shakespeare: The Seven Ages of Human Experience*. 2nd ed. Oxford: Blackwell, 2005.

——, ed. *Antony and Cleopatra*. The New Cambridge Shakespeare. Cambridge: Cambridge University Press, 1990.

——, ed. *The Complete Works of Shakespeare*. 4th ed. New York: HarperCollins, 1992.

Biggins, Dennis. "Sexuality, Witchcraft, and Violence in *Macbeth*." *Shakespeare Studies* 8 (1975): 255–77.

Biggs, Simon. *The Mature Imagination: Dynamics of Identity in Midlife and Beyond*. Buckingham, England: Open University Press, 1999.

Blum, Abbe. "'Strike all that look upon with mar[b]le': Monumentalizing Women in Shakespeare's Plays." In *The Renaissance Englishwoman in Print: Counterbalancing the Canon*. Ed. Anne M. Haselkorn and Betty S. Travitsky. Amherst: University of Massachusetts Press, 1990.

Boose, Lynda E. "The Father's House and the Daughter in It: The Structures of Western Culture's Daughter-Father Relationship." In *Daughters and Fathers*. Ed. Lynda E. Boose and Betty S. Flowers. Baltimore: Johns Hopkins University Press, 1989.

——. "The Father and the Bride in Shakespeare." *PMLA* 97 (1982): 325–47.

Booth, Stephen. *"King Lear," "Macbeth," Indefinition, and Tragedy*. New Haven: Yale University Press, 1980.

Bottoms, Janet. "'Look on her, Look': The Apotheosis of Cordelia." *Shakespeare Quarterly* 55 (2002): 106–13.

Bradford, Alan T. "'Jaques' Distortion of the Seven Ages Paradigm." *Shakespeare Quarterly* 27 (1976): 171–76.

Bradley, A. C. *Oxford Lectures on Poetry.* 1909. Reprint, New York: St. Martin's Press, 1965.

———. *Shakespearean Tragedy: Lectures on "Hamlet," "Othello," "King Lear," and "Macbeth."* 1904. Reprint, New York: St. Martin's Press, 1960.

Braunmuller, A. R., ed. *Macbeth.* The New Cambridge Shakespeare. Cambridge: Cambridge University Press, 1997.

Breight, Curt. "'Treason doth never prosper': *The Tempest* and the Discourse of Treason." *Shakespeare Quarterly* 41 (1990): 1–28.

Bristol, Michael D. "In Search of the Bear: Spatiotemporal Form and the Heterogeneity of Economies in *The Winter's Tale.*" *Shakespeare Quarterly* 42 (1991): 145–67.

Brooks, Peter. *Troubling Confessions: Speaking Guilt in Law and Literature.* Chicago: University of Chicago Press, 2000.

Brooks, Peter, et al. "Responses to 'Forgiveness: An Interview.'" *PMLA* 117 (2002): 296–323.

Brown, Elizabeth A. "'Companion Me with My Mistress': Cleopatra, Elizabeth I, and Their Waiting Women." In *Maids and Mistresses, Cousins and Queens: Women's Alliances in Early Modern England.* Ed. Susan Frye and Karen Robertson. Oxford: Oxford University Press, 1999.

Brown, Paul. "'This thing of darkness I acknowledge mine': *The Tempest* and the Discourse of Colonialism." In *Shakespeare: New Essays in Cultural Materialism.* Ed. Jonathan Dollimore and Alan Sinfield. Manchester, England: Manchester University Press, 1985.

Burckhardt, Jacob. *The Civilization of the Renaissance in Italy.* Trans. Samuel G. C. Middlemore. New York: Harper and Brothers, 1929.

Burrow, J. A. *The Ages of Man: A Study in Medieval Writing and Thought.* Oxford: Clarendon Press, 1986.

Calderwood, James. *If It Were Done: "Macbeth" and Tragic Action.* Amherst: University of Massachusetts Press, 1986.

Cantor, Paul A. "Shakespeare's *The Tempest:* The Wise Man as Hero." *Shakespeare Quarterly* 31 (1980): 64–75.

Carroll, William C., ed. *William Shakespeare, "Macbeth": Texts and Contexts.* New York: Bedford/St. Martin's, 1999.

Cavell, Stanley. "Recounting Gains, Showing Losses: Reading *The Winter's Tale.*" In *Disowning Knowledge in Seven Plays of Shakespeare.* Cambridge: Cambridge University Press, 2003.

——. "The Avoidance of Love." In *Must We Mean What We Say: A Book of Essays.* 1969. Reprint, Cambridge: Cambridge University Press, 1976.

Chaplin, William N. "Form and Psychology in *King Lear.*" *Literature and Psychology* 19 (1969): 31–44.

Chew, Samuel C. *The Pilgrimage of Life.* New Haven: Yale University Press, 1962.

——. "This Strange Eventful History." In *Joseph Quincy Adams Memorial Studies.* Ed. James G. McManaway et al. Washington, D.C.: The Folger Shakespeare Library, 1948.

Clayton, Thomas. "'Is this the promis'd end?': Revision in the Role of the King." In *The Division of the Kingdoms: Shakespeare's Two Versions of "King Lear."* Ed. Gary Taylor and Michael Warren. Oxford: Clarendon Press, 1983.

Coghill, Nevill. "Six Points of Stage-craft in *The Winter's Tale.*" *Shakespeare Survey* 11 (1958): 31–41.

Cook, Carol. "The Fatal Cleopatra." In *Shakespearean Tragedy and Gender.* Ed. Shirley Nelson Garner and Madelon Sprengnether. Bloomington: Indiana University Press, 1996.

Cressy, David. *Birth, Marriage, and Death: Ritual, Religion, and the Life Cycle in Tudor and Stuart England.* Oxford: Oxford University Press, 1997.

Danby, John. *Shakespeare's Doctrine of Nature: A Study of "King Lear."* London: Faber and Faber, 1949.

Daniel, Samuel. *The Complete Works in Verse and Prose of Samuel Daniel.* Ed. Alexander B. Grosart. 1885. Reprint, New York: Russell & Russell, 1963.

Daniell, David. "Shakespeare and the Protestant Mind." *Shakespeare Survey* 54 (2001): 1–12.

Daniell, David, ed. *Julius Caesar.* The Arden Shakespeare. Watson-on-Thames: Thomas Nelson and Sons, 1998.

Delumeau, Jean. *Sin and Fear: The Emergence of a Western Guilt Culture, 13th–18th Centuries.* Trans. Eric Nicholson. New York: St. Martin's Press, 1990.

Derrida, Jacques. *Of Grammatology.* Trans. Gayatri Chakravorty Spivak. Baltimore: Johns Hopkins University Press, 1976.

Dickey, Franklin. *Not Wisely But Too Well: Shakespeare's Love Tragedies.* San Marino: Huntington Library, 1957.

Dolan, Frances E. *Dangerous Familiars: Representations of Domestic Crime in England, 1550–1700.* Ithaca: Cornell University Press, 1994.

Dollimore, Jonathan. "Preface." In *Political Shakespeare: New Essays in Cultural Materialism.* Ed. Jonathan Dollimore and Alan Sinfield. Manchester, England: Manchester University Press, 1985.

——. *Radical Tragedy: Religion, Ideology, and Power in the Drama of Shakespeare and His Contemporaries.* 3rd ed. London: Palgrave, 2004.

———. "Shakespeare, Cultural Materialism, Feminism, and Marxist Humanism." *New Literary History* 21 (1990): 471–91.

Dove, Mary. *The Perfect Age of Man's Life.* Cambridge: Cambridge University Press, 1986.

Duffy, Eamon. *The Stripping of the Altars: Traditional Religion in England c. 1400–c. 1580.* New Haven: Yale University Press, 1992.

Dundes, Alan. "'To Love My Father All': A Psychoanalytic Study of the Folktale Sources of *King Lear.*" *Southern Folklore Quarterly* 40 (1976): 353–66.

Echeruo, Michael. "Tanistry, the 'Due of Birth,' and Macbeth's Sin." *Shakespeare Quarterly* 23 (1972): 444–50.

Egan, Gabriel. *Green Shakespeare: From Ecopolitics to Ecocriticism.* Accents on Shakespeare. London: Routledge, 2006.

Eggert, Katherine. *Showing Like a Queen: Female Authority and Literary Experiment in Spenser, Shakespeare, and Milton.* Philadelphia: University of Pennsylvania Press, 2000.

Elliott, G. R. *Dramatic Providence in "Macbeth": A Study of Shakespeare's Tragic Theme of Humanity and Grace.* Princeton: Princeton University Press, 1958.

Ellison, James. "*The Winter's Tale* and the Religious Politics of Europe." In *Shakespeare's Romances.* Ed. Alison Thorne. New Casebooks. London: Palgrave, 2003.

Enterline, Lynn. "'You speak a language that I understand not': The Rhetoric of Animation in *The Winter's Tale.*" *Shakespeare Quarterly* 48 (1997): 17–44.

Erickson, Peter. *Patriarchal Structures in Shakespeare's Drama.* Berkeley: University of California Press, 1985.

Erikson, Erik H. *Childhood and Society.* 2nd ed. revised and enlarged. New York: W. W. Norton, 1963.

Everett, Barbara. "The New *King Lear.*" *Critical Quarterly* 2 (1960): 325–39.

Ewbank, Inga-Stina. "The Triumph of Time in *The Winter's Tale.*" *Review of English Studies* 5, no. 2 (1964): 83–100.

Farnham, Willard. *Shakespeare's Tragic Frontier: The World of His Final Tragedies.* Berkeley: University of California Press, 1950.

Felperin, Howard. "'Tongue-tied, Our Queen?' The Deconstruction of Presence in *The Winter's Tale.*" In *The Uses of the Canon: Elizabethan Literature and Contemporary Theory.* Oxford: Oxford University Press, 1990.

Finlay, Roger. *Population and Metropolis: The Demography of London, 1580–1650.* Cambridge: Cambridge University Press, 1981.

Foakes, R. A., ed. *King Lear.* The Arden Shakespeare, 3rd series. Walton-on-Thames: Thomas Nelson and Sons, 1997.

Foucault, Michel. *Discipline and Punish: The Birth of the Prison.* Trans. Alan Sheridan. New York: Pantheon Books, 1977.

Fox, Alice. "Obstetrics and Gynecology in *Macbeth.*" *Shakespeare Studies* 12 (1979): 127–41.

Frye, Northrop. "The Argument of Comedy." In *Shakespeare: Modern Essays in Criticism.* Ed. Leonard Dean. New York: Oxford University Press, 1967.

Garber, Marjorie. *Shakespeare After All.* New York: Pantheon Books, 2004.

Gardner, Helen, "The Tragedy of Damnation." In *Elizabethan Drama: Modern Essays in Criticism.* Ed. Ralph J. Kaufmann. New York: Oxford University Press, 1961.

Gash, Anthony. "Shakespeare, Carnival, and the Sacred: *The Winter's Tale* and *Measure for Measure.*" In *Shakespeare and Carnival: After Bakhtin.* Ed. Ronald Knowles. New York: St. Martin's Press, 1998.

Gilbert, Creighton. "When Did a Man in the Renaissance Grow Old?" *Studies in the Renaissance* 14 (1967): 7–32.

Goldberg, Jonathan. "Shakespearean Inscriptions: The Voicing of Power." In *Shakespeare and the Question of Theory.* Ed. Patricia Parker and Geoffrey Hartman. London: Methuen, 1985.

Goldberg, S. L. *An Essay on "King Lear."* Cambridge: Cambridge University Press, 1974.

Grant, Michael. *Cleopatra.* London: Weidenfeld and Nicolson, 1972.

Greenblatt, Stephen. *Hamlet in Purgatory.* Princeton: Princeton University Press, 2001.

———. "Psychoanalysis and Renaissance Culture." In *Literary Theory/Renaissance Texts.* Ed. Patricia Parker and David Quint. Baltimore: Johns Hopkins University Press, 1986.

———. *Shakespearean Negotiations: The Circulation of Social Energy in Renaissance England.* Berkeley: University of California Press, 1988.

Gullette, Margaret Morganroth. *Aged by Culture.* Chicago: University of Chicago Press, 2004.

———. *Declining to Decline: Cultural Combat and the Politics of the Midlife.* Charlottesville: University Press of Virginia, 1997.

Haigh, Christopher. *English Reformations: Religion, Politics, and Society under the Tudors.* Oxford: Clarendon Press, 1993.

Hall, Kim F. *Things of Darkness: Economies of Race and Gender in Early Modern England.* Ithaca: Cornell University Press, 1995.

Haller, William. *The Rise of Puritanism.* New York: Columbia University Press, 1938.

Hamer, Mary. *Signs of Cleopatra: History, Politics, Representations.* London: Routledge, 1993.

Hanawalt, Barbara. "The Child in the Middle Ages and the Renaissance." In *Beyond the Century of the Child: Cultural History and Developmental Psychology*. Ed.Willem Koops and Michael Zuckerman. Philadelphia: University of Pennsylvania Press, 2003.

Harris, Jonathan Gil. "'Narcissus in thy Face': Roman Desire and the Difference it Fakes in *Antony and Cleopatra*." *Shakespeare Quarterly* 45 (1994): 408–25.

Hawkins, Michael. "History, Politics, and *Macbeth*." In *Focus on "Macbeth."* Ed. John Russell Brown. London: Routledge and Kegan Paul, 1982.

Herbert, Mary Sidney. *The Collected Works of Mary Sidney Herbert, Countess of Pembroke*. Ed. Margaret P. Hannay, Noel S. Kinnamon, and Michael G. Brennan. Vol. 1. Oxford: Clarendon Press, 1998.

Holahan, Michael. "'Look, her lips': Softness of Voice, Construction of Character in *King Lear*." *Shakespeare Quarterly* 48 (1997): 406–31.

Holderness, Graham. "*The Winter's Tale*: Country into Court." In *Shakespeare Out of Court: Dramatizations of Court Society*. Ed. Graham Holderness, Nick Potter, and John Turner. New York: St. Martin's Press, 1990.

Holmer, Joan Ozark. "'Draw if You Be Men': Saviolo's Significance for *Romeo and Juliet*." *Shakespeare Quarterly* 45 (1994): 163–89.

Houlbrooke, Ralph A. *The English Family: 1450–1700*. London: Longman, 1984.

Hughes-Hallett, Lucy. *Cleopatra: Histories, Dreams, and Distortions*. New York: Harper & Row, 1990.

Hunter, Robert Grams. *Shakespeare and the Comedy of Forgiveness*. New York: Columbia University Press, 1965.

Huzar, Eleanor Goltz. *Mark Antony: A Biography*. Minneapolis: University of Minnesota Press, 1978.

Jaffa, Harry V. "The Limits of Politics: *King Lear*, Act I, Scene I." In Allan Bloom with Harry V. Jaffa. *Shakespeare's Politics*. New York: Basic Books, 1964.

Jankowski, Theodora A. *Women in Power in the Early Modern Drama*. Urbana: University of Illinois Press, 1992.

Johnson, Nora. "Body and Spirit, Stage and Sexuality in *The Tempest*." *ELH* 64 (1997): 683–701.

———. "Ganymedes and Kings: Staging Male Homosexual Desire in *The Winter's Tale*." *Shakespeare Studies* 26 (1998): 187–217.

Jordan, Constance. *Shakespeare's Monarchies: Ruler and Subject in the Romances*. Ithaca: Cornell University Press, 1997.

Jorgensen, Paul A. *Lear's Self-Discovery*. Berkeley: University of California Press, 1967.

———. *Our Naked Frailties: Sensational Art and Meaning in "Macbeth."* Berkeley: University of California Press, 1971.

Kahn, Coppélia. *Man's Estate: Masculine Identity in Shakespeare.* Berkeley: University of California Press, 1981.

———. "The Absent Mother in *King Lear.*" In *Rewriting the Renaissance: The Discourses of Sexual Difference in Early Modern Europe.* Ed. Margaret W. Ferguson, Maureen Quilligan, and Nancy Vickers. Chicago: University of Chicago Press, 1986.

———. "The Providential Tempest and the Shakespearean Family." In *Representing Shakespeare: New Psychoanalytic Essays.* Ed. Murray M. Schwartz and Coppélia Kahn. Baltimore: Johns Hopkins University Press, 1980.

Karp, David A. "A Decade of Reminders: Changing Age Consciousness Between Fifty and Sixty Years Old." *The Gerontologist* 28 (1988): 727–38.

Kermode, Frank, ed. *The Tempest.* The Arden Shakespeare. 1954. Reprint, London: Routledge, 1994.

Kinney, Clare. "The Queen's Two Bodies and the Divided Emperor: Some Problems of Identity in *Antony and Cleopatra.*" In *The Renaissance Englishwoman in Print: Counterbalancing the Canon.* Ed. Anne M. Haselkorn and Betty S. Travitsky. Amherst: University of Massachusetts Press, 1990.

Kitch, Aaron. "Bastards and Broadsides in *The Winter's Tale.*" *Renaissance Drama* 30 (1999–2000): 43–71.

Knight, G. Wilson. *The Imperial Theme: Further Interpretations of Shakespeare's Tragedies Including the Roman Plays.* 1931. Reprint, London: Methuen, 1954.

———. *The Wheel of Fire: Interpretations of Shakespearean Tragedy with Three New Essays.* 1930. Reprint, London: Methuen, 1965.

Kotre, John. *Outliving the Self: Generativity and the Interpretation of Lives.* Baltimore: Johns Hopkins University Press, 1984.

Krier, Theresa M. *Birth Passages: Maternity and Nostalgia, Antiquity to Shakespeare.* Ithaca: Cornell University Press, 2001.

Kristeva, Julia. "Forgiveness: An Interview." *PMLA* 117 (2002): 278–95.

Kuriyama, Constance Brown. "'The Mother of the World': A Psychoanalytic Interpretation of Shakespeare's *Antony and Cleopatra.*" *ELR* 7 (1977): 324–51.

Kurland, Stuart M. "'We need no more of your advice': Political Realism in *The Winter's Tale.*" *Studies in English Literature: 1500–1900* 31 (1991): 365–86.

La Belle, Jennijoy. "'A Strange Infirmity': Lady Macbeth's Amenorrhea." *Shakespeare Quarterly* 31 (1980): 381–86.

Laird, David. "Competing Discourses in *The Winter's Tale.*" *Connotations* 4 (1994–95): 25–43.

Laslett, Peter. *The World We Have Lost.* London: Methuen, 1965.

———. *The World We Have Lost—Further Explored.* London: Methuen, 1983.

Latham, Agnes, ed. *As You Like It.* The Arden Shakespeare. 1967. Reprint, London: Routledge, 1993.

Leggatt, Alexander. *King Lear.* Twayne's New Critical Introductions to Shakespeare. Boston: G. K. Hall & Co., 1988.

Levin, Richard A. *Shakespeare's Secret Schemers: The Study of an Early Modern Dramatic Device.* Newark: University of Delaware Press, 2001.

Levin, Richard. "Unthinkable Thoughts in the New Historicizing of English Renaissance Drama." *New Literary History* 21 (1990): 443–47.

Levine, Laura. *Men in Women's Clothing: Anti-Theatricality and Effeminization, 1579–1642.* Cambridge Studies in Literature and Culture 5. Cambridge: Cambridge University Press, 1994.

Levinson, Daniel, et al. *The Seasons of a Man's Life.* New York: Alfred A. Knopf, 1978.

Lewis, C. S. *English Literature in the Sixteenth Century Excluding Drama.* The Oxford History of English Literature. Vol. 3. Oxford: Clarendon Press, 1954.

Lindley, David, ed. *The Tempest.* The New Cambridge Shakespeare. Cambridge: Cambridge University Press, 2002.

Loughrey, Bryan, and Neil Taylor. "Ferdinand and Miranda at Chess." *Shakespeare Survey* 35 (1982): 113–18.

Lupton, Julia Reinhard. *Afterlives of the Saints: Hagiography, Typology, and Renaissance Literature.* Stanford: Stanford University Press, 1996.

MacDonald, Joyce Green. *Women and Race in Early Modern Texts.* Cambridge: Cambridge University Press, 2002.

Mack, Maynard. *"King Lear" in Our Time.* Berkeley: University of California Press, 1965.

Mares, F. H., ed. *Much Ado About Nothing.* Cambridge: Cambridge University Press, 2003.

Marshall, Cynthia. "Man of Steel Done Got the Blues: Melancholic Subversion of Presence in *Antony and Cleopatra.*" *Shakespeare Quarterly* 44 (1993): 385–408.

Matchett, William H. "Some Dramatic Techniques in *King Lear.*" In *Shakespeare: The Theatrical Dimension.* Ed. Philip C. McGuire and David A. Samuelson. New York: AMS Press, 1979.

Mazzio, Carla, and Douglas Trevor. "Dreams of History: An Introduction." In *Historicism, Psychoanalysis, and Early Modern Culture.* Ed. Carla Mazzio and Douglas Trevor. London: Routledge, 2000.

McAdams, Dan P., and Regina L. Logan. "What Is Generativity?" In *The Generative Society: Caring for Future Generations.* Ed. Ed de St. Aubin et al. Washington, D.C.: American Psychological Association, 2004.

McCabe, Richard A. *Incest, Drama, and Nature's Law, 1550–1700.* Cambridge: Cambridge University Press, 1993.

McLuskie, Kathleen. "The Patriarchal Bard: Feminist Criticism and Shakespeare: *King Lear* and *Measure for Measure.*" In *Political Shakespeare: New Essays in Cultural Materialism.* Ed. Jonathan Dollimore and Alan Sinfield. Manchester, England: Manchester University Press, 1985.

Miller, David Lee. *Dreams of the Burning Child: Sacrificial Sons and the Father's Witness.* Ithaca: Cornell University Press, 2003.

Morse, William R. "Metacriticism and Materiality: The Case of Shakespeare's *The Winter's Tale.*" *ELH* 58 (1991): 283–304.

Muir, Kenneth, ed. *Macbeth.* The Arden Shakespeare. 1951. Reprint, London: Routledge, 1995.

Neeley, Carol Thomas. *Broken Nuptials in Shakespeare's Plays.* Urbana: University of Illinois Press, 1993.

Neill, Michael. *Issues of Death: Mortality and Identity in English Renaissance Tragedy.* Oxford: Clarendon Press, 1997.

———. "Remembrance and Revenge: *Hamlet, Macbeth,* and *The Tempest.*" In *Jonson and Shakespeare.* Ed. Ian Donaldson. London: Macmillan, 1983.

———, ed. *Anthony and Cleopatra.* The Oxford Shakespeare. Oxford: Oxford University Press, 1994.

Neugarten, Bernice, ed. *Middle Age and Aging.* Chicago: University of Chicago Press, 1968.

Nevo, Ruth. *Shakespeare's Other Language.* London: Methuen, 1987.

Norbrook, David. "*Macbeth* and the Politics of Historiography." In *Politics of Discourse: The Literature and History of Seventeenth-Century England.* Ed. Kevin Sharpe and Steven N. Zwicker. Berkeley: University of California Press, 1987.

Nostbakken, Faith. "Cultural Materialism." In *Encyclopedia of Contemporary Literary Theory: Approaches, Scholars, Terms.* Gen. ed. and comp. Irena R. Makaryk. 1993. Reprint, Toronto: University of Toronto Press, 1997.

Nuttall, A. D. *Why Does Tragedy Give Pleasure?* 1996. Reprint, Oxford: Clarendon Press, 2001.

Orgel, Stephen. "The Poetics of Incomprehensibility." *Shakespeare Quarterly* 42 (1991): 431–37.

———, ed. *William Shakespeare: "The Winter's Tale."* The Oxford Shakespeare. Oxford: Oxford University Press, 1996.

Paster, Gail Kern. *The Body Embarrassed: Drama and the Disciplines of Shame in Early Modern England.* Ithaca: Cornell University Press, 1993.

Peat, Derek. "'And that's true too': *King Lear* and the Tension of Uncertainty." *Shakespeare Survey* 33 (1980): 43–53.

Phelan, William Jeffrey. "The Vale of Years: Early Modern Aging, Gender, and Shakespearean Tragedy." Ph.D. dissertation, University of California, Los Angeles, 1997.

Pollock, Linda A. *Forgotten Children: Parent-Child Relations from 1500 to 1900.* Cambridge: Cambridge University Press, 1983.

Poole, William. "False Play: Shakespeare and Chess." *Shakespeare Quarterly* 55 (2004): 50–70.

Ray, Ruth E. *Beyond Nostalgia: Aging and Life Story Writing.* Charlottesville: University Press of Virginia, 2000.

Rossiter, A. P. *Angel with Horns and Other Shakespeare Lectures.* New York: Theater Arts Books, 1961.

Rowell, Geoffrey. "The Anglican Tradition: From the Reformation to the Oxford Movement." In *Confession and Absolution.* Ed. Martin Dudley and Geoffrey Rowell. London: SPCK, 1990.

Ryan, Kiernan. "*King Lear:* A Retrospect, 1980–2000." *Shakespeare Survey* 55 (2002): 1–11.

———. "Introduction." In *Shakespeare: The Last Plays.* Ed. Kiernan Ryan. London: Longman, 1999.

Sanders, Wilbur. *The Dramatist and the Received Idea: Studies in the Plays of Marlowe and Shakespeare.* Cambridge: Cambridge University Press, 1968.

Schalkwyk, David. "'A Lady's "Verily" Is as Potent as a Lord's'": Women, Word, and Witchcraft in *The Winter's Tale.*" *ELR* 22 (1992): 242–72.

Schmidgall, Gary. "The Discovery at Chess in *The Tempest.*" *English Language Notes* 23, no. 4 (1986): 11–16.

Schwartz, Murray M. "Leontes' Jealousy in *The Winter's Tale.*" *American Imago* 30 (1973): 250–73.

———. "*The Winter's Tale:* Loss and Transformation." *American Imago* 32 (1975): 145–99.

Sears, Elizabeth. *The Ages of Man: A Study in Medieval Writing and Thought.* Oxford: Clarendon Press, 1986.

Sharpe, J. A. "'Last Dying Speeches': Religion, Ideology, and Public Execution in Seventeenth-Century England." *Past and Present* 107 (1985): 144–67.

Sheehy, Gail. *Understanding Men's Passages: Discovering the New Map of Men's Lives.* New York: Random House, 1998.

Shell, Marc. *The End of Kinship: "Measure for Measure," Incest, and the Ideal of Universal Siblinghood.* Stanford: Stanford University Press, 1988.

Shelley, Percy Bysshe. *The Complete Poetical Works of Percy Bysshe Shelley.* Ed. Neville Rogers. 4 vols. Oxford: Clarendon Press, 1975.

Shuger, Debora K. *Political Theologies in Shakespeare's England: The Sacred and the State in "Measure for Measure."* Houndmills: Palgrave, 2001.

———. "Subversive Faiths and Suffering Subjects: Shakespeare and Christianity." In *Religion, Literature, and Politics in Post-Reformation England, 1540–1688.* Ed. Donna B. Hamilton and Richard Strier. Cambridge: Cambridge University Press, 1996.

Sinfield, Alan. "*Macbeth,* History, Ideology, and Intellectuals." *Critical Quarterly* 28 (1986): 63–77.

Smiley, Jane. *A Thousand Acres.* New York: Random House, 1991.

Smith, Lacey Baldwin. "English History Trials and Confessions in the Sixteenth Century." *Journal of the History of Ideas* 15 (1954): 471–98.

Snyder, Susan. "Mamillius and Gender Polarization in *The Winter's Tale.*" *Shakespeare Quarterly* 50 (1999): 1–8.

———. "Patterns of Motion in *Antony and Cleopatra.*" *Shakespeare Survey* 33 (1980): 113–22.

Sokol, B. J. "*The Tempest,* 'All Torment, Trouble, Wonder, and Amazement': A Kleinian Reading." In *The Undiscover'd Country: New Essays on Psychoanalysis and Shakespeare.* Ed. B. J. Sokol. London: Free Association Books, 1993.

———. *Art and Illusion in "The Winter's Tale."* Manchester, England: Manchester University Press, 1994.

Spencer, T. J. B., ed. *Shakespeare's Plutarch.* London: Penguin, 1964.

Stampfer, Judah. "The Catharsis of *King Lear.*" *Shakespeare Survey* 13 (1960): 1–10.

Stern, Jeffrey. "*King Lear:* The Transference of the Kingdom." *Shakespeare Quarterly* 41 (1990): 299–308.

Stewart, J. I. M. *Character and Motive in Shakespeare: Some Recent Appraisals Examined.* London: Longmans, Green and Co., 1949.

Stirling, Brents. "Cleopatra's Scene with Seleucus: Plutarch, Daniel, and Shakespeare." *Shakespeare Quarterly* 15 (1964): 299–311.

Summers, Joseph H. "The Anger of Prospero." *Michigan Quarterly Review* 12 (1973): 116–35.

Tambling, Jeremy. *Confession: Sexuality, Sin, the Subject.* Manchester, England: Manchester University Press, 1990.

Tentler, Thomas. *Sin and Confession on the Eve of the Reformation.* Princeton: Princeton University Press, 1977.

Thompson, Ann. "Are There Any Women in *King Lear*?" In *The Matter of Difference: Materialist Feminist Criticism of Shakespeare.* Ed. Valerie Wayne. Ithaca: Cornell University Press, 1991.

———. "'Miranda, Where's Your Sister?' Reading Shakespeare's *Tempest.*" In *Feminist Criticism: Theory and Practice.* Ed. Susan Sellers. London: Harvester Wheatsheaf, 1991.

Thompson, Stith. *Motif-Index of Folk-Literature.* Bloomington: Indiana University Press, 1957.

Thorne, Alison. "Introduction." In *Shakespeare's Romances.* Ed. Alison Thorne. New Casebooks. London: Palgrave, 2003.

Vaillant, George E. *The Wisdom of the Ego.* Cambridge, Mass.: Harvard University Press, 1993.

Van Elk, Martine. "'Our praises are our wages': Courtly Exchange, Social Mobility, and Female Speech in *The Winter's Tale.*" *Philological Quarterly* 79 (2000): 429–57.

Vanita, Ruth. "Mariological Memory in *The Winter's Tale* and *Henry VIII.*" *Studies in English Literature: 1500–1900.* 40 (2000): 311–37.

Wakefield, Jerome C. "Immortality and the Externalization of the Self: Plato's Unrecognized Theory of Generativity." In *Generativity and Adult Development: How and Why We Care for the Next Generation.* Ed. Dan P. McAdams and Ed de St. Aubin. Washington, D.C.: American Psychological Association, 1998.

Walker, Roy. *The Time is Free: A Study of "Macbeth."* London: Andrew Dakers Ltd., 1949.

Walton, J. K. "Lear's Last Speech," *Shakespeare Survey* 13 (1960): 11–19.

Watson, Robert N. *The Rest is Silence: Death as Annihilation in the English Renaissance.* Berkeley: University of California Press, 1994.

——. *Shakespeare and the Hazards of Ambition.* Cambridge, Mass.: Harvard University Press, 1984.

Weber, Max. *Max Weber on Charisma and Institution Building: Selected Papers.* Ed. S. N. Eisenstadt. Chicago: University of Chicago Press, 1968.

Willbern, David. "Phantasmagoric *Macbeth.*" *ELR* 16 (1986): 520–49.

Woodward, Kathleen. *Aging and Its Discontents: Freud and Other Fictions.* Bloomington: Indiana University Press, 1991.

Wrightsman, Lawrence S. *Adult Personality Development,* vol. 1: *Theories and Concepts.* Thousand Oaks, Calif.: Sage Publications, 1994.

Wrigley, E. A., et al. *English Population History from Family Reconstitution.* Cambridge: Cambridge University Press, 1997.

Zender, Karl F. "Isabella's Choice." *Philological Quarterly* 73 (1994): 77–93.

——. "The Politics of Incest." In *Faulkner and the Politics of Reading.* Baton Rouge: Louisiana State University Press, 2002.

Index